CADDY
FOR
LIFE

ALSO BY JOHN FEINSTEIN

Open

The Punch

The Last Amateurs

The Majors

A March to Madness

A Civil War

A Good Walk Spoiled

Play Ball

Hard Courts

Forever's Team

A Season Inside

A Season on the Brink

Running Mates
(A Mystery)

Winter Games
(A Mystery)

CADDY
FOR
LIFE

The Bruce Edwards Story

JOHN
FEINSTEIN

Little, Brown and Company
New York   Boston

Little, Brown and Company
Time Warner Book Group
1271 Avenue of the Americas, New York, NY 10020
Visit our Web site at www.twbookmark.com

First Edition

Library of Congress Cataloging-in-Publication Data

Feinstein, John.
    Caddy for life : the Bruce Edwards story / John Feinstein.—1st ed.
        p.   cm.
    Includes index.
    ISBN 0-316-77788-9
        1. Edwards, Bruce, 1954–   2. Caddies—United States—Biography.
    3. Watson, Tom, 1949–   I. Title.

GV964.A2E394   2004
796.352'092—dc22   2003027136

10 9 8 7 6 5 4 3 2 1
Q-FF
Printed in the United States of America

*This is for all those who have suffered because of ALS:
victims, family, friends. And for all those working
through fund-raising or research to find the cure.
May their prayers be answered and their hopes
and dreams become reality very, very soon.*

Introduction

IN MAY OF 1981, when I was still the kid on the sports staff of the *Washington Post*, I was given a dream assignment. "Go on up to the Memorial Tournament next week," sports editor George Solomon told me. "Bring back some stories we can use Kemper week."

The Kemper Open had moved a year earlier from Charlotte, North Carolina, to Congressional Country Club, which is a few miles from downtown Washington. That made it, as far as the *Post* was concerned, the fifth major. Since I had been pleading with George for the chance to cover golf for most of two years, he decided this was a good time to get me off his back. No one else on staff really wanted to spend a week outside Columbus, Ohio, on a vague quest to "bring back some stories," except for me. I was single, I loved golf, I was more than happy to spend a few days at Jack Nicklaus's tournament, although I wouldn't dare tell anyone there that the Memorial (which they thought was really the fifth major) was just a warm-up for the Kemper.

I had grown up working in the pro shop at a small golf club on the eastern end of Long Island and had developed a great passion for the game even though I had serious deficiencies actually playing it. I could tell you off the top of my head who had won almost every major played in my lifetime, and I knew the bios of most of the top players on the tour. Of course I had never met any of them and none of them knew me. In that sense, the assignment was somewhat daunting. I arrived at Muirfield Village Country Club late on Tuesday afternoon, excited but nervous.

I collected my credential in the pressroom and walked outside the clubhouse, wondering if anyone was still around I could talk to. I had no idea what kind of stories I wanted to bring home. As I rounded the corner leading from the clubhouse to the putting green, I spotted a lone figure sitting on a low stone wall that divides the putting green in half. He was smoking a cigarette, clearly relaxing after a long day before he went home.

Bruce Edwards.

I recognized him instantly, just as any golf fan back then would. He was Tom Watson's caddy, and Watson was the number one player in the world. Six weeks earlier, he had won his second Masters to go with the three British Opens he had won. That gave him five majors at age thirty-one, two of those wins coming in classic duels with Nicklaus. If you followed golf, you knew who Bruce was — he was the guy who walked the fairways stride for stride with Watson, the two of them seemingly in lockstep, usually smiling and laughing, clearly enjoying each other's company. Watson had short reddish-brown hair and a quick smile. Bruce had long brown hair and an equally quick smile. They always looked to me like they belonged together.

There was a sign next to the green which said PLAYERS, CADDIES, AND OFFICIALS ONLY. There was also no one around. If anyone said something, I'd just pretend I hadn't seen the sign. I walked over to Bruce, introduced myself, and asked if he had — as we reporters like to say — a couple of minutes to talk.

"Sure," he said. "Sit down."

I quickly confessed that this was the first time I'd been sent to cover a golf tournament and that I might ask some seriously stupid questions. "Don't worry about it," Bruce said. "You must know something about golf. You recognized a caddy."

Not just any caddy, I pointed out. Bruce laughed. "I don't work for just any player, do I?" he said.

We went from there. I asked the usual questions about his background, and Bruce told me about growing up in Connecticut, the son of a dentist, and of his passionate desire as a teenager to caddy. He re-created — as he had done many times before — the day in St. Louis when he first met Watson. He talked about what made Watson special. "Watch him when things go wrong," he said. "He gets better. Never whines or makes excuses. Just keeps playing. That's what I love about working for him."

We talked about other players — good guys, bad guys, funny guys. Bruce gave me the names of other caddies I should talk to who had interesting stories to tell. At some point I noticed a chill in the air. We had been talking for close to two hours. Not once had Bruce looked at his watch or asked how much longer the "couple of minutes" was going to drag on. Finally I thanked him and we both stood up.

"Hey, anytime," Bruce said. "Good luck."

As a reporter, you rarely get as lucky as I did that day. Bruce essentially gave me a road map for the entire week, telling me stories that would lead me to other stories. He became, you could say, my first tour guide. I had stumbled smack into what we call a go-to guy in my first five minutes covering golf. It wasn't until 1993 that I began to cover golf on a regular basis, but in the years that intervened, whenever I did cover golf, I always looked for Bruce. He wasn't just a bright caddy, he was one of the brighter people I knew in any walk of life. After I began to cover the tour more regularly, Bruce became someone I depended on for a story, a quote, an anecdote, or just a few minutes of laughter.

It may not have been until 1998 that I first really felt I understood what made him special as a caddy. I had always noticed his demeanor, his upbeat approach, and his enthusiasm. But one Monday afternoon, I found out there was more to it than that. I was walking with Watson, Fred Couples, and Chris DiMarco during a practice round prior to the U.S. Open, held that year at the Olympic Club, outside San Francisco. I had bought a yardage book for the week, the orange book all the caddies now buy that shows them exact yardages from various spots on each hole and where hidden trouble may be. Walking onto one of the greens, I noticed Bruce looking at two yardage books, one bright and brand-new, the other beaten up.

"This one's from the last time we were here," he said, showing me a 1987 Olympic yardage book. "I keep all my yardage books so I can compare when we go back to places to see if anything's changed. Sometimes I'll notice that I've written down a correction in the old book and I'll check to see if the new one has it right or wrong. Of course if I have any doubt, I just walk it off myself."

He showed me where he had scribbled notes about ridges on greens or breaks he hadn't actually seen the first time Watson had putted from a particular spot. He would suggest that Watson putt from those places during the practice rounds to see if the unseen break might still be there. No detail too small. "You never know where it might make a difference," he said. "I actually liked it better when I first came out, when there were no yardage books. That way the caddies who took the time to walk the golf course and check everything out had an advantage. The yardage books are an equalizer, because they're usually right. So you look for small things that they don't have in them. Maybe in a week, you might save your guy one shot someplace. But that shot could be the difference between winning and losing."

A little more than a year after the 1998 Open, Watson turned fifty and moved over to the Senior Tour. Bruce went with him. He had left Watson once — after being encouraged by Watson to do so — to work for Greg Norman for three years. He had made a lot of money working for Norman, but it simply wasn't the same as being with Watson, who was both his boss and his friend. He had returned to Watson in 1992 and, even though he had plenty of other chances to leave, he had made it clear he would finish his caddying career — whenever that day came — carrying the same bag he had carried since his first month on tour.

He missed the regular tour. At the Masters in April of 2000, he walked up the hill on the first practice day from the bag room, stood under the famous tree outside the clubhouse, and spread his hands wide, his palms turned upward, his face turned toward the sky. "Real tour air," he said, grinning broadly. "I feel like I can breathe again!"

I was standing there at that moment, and we joked about the differences between the Senior Tour and the PGA Tour. "I miss it," he said. "I miss a lot of my guys." He smiled. "But this is where Tom and I are right now. I guess I'll just ride off into the sunset with him."

That sounded about right to me. Tom and Bruce were to golf what George and Gracie were to comedy, Woodward and Bernstein were to journalism, Fonteyn and Nureyev were to dancing. They were partners for life, linked in our minds forevermore.

It was a routine conversation with a close friend on a winter afternoon. It was snowing, as it had almost every other day in the winter of 2003, and I was asking my friend Dave Kindred if he wanted to drive with me to Lewisburg, Pennsylvania, the next day to watch Holy Cross and Bucknell play basketball. This is a running joke between us. Like a lot of my friends, Kindred, who writes for *Golf Digest* and the *Sporting News,* finds my fascination with basketball in the Patriot League both amusing and confusing, especially when it involves driving through snowstorms on back roads in February. Naturally, I always offer him the chance to make the drive with me — "You might learn something" is my usual line — and he always thanks me profusely for the opportunity and then says something about having to reorganize his sock drawer that day. "Otherwise," he will say, "I'd be right there with you. You know that."

This time, though, his answer was different. He still turned me down, but the subject of his sock drawer never came up.

"I have to go to Florida tomorrow," he said.

"*Have* to go?" I said. "Sounds like tough duty this time of year. What are you going down there for?"

"To see Bruce Edwards."

The mention of Bruce's name put a smile on my face. "You doing a column on him?" I asked. "That's one of your rare good ideas. Be sure to tell him I said hello and ask him to tell you how he launched my career as a golf writer."

I was a little bit surprised when Kindred didn't respond with a wisecrack. There was nothing funny in his voice when he answered by saying, "You don't know, do you?"

That brought me up short.

"Don't know what?"

Kindred paused for a moment. He knew that Bruce and I were friends.

"He's got ALS," he said finally.

For once in my life I was completely speechless. Maybe I had heard wrong. Three letters. Maybe one was incorrect and it was something else, some disease I'd never heard of. When I found my voice, I said quietly, almost praying that Dave was going to assuage my fears with his answer, "You mean ALS — as in Lou Gehrig's disease?"

"Yes."

I know now, having talked to dozens of people in the past few months who know and love Bruce, that my reaction at that moment was virtually identical to theirs when they heard the news: I felt sick to my stomach. My heart was pounding and I could feel myself starting to shake. "When?" I asked. "When was it diagnosed?"

"Last month," Kindred said. "People didn't really know until last week. *Golf Digest* wants me to go down and talk to him. I talked to his father last night. It doesn't sound very good at all."

There is absolutely nothing good about amyotrophic lateral sclerosis — which has been known to people as Lou Gehrig's disease since it killed the great Yankee first baseman back in 1941. Now, as then, there is no cure for ALS, which is described as a neuro-degenerative disease that attacks nerve cells and pathways to the brain and spinal cord. ALS victims die from asphyxiation when the paralysis spreads to the diaphragm. In simple terms, the disease gradually destroys the muscles throughout your body. Your brain is unaffected, which means you watch helplessly as your body collapses one step at a time.

"His father says he has the more aggressive kind," Kindred added. "That usually means one to three years."

One to three years, I thought. Bruce wasn't much older than I was, not yet fifty, I knew for sure. "He's forty-eight," Kindred said, as if reading my mind.

"Just tell him I'm thinking of him, okay?" I said, feeling guilty that I hadn't known sooner.

I hung up the phone and sat staring at the snow for a good long while.

When I came out of my trance, I went on the Internet to find out more about ALS. I knew what most people know: It had killed Gehrig, and there's no cure. I wondered what Kindred meant about the more aggressive kind. I found that out fairly quickly. Bruce apparently had what is called bulbar ALS, as opposed to peripheral ALS. The life expectancy for peripheral ALS is longer — three to five years. Bulbar ALS tends to attack the throat first, the legs later. I remember thinking, "Well, at least he should be able to keep caddying for a while."

After a few minutes, I knew more than I wanted to know about ALS. I could find nothing encouraging, no sign that anyone was close to finding a cure. There were about 30,000 people suffering with ALS in the United States, a tiny slice of the population compared with some other diseases. I would soon find out that was one of the reasons so little progress has been made in research. Pharmaceutical companies understandably focus their money and time on diseases that afflict the most people. One of the reasons there are so few people with ALS is both simple and chilling: Very few people live long once diagnosed. It is a fast and brutal killer.

Feeling even worse after my research than I had before, I started to compose a letter to Bruce. For quite a while, I stared at a blank screen. What could I possibly say? Hang in there? Sure, easy for me to say. Finally I remembered the first day we had met. I reminded Bruce about that day and told him how much I thought it said about him that he had been willing to sit there for so long and help out a complete stranger. I told him how much our friendship had meant to me through the years.

A few days later, I got an e-mail. "Thanks so much for reminding me about 1981," Bruce wrote. "I've always believed that family and friendships are the two most important things in a man's life. Reminding me that I did something good (at least once!) made my day." He went on to say that he was feeling okay — "even though I often sound like the town drunk" — and that he had a brand-new family, since he had just remarried and his new wife, Marsha, had a nine-year-old son and an eight-year-old daughter. "It's different," he wrote, "but a lot of fun." Only later would I learn that he had proposed to Marsha on New Year's Eve — fifteen days before he was diagnosed. He closed by saying he would see me in Augusta. "I just hope," he wrote, "that these tired legs can handle those hills."

The last line was frightening. Already he was feeling the disease in his legs.

If you are a golf fan, you probably watch the Masters on television each year. If you watched in 2003, you no doubt saw Dick Enberg's essay on caddies, focusing on Bruce and his relationship with Watson and his battle with ALS. The piece ended with Bruce coming off the 18th green on Saturday morning after Watson had finished his rain-delayed second round and collapsing in tears on Hilary Watson's shoulder. Tom had missed the cut, and Bruce came off the green thinking that he had very possibly worked at the Masters for the last time.

What you didn't see was Bruce hand-in-hand with Marsha, walking up the hill to the clubhouse, the tears gone, just wanting to get someplace quiet. He had been doing interviews all week, the subject of dozens of columns around the country, all of them sympathetic. I had walked a number of holes with the group of Watson, Mike Weir, and Padraig Harrington on Friday, but hadn't been around when play was called for darkness on Friday because I had to be inside the pressroom writing at that hour. I hadn't yet had a chance to see Bruce, and I knew he would be leaving soon since Watson had missed the cut.

I walked around to the front of the clubhouse, where the caddies usually hang out, figuring he would go there to see his friends before leaving. I found him standing on the porch outside the locker room with Marsha. Bruce was fighting tears again. It had been just under twenty-two years since we had first met, but I wasn't sure if this was a moment when I should leave him alone or go over to say hello. Bruce, as always, made it easy.

"John," he said, waving me over when he saw me. "I want you to meet Marsha."

He had the old smile on his face, even though his words were slurred and the tears were still on his cheeks. He hugged me, then introduced his wife to me. We joked about his speech for a moment — "You don't sound a lot different than you sounded after about nine o'clock in the old days," I said when he tried to apologize for the way he sounded. Then I turned serious for a minute.

"You okay?" I asked.

"Yeah," he said. "Tired. We should have made the cut. Four-putted the sixth. That killed us." He paused. "Next year we'll win."

That started him crying again. I couldn't think of anything clever or funny to say. Finally he looked at me and said, "You know, a number of people have suggested to me that I do a book about my life on the tour and with Tom."

I felt myself cringe inwardly. First, I was appalled that anyone would approach him about such a thing under the current circumstances. Second, I knew what was coming next. "I'd like to do it," he continued. "But only if you write it."

Oh God, this was awkward. For about sixty seconds or so, I was in full, 100 percent selfish mode. I had just finished one book, which was about to be published, and I was working on another one. I had promised Mary, my wife, that I would take the summer off to spend some serious time with her and our two children. Plus, doing a book on Bruce would inevitably mean spending time with him as his health deteriorated. I was searching for a way out almost before he finished what he was saying.

"Bruce, I'm unbelievably flattered," I said — meaning it. "But, well, this is a tough time. I've got two books working and I promised my wife I'd take a break. But if you really want to do it, I can help you find someone who would do a really good job." I was actually thinking at that moment of Kindred.

The look on his face told me he knew a blow-off when he heard it. "I understand," he said. "It's not a problem."

If he had punched me in the stomach, I think I would have felt better than I did at that moment. In that instant, one thought ran through my mind: *You have to do this*. In the next, the entire book suddenly crystallized in my mind. It was a love story in three parts: Bruce and Watson, Bruce and the life on tour, and Bruce and this gutsy young woman standing next to him. "You know what," I said. "I'll figure something out. We can do this. Give me a few days to talk to my publisher."

Not surprisingly, he was confused by my complete turnaround. "Listen," he said, "don't do anything that will mess up your family."

It's okay, I told him. I then explained the way I had just envisioned the book. His eyes lit up. Marsha then asked how old my children were, and we spent the next few minutes comparing notes on kids. "I'll call you in a few days," I said.

"You sure?" he said.

"I'm sure."

If I had any remaining doubts, they went away a few minutes later, when I called Mary. I expected her to remind me that the word *no* existed for a reason, that she understood why I would want to do the book but there were other people who could do it. Once I finished telling her the story, she said simply, "You have to do this."

And so I did. To say that there have been difficult moments these past few months would be an understatement. Bruce and Marsha and their families and friends have been through moments of hope and seen those hopes turn up empty. They have been through extraordinary moments of joy, none more remarkable than the day Watson shot 65 to lead the U.S. Open and the entire golf world stopped to cheer for him and for Bruce.

Through it all, Bruce's health has obviously worsened. All of us who care about him have had a tough time watching him get thinner and weaker, seeing him forced into a golf cart while caddying and end 2003 knowing he would not be able to caddy at all in 2004. But I can honestly say now that I would not have missed these last few months for anything. In 1981 Bruce patiently gave me lessons in golf and about life on the PGA Tour. This past year, he has given me lessons in courage, in grace under pressure, in generosity of spirit, and in how to live life even when time is short.

In my last conversation with Tom Watson at the end of the year, we talked at length about what Bruce was going through, about what the year had meant to him, and about all he had learned about ALS and the research that is ongoing. Watson talked with great passion about various drug trials being conducted, about the hope that a way to at least slow down the disease may not be that far off.

"If we can just keep Bruce in working order for another year, there may be something," he said, his voice trailing away.

A year for someone with ALS might be too long. Watson knew that. He had seen up close what the disease had done to his friend in a year.

"What I think has amazed everyone this past year, even me, someone who knows him so well, is his attitude and spirit," Watson said, the words coming slowly. A moment earlier, talking about research and drug trials and hope for the future, his voice had been strident, full of life. Now his voice was almost a whisper. "He simply won't give in mentally or emotionally, no matter what happens," he continued, beginning to choke up. "He's an extraordinary person. I can't tell you how much I admire him. He's been such an inspiration to people in the last year." Watson was crying now, the tears running down his cheeks. "And to me."

And to all of us lucky enough to know him.

CADDY
FOR
LIFE

1

The Reunion

TO BE IN NEW ENGLAND on the first Saturday in September when the Red Sox are in a pennant race, when college football is beginning again and the first hints of fall are in the air, is to be about as close to heaven as one can come while still on earth.

On just such a day in 2003, on a morning when the sky was brilliantly blue and the temperature at sunrise was in the low 60s, a far-flung family gathered at 416 Brenda Lane in Franklin, a Boston suburb about twenty-five miles southwest of Kenmore Square and Fenway Park. Jay and Natalie Edwards had driven from their retirement home in Vero Beach, Florida, stopping in Annapolis on the way to spend a little extra time with their daughter Chris, her husband, John, and their two children. Chris, the oldest of the four Edwards children, is, like her husband, a retired Navy veteran. After Jay and Natalie continued their drive north, Chris and her family flew into Boston on Friday night.

Brian, the second son, and his wife, Laurie, had the longest trip, coming from their home in Steamboat Springs, Colorado. They had flown east on Wednesday and had spent time on Cape Cod riding bicycles and roller-blading. Rare was the day in their lives when they didn't bike or run or blade or look for something new and different to attempt. Gwyn and Lenny were the only ones who didn't have to travel, because they were the hosts, which meant they had the most work to do. That was how they wanted it, though, especially Gwyn, the baby in the family. She had retired from a successful career in public relations to raise their three children, who now ranged in age from five and a half to two and a half. It was Gwyn who had first come up with the idea to get everyone together and Gwyn who had pushed everyone else to make sure it happened.

Technically this was not a reunion but a chance to celebrate the wedding of Jay and Natalie's son Bruce. Bruce, the second child and the first son, had married Marsha Cummins Moore on a beach in Hawaii in February, almost thirty years after they first met and five weeks after they had become engaged.

The engagement had caught the family a little off guard; they hadn't known there was someone serious in Bruce's life. The wedding had been a complete surprise, because it had all happened in less than a week. Hilary Watson, whose husband, Tom, had been Bruce's boss for almost his entire adult life, had suggested it to Marsha on a Monday and the ceremony had taken place six days later on the beach. Friends had commented that it was typical of Bruce to find a way to get married in his bare feet.

Tom Watson was Bruce's best man. In his toast to the bride and groom he had commented that this was a marriage that was beginning under very difficult circumstances. "The groom," he said, "is a lifelong Eagles fan. The bride is a devoted Cowboys fan. That's why it took so long for them to finally get together. Clearly, they are going to have a lot of work to do."

When the rest of the family heard about the wedding, they were taken by surprise, but they also understood. Everyone talked about getting together at some point at Bruce and Marsha's home in Florida to celebrate. But there was no specific date or plan. Late in March, as was almost always the case on weekends, Gwyn and Lenny had the TV tuned to that week's golf tournament. It was the Players Championship. Gwyn was walking through the living room when she heard NBC's Jimmy Roberts mention the name Bruce Edwards. She stopped and sat down. A moment later her big brother was on the screen. She took a deep breath when she saw him and tried not to cry.

Bruce's voice was thick, his words difficult to understand, almost as if he'd been drinking. That wasn't a surprise, because she'd talked to him on the phone frequently in the weeks since the wedding and knew that was how he sounded now. "But I hadn't seen him," she said. "When I saw how thin he was, when I saw how different he looked in just a few weeks, that's when it really hit me. That was when I first thought to myself, 'We have to get everyone together — soon.'"

Months later, sitting on a couch in the living room with Lenny next to her, she still found it difficult to say exactly why the thought had crossed her mind that day. "I don't honestly remember if I thought it specifically," she said. "But obviously it was somewhere in my mind."

Somewhere in her mind was the thought that couldn't be avoided — not on that afternoon in March nor on that spectacular Saturday in September: If we don't get the family together soon, the next time might be at Bruce's funeral.

Three weeks before Bruce's wedding, at the age of forty-eight, an unsmiling doctor at the Mayo Clinic had said to him, "Do you know what ALS is? It's also known as Lou Gehrig's disease. In all likelihood, you have one to three years to live."

Just like that. No ifs or ands or buts. He had issued what was, essentially, a death sentence, almost as if he were a judge telling a criminal his decision based on the facts before him.

That had been on a cold, snowy January day in Minnesota. A lot had happened since then, much of it good, some of it extraordinary. Bruce had been to many different doctors and had been told many different things about how he could get better. But the disease was still progressing. Bruce knew it, Marsha knew it, the family knew it. When Bruce and Marsha arrived at Gwyn and Lenny's house that

Friday night in September, there was a plate of mussels, courtesy of Brian and Laurie, sitting on the table on the back patio that Lenny had managed to finish building in time for the weekend.

"Try a couple," Brian advised his older brother. "They're delicious."

"Great," Bruce said with the wicked smile that was his trademark. "Can they cure ALS?"

Everyone laughed. It was a funny line, typical Bruce.

And then everyone sat back and the cool evening was completely silent for a moment.

In all there were seventeen of them gathered at 416 Brenda Lane, the house that Gwyn and Lenny had moved into ten months earlier. In addition to Jay and Natalie Edwards, the patriarch and matriarch, and their four children and their spouses, there were seven children, ranging in age from fifteen-year-old Natalie, John and Chris's oldest, down to little Jay, Lenny and Gwyn's youngest. Gwyn and Lenny had rented a moon-bounce for the weekend, and it proved to be a masterstroke, keeping the kids busy with little squabbling. That left the adults time to sit on the patio, enjoy the spectacular weather, wonder if the Red Sox might finally be for real, and of course reminisce and remember.

"Thank God Bruce was always the kind of kid who stuck to his guns," Jay Edwards said on Friday evening, shortly before Bruce arrived. "Those first few years, we kept waiting for him to say 'enough,' and come home and go to college. Who knows, if he hadn't ended up with Tom Watson maybe he would have come home, but I'm not sure. He loved the life out there. He made lots of friends, good friends, and he really found a niche doing what he was doing. He was right, we were wrong. I'm really proud of what he has become."

Bruce Edwards would have loved hearing his father say those words. For years, he was convinced that he would never hear them, because his father was incapable of believing them. One of the jokes among the Edwards children, even after Bruce turned forty, even after he had made himself an excellent living as a caddy on the PGA Tour for years and years, was that Mom and Dad were still waiting for him to grow up, go to college, and find a real job. It was almost like the old joke about the mother of the first Jewish president, who leans over to the person sitting next to her during the inaugural address and says, "You know, my other son's a doctor."

Their son had become the king of the caddies. He was the best in the world at a profession that had earned respectability in large part because of the work done by him and his contemporaries. They had changed the image of the tour caddy from irresponsible hanger-on to respected partner. And yet Jay and Natalie were still waiting for him to come home and become a doctor. Or a lawyer. Or a dentist.

In fact Bruce often told people that his parents' proudest moment watching him caddy had not come at the 1982 U.S. Open, when Watson beat Jack Nicklaus with what might have been golf's most famous shot, holing an impossible chip at the 17th hole — after which Watson pointed his finger at Bruce and said, "I told you I was gonna make it!" Their proudest moment came two years later, at the 1984 U.S. Open. Walking outside the ropes, the Edwardses were there when someone pointed at Tom Watson and said, "It's him."

"Not it's *him*," Bruce Edwards corrected. "It's *he*." Then he paused for a second, glanced at his parents, and said, "And I'll bet you never thought you'd hear *that* from a caddy."

There had never been anything very typical about Bruce as a caddy. His relationship with Watson had been built on many things, not the least of which was his willingness to disagree with his boss, even challenge him on occasion. Watson had enough self-confidence that he didn't mind being told he was wrong. The two of them argued often but almost never really fought. Bruce always gave most of the credit for that relationship to Watson. "He let me be wrong," he said. "I never said anything thinking that if I was wrong, I'd get fired or yelled at. Sometimes he listened to me, sometimes he didn't. But once he made his decision, he always took responsibility for the outcome."

"I'm not much of a whiner and Bruce isn't a whiner," is how Watson describes the way they worked together. "We just both go out there and do our jobs."

From 1973 until the middle of 1989, they had done their jobs together, appearing to most in golf to be a matched set. Sometimes when they walked the fairways side by side, it appeared they were connected by an invisible string. Their walking paces were identical — fast — and neither one ever seemed to get his head down or pout on days when things didn't go well. Watson almost never lost his bouncy step, even in the wake of some difficult defeats, and his caddy matched him every step of the way. They had separated for three years when Watson cut back on his playing schedule and encouraged Bruce to accept an offer from Greg Norman, then the number one player in the world.

But in '92 Bruce had returned, and they'd worked together ever since — more than twenty-five years as partners. "It really wasn't the same without him," Watson said years later, looking back at their three-year separation. "I missed his personality and I missed having someone there who knew me so well I didn't even have to think before I did anything."

Bruce came back in the fall of '92 and, in many ways, it was as if he had never been away. They fell back into their same old arguments: Watson's Royals vs. Edwards's Phillies; Watson's conservative politics vs. Edwards's far more moderate views; the annual bet on the NCAA basketball tournament. They really were the old couple that has been together for so long that they finish each other's sentences and know one another's thoughts.

When Watson turned fifty in 1999 and moved over to the Senior Tour, Bruce had plenty of chances to work for other top players on the more lucrative and far more enjoyable PGA Tour.

In truth Bruce, like Watson, would have loved to stay on the PGA Tour forever. The Senior Tour is a shadow of the "real" tour. Most of its tournaments are 54 holes with no cut, as opposed to the PGA Tour's 72 holes with a 36-hole cut. The crowds most weeks are little more than a handful and there is a heavy emphasis on pro-ams, because the tour is so dependent on corporate America to keep the dollars flowing. What's more, most of the golf courses are set up short and easy to create the illusion that the over-fifty set can still score the way they did when they were younger. Watson has never been a short and easy sort of golfer. He likes golf courses difficult and conditions tough. He is famous for playing his best golf in the worst possible conditions — one of the reasons he won the often weather-challenged British Open five times.

Watson was still good enough to win on the regular tour a few months before he turned forty-nine. He still craves going out and competing with the kids, but his post-fifty body won't let him practice and grind the way he did when he was younger. That makes it unrealistic for him to tee it up with the youngsters on a regular basis, and playing with the seniors week in and week out doesn't motivate him the way he was motivated when he was younger. "There's nothing wrong with the Senior Tour," Watson insists. "I like it fine. But I'm not able to practice and work like I did when I was younger, so it's different than it was back then. I have to approach it differently simply because it is different."

Bruce could have left Watson when he turned fifty for almost any player out there. He is that highly thought of by the men on tour. He would have made more money, and, again, Watson would have understood, because Watson is both a businessman and an older brother figure to Bruce. "When he told me about having the chance to go work for Greg, I told him, 'Go for it,'" Watson said. "It was like a father pushing a son out of the nest. There was too much money on the table potentially to pass it up."

Bruce remembers Watson being even more direct back then: "'You need to do this,' he said. 'I can't win for you anymore.'"

That was at a low point of Watson's career, when the swing and putting stroke that had made him the world's best player had deserted him. If Bruce had left again in 1999 or 2000, not wanting to go the Senior Tour route, Watson would have understood again.

But there was absolutely no way Bruce was leaving Watson, whether Watson played the Senior Tour, a mini-tour in Florida, or decided to try to win all the state championships of the Midwest. He had left home once. He had no intention of leaving him again.

"As long as Tom wants me, I'll never leave him," he said once. "He's a lot more than just my boss. He's my friend, he's my best adviser." He smiled. "Of course I don't always listen to him, sort of like I didn't always listen to my dad. But I'm not leaving Tom Watson. He'll have to fire me to get rid of me again."

Of course Watson would never fire Bruce. Each had been the constant — except for that three-year window — in the other's adult life. Each had been married and divorced and remarried in the thirty years that they had known one another. Bruce had watched Watson's children grow up, and Watson, after joining Edwards's parents in pushing Bruce to go to college, had come to realize it wasn't going to happen. "He's a gypsy at heart," Watson liked to say. "There wasn't anything I was going to say, or his mom and dad were going to say, that would change that."

They had faced all sorts of crises, some big and some not so big, together. Bruce had watched Watson struggle, first with his swing, later with his putting, and remained resolute that it would all get better, even at times when Watson wasn't so sure. Watson had understood Bruce's departure and his return. He had worried openly about Bruce's choice when he married for the first time — so had his family — and then had been there to help Bruce pick up the pieces when the marriage ended horribly.

Now, though, Watson and Bruce were going through a crisis unlike any other, one neither man could possibly have imagined. Watson had worried for years about Bruce's constant smoker's cough, a hacking that probably dated back to shortly after he started smoking as a teenager. Periodically he had urged Bruce to see a doctor, to get a full checkup, to have his throat and lungs examined. Bruce always laughed him off, in part because he was young and felt invulnerable, in part because — like most in his profession — he had no medical insurance and wasn't willing to pay the cost of a full checkup himself.

But during 2002, a series of problems finally got Bruce's attention. In the spring he began noticing that his speech was sometimes slurred. People had noticed, but no one said anything. They figured he was tired or maybe he'd had a little too much to drink. Greg Rita, a longtime caddying pal whose mother had suffered a stroke, wondered if Bruce had suffered a minor stroke without knowing it. In October Bruce had walked into a bar in Las Vegas and ordered a glass of wine.

"I'm sorry sir, I can't serve you," the bartender said. "You've had too much to drink."

Bruce hadn't had a single drink that day.

He began having trouble with his left hand, noticing a cleft between his thumb and index finger. Then, one night in early January, he woke up in the middle of the night having an uncontrollable coughing fit. When Watson heard about the coughing fit, he called his own doctor at the Mayo Clinic and explained Bruce's symptoms. The doctor, Ian Hay, later told Bruce that his words to Watson were direct: "He needs to be up here yesterday."

Bruce made the trip to the Mayo on a snowy Tuesday in January. Marsha Cummins Moore went with him. Two weeks earlier, almost thirty years after they had first met, Bruce had proposed to her. Having Marsha there was comforting for Bruce. He wasn't scared, but he was concerned. Like Watson, he worried the doctors were going to find something wrong with his lungs. He knew better than anyone how much he smoked.

He never dreamed even for an instant that the diagnosis would be ALS — amyotrophic lateral sclerosis, commonly known as Lou Gehrig's disease. When Eric Sorenson, the neurological specialist Doctor Hay had brought in to test him, delivered the news, he asked Bruce if he knew what ALS was. Bruce knew. "I would advise," Sorenson said, matter-of-factly, "that you go home and get your affairs in order."

Eight months had passed since that nightmarish day. Bruce had dealt with having to tell his family and then his close friends. He had dealt with all the publicity surrounding his illness and had been interviewed more in a few months than in the past thirty years. He had done the interviews and accepted all that came with what he was dealing with, in part because it is not in his nature to say no to people, but also because he hoped he could raise awareness about the disease and, in doing so, help raise money for research — if not in time to save him, then perhaps to save others. He had done all this with a kind of grace and courage that had made him into a heroic figure to many, not a role Bruce wanted or felt he deserved. But he had accepted it as part of what he was going through.

The cheers for him, especially at the U.S. Open in June, had been both heartwarming and heartbreaking. "I loved what they were doing for me," he said. "I hated the reason they felt compelled to do it."

Watson had heard cheers throughout his career. They were almost second nature to him as an icon of the game. But never cheers like this, never cheers that brought him to tears. "As much as I was thrilled for Bruce that so many people cared," he said, "the cheering broke my heart. A lot of people have described the last few months as bittersweet for Bruce and me. I can honestly say it's a lot more bitter than sweet. A lot more."

Now, in September, in Gwyn and Lenny's backyard, surrounded by people who had loved him long before he got sick, Bruce was doing everything he could to make the weekend as sweet as possible. He sat and listened to all the old stories, cracking up when his father described going to pick Bruce up after his first day of kindergarten only to be told Bruce had been kept after school for misbehaving.

"How many kids get in trouble on their *first* day of kindergarten?" Jay Edwards asked, laughing now at the memory.

"I was framed," Bruce insisted.

"You were framed your entire life," his mother said.

"Damn right," he said.

Gwyn had arranged for a photographer to come in on Saturday

morning to take family photos. Patiently, they went through their paces: a group photo of all seventeen of them — not easy with the younger kids squirming to go back and play — then breakdown pictures of each couple, each couple with their kids, the grandparents with the grandchildren. Finally Jay and Natalie's four kids all together.

"They all turned out pretty damn well," Jay Edwards said softly as he saw Chris, Bruce, Brian, and Gwyn smiling for the camera.

The photographer worked swiftly and was back a few hours later with images that Lenny was able to bring up on the computer for everyone to look at so they could decide which ones they wanted printed. Lenny had even gone so far as to set up soft background music as the sixty images came up on the computer screen. The kids were busy playing, so the adults went inside to look. There they all were, wearing happy smiles, a handsome, successful family spending a gorgeous weekend with one another, enjoying every shared moment.

That was when Bruce lost it. Seeing the photos of all the people he loved so much was simply more than he could bear. He fought the tears for a while, leaned on Marsha to try to stop, and then gave up. He had to go outside and get away. Marsha followed, and he cried on her shoulder for several minutes to compose himself.

"I just couldn't stop thinking of the sadness I knew my dying was going to bring to all of them," he said later. "I'm not afraid to die, I'm really not. But I know my death is going to bring the people I care about the most a lot of pain. When I saw those pictures, everyone together, enjoying one another so much, enjoying *life* so much, it all caved in on me."

Naturally Bruce felt guilty about getting so emotional. Just as he had somehow felt guilty when he had to tell his parents about his illness. "I'm so sorry," he had said that night, "to have to tell you this."

Of course guilt was the last thing he should have felt. What he should have felt was pride, because that was what his family members felt when they thought about him. They were proud of what he had accomplished, proud of the man he had become, and proud that he had always done it on his own terms. More than anything, they had been proud — and amazed — by his ability to keep his sense of humor and his upbeat approach to every day, even at a time when so much of the future looked so terribly bleak.

"When I first heard, I felt compelled to sit down and write him," Gwyn said. "I knew if I got on the phone with him and tried to tell him how I felt, I'd just lose it and that would make things worse. So I sent him an e-mail, telling him how much I loved him and reminding him that we were all here for him anytime, any way he needed us. I signed the note, 'love and prayers.' When he wrote me back, he signed his note, 'love, prayers . . . and the Eagles.' It made me laugh and it made me cry, because it was just so Bruce."

If nothing else, Bruce would never stop being Bruce.

2

The Black Sheep

THE WAY JAY EDWARDS likes to tell it, it began in "crown and bridges," which may sound like the name of an English pub but was actually a dental class he was taking at the University of Pennsylvania. He was only twenty, but he was already a third-year dental student, having enrolled at Penn at the age of sixteen as part of a six-year dental program — two years of undergraduate work followed by four years of dental school.

It surprised no one that Jay Edwards would go to dental school. His father, Jonas Edwards, was a smalltown dentist, practicing in Riverside, a mill town in the New Jersey suburbs of Philadelphia. The family lived one town over in Delanco, which sits on the Delaware River about thirteen miles north of Philadelphia. Jay was his parents' third and last child, but their only son. His grandfather had been a physician, his father a dentist, so it only made sense that he follow in their footsteps in some way. "I grew up being very organized and very careful. It just seemed to be the right way to do things," he said. "I've always described myself as a belt-and-suspenders guy."

Belt and suspenders in hand, he went off to Penn shortly after the end of World War II, having been skipped ahead twice in grade school, and found himself in classes with men many years older than he was. "Guys back from the war going to school on the GI Bill," he said. "In fact my third year in dental school, I was still the youngest person in the entire school."

It was in that third year that he met Natalie Oberhaus, an aspiring dental hygienist, who was also a Penn undergrad. The hygienists were assigned to different dental classes to work with the future dentists, and Natalie walked into Jay's crown and bridges class one day and left him feeling as light-headed as if he had been given laughing gas. "Love at first sight," he said. "She was assigned to help me with something. I took one look at her and said, 'This is it.'"

"He was very definitely the aggressor," his wife said with a smile more than fifty years later.

Aggressiveness led to dating, which led to engagement, which led to marriage in December of 1951, soon after Jay had graduated with his dental degree. The following summer, Jay, who was now in the Army dental corps, was sent to Great Britain. By then, Natalie was pregnant with their first child, Chris, who arrived in January. Six weeks later, Natalie and the baby flew over to the United Kingdom so Chris could meet her father. "She was a colicky baby," Natalie Edwards remembered. "By the time I got over there, I was completely worn out. The first night after we got there I said to Jay, 'She's all yours, I'm going to bed.' Jay made it about halfway through the night before he fired a cigarette lighter against a wall in frustration because Chris simply wouldn't stop crying. "I said, 'There has got to be more to life than this!'" he remembered.

Chris got over the colic and quickly became a model child: smart, well behaved, neat, always on time, great grades, adored by all her classmates in school. If you were to order a kid from a mail-order catalog, you would have ordered Chris. "She was always the perfect kid," said Gwyn, a description that makes Chris cringe.

"I wasn't close to perfect," she said. "But I guess I was a fairly typical first kid. I followed rules. I listened to what I was told. To this day if there's a sign somewhere that says don't walk on the beach, my instinct is to not walk on the beach. My husband will walk right past the sign, and I'll be standing there saying, 'John, the sign says you aren't supposed to walk there.' "

Soon after Jay finished his two-year Army stint, he and Natalie and their daughter settled in Wethersfield, Connecticut, a rapidly growing suburb a few miles south of Hartford. Jonas Edwards would have liked to see his son join his practice, but Jay didn't want to work in a mill town in New Jersey and Natalie had grown up in Farmington, about ten miles from Wethersfield. He decided to set up practice in Wethersfield.

"We liked the town, it seemed like a good place to raise kids," he said. "We were able to find a house that was perfect to build an office onto. I always had my office right there in the house. It ended up working out very well."

The only drawback to having Dad's office at home, according to the kids, was when he had a cancellation. "He'd walk over and say, 'My four o'clock canceled, let's take care of that molar,' " Chris remembered. "If we saw him coming over during the day, we all scrambled for cover."

By the time Jay and Natalie were settled in Wethersfield, Chris was two and Natalie was pregnant with child number two. He arrived on November 16, 1954, with a shock of brown hair and a quick, easy smile that was a part of his personality almost from the day he was born. They named him Bruce Jay Edwards and were extremely relieved when he wasn't the least bit colicky. "I'm not sure either of us could have lived through that again," Jay said with a laugh.

It wasn't long after he began walking and talking that Bruce began to provide his parents with an entirely different kind of challenge. They had more or less expected their son to be a male version of Chris. "We got spoiled by Chris," Natalie said. "She was just about as easy a kid to raise as you could ever hope to have. So we got fooled. When Bruce wasn't the same way, instead of seeing him as different, I think we probably thought something was wrong."

Bruce was independent, always in some kind of trouble in school, anything but a model student, and rebellious. Everyone in the family remembers Jay and Natalie telling Bruce he had to come inside in the evening as soon as the streetlights came on. Then they would walk outside and find Bruce firing rocks at the streetlights to knock them out of commission. "If they didn't come on," he said, "I didn't have to come in. I'd usually miss with the first three or four, but sooner or later, I'd get them."

With the benefit of twenty-twenty hindsight and medical knowledge that didn't exist in the 1950s, Jay and Natalie are convinced now that their first son had attention deficit disorder (ADD). In those days ADD was unknown, and smart kids like Bruce who couldn't concentrate in school were often accused of not trying hard enough and of failing to live up to their potential. That's what made it tough for Jay and Natalie. They knew Bruce was smart, he simply refused — or so they thought — to apply himself.

"Of course knowing what we know now, we would have handled things entirely differently," Jay said, shaking his head. "We always thought Bruce was testing us, that he was simply being stubborn. I'm convinced now it wasn't nearly that simple."

Brian was born three years after Bruce, in September of 1957, and Gwyn came along in 1962. By then the family hierarchy was pretty much set: Chris was the good child; Bruce was the bad child. Brian and Gwyn became observers of the family dynamic as they grew up. "We probably shortchanged both Brian and Gwyn growing up because we were so focused on Bruce," Jay said. "Almost everything that happened in the family seemed to center on Bruce and his behavior. Whenever we traveled, we gave him a pill that was supposed to help him sleep. Sometimes it worked, sometimes it didn't. But it was always the same: If he slept, the others slept; if he was awake, they all stayed awake."

It is not at all unusual in today's world for a family with an ADD child to be ruled by the whims and moods of that child. Many ADD kids today take medication to modify their behavior and to help them concentrate in school. When Bruce was growing up, there was no diagnosis, no medication, and no relief for anyone in the family. "I think I challenged them and tested them almost every day," Bruce said. "It was never easy."

It certainly wasn't easy on Bruce, who was keenly aware of what his family perceived as his shortcomings. He was sent to different child psychologists, which angered and frustrated him. Brian remembers Bruce coming home from one psychologist's where he had run into one of his classmates. "That kid is crazy," he told Brian. "I'm not perfect, but I'm *not* crazy."

Chris and Bruce may have had different personalities, but they were similar physically: slender, dark-haired, with easy smiles, and good at any sport that involved speed. Brian and Gwyn were both stockier, Brian with sandy hair and Gwyn with the same brown hair as Chris and Bruce but swimmer's shoulders. In fact she swam in high school and briefly in college at Lafayette. When she stopped swimming, she played women's rugby briefly. "I played until we went up to play Rutgers," she said. "I was a pretty big kid, five seven, a hundred and forty pounds, but these women were *huge*. I was the biggest girl on our team, and I was smaller than anyone playing for them. They were mean too. They just beat us to a pulp. That, and knee surgery, ended my rugby career."

Brian was always a runner. He ran cross-country in both high school and college and still runs today. He has run in several Boston Marathons, with a best time of 3:07. "Brian likes to do anything that's hard," Bruce said. "Marathons, white-water rafting. If it isn't hard or dangerous, he isn't interested in it."

Bruce and Brian were roommates briefly as kids before Brian decided to turn the family's sunroom into his room. Gwyn, always the observer, didn't think Brian moved out of the room because he needed more space but because he wanted to get away from the crossfire between Bruce and their parents.

In spite of Bruce's frustrations with his parents and theirs with him, the family remained close-knit as the kids grew up. Gwyn, eight years younger than Bruce, adored him because to her, "he was always so cool." Jay and Natalie had a strict rule on school nights that all four children had to spend the hours between seven o'clock and nine o'clock in their rooms, either working on homework or, if they finished their homework, reading a book. There was absolutely no way Bruce was going to spend two hours in his room studying or reading. Most nights he would climb out his window, onto a balcony that he shared with Gwyn, wave goodbye to her, climb down the balcony, and come back just before nine. He would smoke a final cigarette on the balcony, flip the butt away, and climb back inside just before quiet time, as it was called, came to an end.

His study habits had to catch up with him sooner or later, and when they did, it created more tension. Chris was reeling off A's in high school, en route to Bucknell, where she would major in French and international relations. Brian and Gwyn were both good students who rarely got into any kind of serious trouble. Bruce was always the one with the bad report cards and the calls coming home from teachers about his behavior.

"Looking back, I think following Chris was going to be tough for Bruce under any circumstances," Gwyn said. "My parents saw her as the norm, as what you would expect in a child. In her own way, she was just as abnormal as Bruce, because she was *so* perfect. If Bruce had been an average student, an average kid, my parents probably would have thought something had gone wrong. But when he was completely the opposite, they were convinced that something was terribly, terribly wrong. There was really nothing seriously wrong with Bruce, he was just *different* from Chris."

When Bruce got to high school, Jay and Natalie decided a change of scenery might help him. They sent him to a prep school called Watkinson for a year, and things did not improve. Bruce's grades were no better, he didn't like the school, and the school didn't like him. "Watkinson didn't work for Bruce," his father recalled. "So we decided to try Marianapolis."

Marianapolis was a small Catholic boarding school in Thompson, Connecticut, near the Massachusetts border. Perhaps because it was so small — there were thirty-nine boys in Bruce's graduating class — Bruce did better there. The teachers were able to give him more attention. His grades improved and so did his behavior. He even took the SAT's and got 1,130, a solid score that would have gotten him into plenty of colleges.

But the thought of going to college never crossed Bruce's mind — except when his parents brought it up. To Jay and Natalie, college was an automatic, no different than going to first grade. It was simply something that you did. Bruce didn't see it that way. For one thing, he couldn't think of a single thing he wanted to study in college or a career that would follow college. "There was a bus stop right across the street from where we lived," he said. "Every morning when I was a kid, I would watch all the men from our neighborhood walk over to the bus with their briefcases to take the bus into Hartford to go to their offices. Most of them were in insurance, but there were some lawyers, probably a couple of doctors. I remember thinking back then there was no way that was going to be my life, getting up every day and going to an office from nine to five. I knew that wasn't for me. I just would have felt cooped up doing something like that."

Back then, watching the men line up for the bus, Bruce had no idea what he might do as an alternative. By the time he was in high school, that had changed. Golf had come into his life. More specifically, caddying had come into his life.

Growing up in New Jersey, Jay Edwards hadn't played much golf. His father played golf, but Jay was a lot more interested in baseball. Often when Jonas Edwards would go over to Riverton Country Club to hit golf balls, Jay and his dog would tag along. "He would hit flies to me in between golf shots," Jay remembered. "I thought that was a lot more fun than playing golf." He began to play a little bit while in college and then, after starting his dental practice, began playing with friends on the public courses in the Wethersfield area. By the time the kids were born, he and Natalie were both playing a lot of golf and they were looking for a place where the kids could spend time in the summer. So they decided to join Wethersfield Country Club.

Wethersfield wasn't a rich man's club by any means, but it was a comfortable place with a very good golf course, one good enough to host a PGA Tour event. The Insurance City Open had been launched in 1952 at Wethersfield and, under different names it would stay at Wethersfield until 1983. When the Edwards family joined the club in the mid-1960s, it had become the Greater Hartford Open. Soon after the family joined the club, Bruce began to caddy there during the summer. He played golf too, but right from the start it was caddying that he enjoyed the most.

"Part of it was the money," he said. "When I first started, you could carry double at four dollars a bag. Throw in a dollar tip for each bag and you made ten dollars a round. Some days, if there were enough people there, I'd go thirty-six. That added up to pretty good money for a thirteen-year-old kid. Plus I met a lot of guys that I really liked, other caddies. Most of them weren't the kids of club members, and I felt very comfortable around them right from the start. Maybe if I'd been bitten by the playing bug it would have been different, but I never was."

Jay Edwards thinks both his sons — Brian followed Bruce into the caddy program — might have been more interested in playing if Wethersfield's pro had encouraged juniors more. But he didn't, and both Edwards boys ended up spending most of their summers as caddies.

"What really made it fun, though, was knowing that there was that huge bonus waiting for you at the end of the summer if you did a good job," Bruce said. "That was what we all really pointed for, because it was such a cool thing."

"That bonus" was the Greater Hartford Open. In the 1960s, there were only a handful of full-time tour caddies. Most clubs that hosted tour events didn't allow them to work anyway, especially the summer tournaments, where one of the allures of the caddy program was the chance to work in a tour event. The GHO was always held in those days on Labor Day weekend. That's what made it the end-of-the-summer bonus for the Edwards brothers and the other Wethersfield caddies.

Bruce's first GHO was in 1967, a few months prior to his thirteenth birthday. He was assigned the bag of Dick Lotz, a solid pro who would go on to win three times on tour. "I was only in my third year on the tour, and I couldn't afford a full-time caddy," Lotz remembered. "So at most of the clubs I would go to the caddymaster and ask for a local caddy, preferably someone who played golf. At Hartford, the caddymaster told me he would find me someone and I went out to practice. When I came back, he said, 'I've got someone for you,' and brought this very slight youngster out to me. I looked at him and said, 'Young man, I don't think you're any bigger than my bag.' He looked at me and said, 'Don't worry, sir, I can do the job.' I told him we'd try it in the practice round the next day and see how he did. Well, a few holes in I knew I had someone special."

What Lotz remembers most is Bruce's passion for the job. "He knew exactly what he was doing and what was expected of a caddy," he said. "Clearly he loved doing it. And he was such a nice kid. I met his family during the week and we really struck up a friendship. They were good people."

Lotz played well during the week, finishing in a tie for twelfth place. That earned him a check of $1,200. From that he generously paid his caddy 5 percent — the going rate at the time was 3 percent. Bruce took the $60 check, had it framed, and put it on the wall in his room.

From that weekend forward, there was no doubt in his mind about what he wanted to do when he finished high school. He had no interest in college, no interest in any kind of "profession," as his parents would call it — not law, not medicine, not insurance, not even dentistry. "I wanted to caddy on the PGA Tour full-time," he said. "I knew it the first time I stepped inside the ropes. I just loved the way it felt. I loved being a part of the action, of knowing what was really going on and being a part of what was going on. I wasn't nervous doing it, I was having fun."

He also had a natural affinity for the job. Even though he hadn't played that much golf, he had a natural feel for the game. He was always good at reading greens, even though in those years players rarely asked a caddy to read greens. Caddying was completely different in the 1960s from the way it is now. "Basically your job was to carry the bag," Bruce said. "Carry the bag, maybe be encouraging at the right time, have a sense of humor. And never be late. If you could do those things, you could caddy."

Bruce could do those things. When Lotz returned to Hartford a year later, he requested that Bruce caddy for him. He continued to do so whenever he came to Hartford. By then Brian was caddying too. He also enjoyed it — especially the money — but he wasn't as passionate about it as Bruce. Jay and Natalie were thrilled to see that Bruce had found a niche, something he enjoyed, something that carried some responsibility, that kept him out of trouble.

"We always knew where he was during the summer," Jay Edwards said. "There were a lot worse places he could have been instead of Wethersfield working as a caddy. We were delighted with it."

Two of Bruce's closest friends in those days were Gary Crandall and Bill Leahey. Crandall's family also had a membership at Wethersfield, and he lived, by his description, "a half a block and a field I could cut through" away from the club. Leahey's parents weren't members, and he played most of his golf at Goodwin Park, a public course that wasn't far from Wethersfield. But he also spent a lot of time at Wethersfield, which was about two miles from his house, working as a caddy. The three boys had met earlier, competing with and against one another as athletes in grammar school and junior high, and they enjoyed spending time together. All three had played soccer — Wethersfield was one of the first communities in the country to seriously embrace youth soccer in the '60s — and Bruce and Bill had played Little League baseball against each other.

"Bruce was always a good athlete," Leahey remembered. "Very fast. Soccer might have been his best sport. I think one of his big disappointments when his parents sent him to prep school was that he didn't get to play soccer at Wethersfield, which was one of the real high school powerhouses in the state at the time."

Crandall and Bruce were teammates briefly on the Wethersfield High School golf team before Bruce went to boarding school. They also conspired to run away together one year. Crandall is only four months older than Bruce, but he was a year ahead of him in school.

During his senior year, he was confused about what direction his life might be going in when he graduated and upset about the divorce his parents were going through. Bruce didn't have any parental marital problems to deal with, but he was locked in a constant battle with his parents about his grades, his behavior, and his future. So the two of them decided to escape — specifically, escape to Orlando.

"I had saved a fair bit of money from caddying, so I bankrolled the deal," Crandall remembered. "We bought a couple of plane tickets to get down there. I had no idea what I was going to do, but Bruce had decided he was going to work at Disney World."

They left early one morning, Gary showing up at the house to meet Bruce at 5:30 a.m. The only hitch was when Jay caught Bruce climbing out the window and demanded to know what the hell was going on. "I think I told him we were going to play some golf at sunrise, something like that," Bruce said. "I'm sure he didn't buy it, but I know he didn't think we were running away."

They made it to Orlando, and Bruce went to apply for a job at Disney World. He filled out all the application forms and was told there were jobs available, but if he wanted to work for Disney, he would have to cut his shoulder-length brown hair to conform to the neat, trim Disney look. Right there the Disney dream ended for Bruce.

They slept in the airport the first couple of nights, the better to save Crandall's money. "In the morning a security guard would come around at six a.m., wake us up, and tell us we had to leave because people were going to start showing up for flights," Bruce remembered. "But he let us stay there until then."

They soon came up with a Plan B. The PGA Tour was in Greensboro, North Carolina, that week. They would use the last of Crandall's money on tickets to fly there, then round up a couple of bags for the week. They arrived in Greensboro on Monday, and by Tuesday they had secured bags for the two pro-ams. But neither of them was able to find a bag for the tournament. After one night sleeping in the grandstands near the 18th green — "very uncomfortable," Crandall remembered — they spent two nights in an $8-a-night motel. With almost no money left and no work on the horizon, they decided this wasn't working out and went home.

Crandall had missed a week of school and almost didn't graduate. Jay and Natalie were so relieved when Bruce came home safely that he escaped serious punishment. "It was actually one of our better talks," he remembered. "They told me why they were so frightened and why it was wrong, and I for once realized they were right." After that trip, Bruce forgot about working at Disney World. But caddying remained an important part of his life.

Bruce and some of the other caddies even started showing up at Westchester and Pleasant Valley, summer events just a couple of hours away, looking for bags. One year Lotz's caddy left his clubs sitting outside the clubhouse after the first round at Westchester and they were stolen. Jay and Bruce had driven down to watch Lotz play, and Lotz told Bruce that if his caddy didn't recover the clubs by the next morning, he was going to fire him. Would Bruce be willing to drive back down and work? Absolutely. Bruce made Jay get out of bed at 5:30 a.m. so he could drive him to Westchester in time for Lotz's tee time. The clubs hadn't shown up. Lotz borrowed an extra set from Dale Douglass and handed the bag to Bruce.

Caddying, especially in the GHO, became Bruce's raison d'être. In the 1973 Marianapolis yearbook there was a question next to the photo of each graduating senior: "What makes you happiest?" Bruce's answer: "Caddying on the PGA Tour."

Even though they could see how much Bruce loved to caddy, Jay and Natalie had never once thought it was something he would consider doing as anything more than a summer job. They knew he wasn't the best student in the world, but his grades as a senior and his SAT's were certainly good enough to get him into a number of colleges. Problem was, Bruce never bothered applying anyplace, because he had already made his postgraduation plans: As soon as he finished school he was planning to head out to the PGA Tour. He was already trying to convince Crandall and Leahey to go along with him. Crandall was a year out of school and working at a job he hated in a drugstore, but he wasn't certain the caddying life was the way to go. Leahey, who was two years ahead of Bruce in school, had already finished his first two years at Upsala College, in New Jersey. The idea of spending the summer traveling the country appealed to him. He told Bruce that as soon as he was finished with spring semester — Upsala had classes until late in June — he would meet him on tour. In the meantime, Bruce would start off on his own. It didn't daunt him in the least.

Needless to say, when Bruce came home on a visit from school and announced this plan, it was not greeted enthusiastically. Jay and Natalie didn't blow up and scream and yell and tell him the plan was unacceptable. "For one thing," Jay said, "if we had, we would have lost him. I wasn't happy, but it was a fight we weren't going to win. I told him, though, that I wasn't going to make it easy for him, that I didn't want him calling me from the road for money. If he wanted to do this, okay, but he was going to be on his own."

"We thought if he did it for a year, he would get it out of his system," Natalie said. "Once it was a job and he had to work at it week after week, it wouldn't seem quite so glamorous. He would come home and go to college after a year and that would be that."

To some degree that was also the way Bruce was thinking. Even though he had battled his parents — particularly his father — throughout his boyhood, he was still very much their son. Jay Edwards, with his Philadelphia roots, had always been a fan of all Philadelphia teams — "Hell, I still root for the Athletics because they're originally from Philly," he said — and was especially passionate about the Phillies and Eagles. To this day, Bruce is passionate about the Phillies and Eagles, far more so than any of his siblings. Brian grew up rooting for the New York Mets and the Green Bay Packers ("He's a front-runner," Bruce likes to point out. "They were both at the top when we were kids."), but Bruce adopted his father's teams and took on his passion for them.

And being Jay and Natalie's son, there was part of him that figured college *was* what you did after high school. He had been the only member of the thirty-nine-man Marianapolis class of '73 who had not applied to college and was not going to college. When he presented his plan to his parents he told them it was just for a year. He wanted to travel, see places he had never seen, have some fun as an eighteen-year-old away from home for the first time (without his boarding school jacket and tie), and learn more about the golf tour, a place that fascinated him. Jay and Natalie knew they had no choice. They would suck it up for a year and wait for him to come home, go to college, and find a real job.

One person who did try to talk Bruce out of pursuing caddying was the person most convinced he would be an excellent caddy: Dick Lotz. "It had nothing to do with him and everything to do with the lifestyle," he said. "There just wasn't very much money to be made out there at the time unless you got very lucky. Most guys were like me, they couldn't afford to pay that much. I knew Jay and Natalie wanted him to go to college, and I thought it was the right thing to do too. But he was absolutely determined and asked me if I would help him. When I realized he was going out there one way or the other, I told him I would."

The day after he graduated from high school, Bruce bought a plane ticket and headed for Charlotte, North Carolina. Lotz had a full-time caddy by then, but he had put Bruce in touch with David Graham, a twenty-seven-year-old Australian who had already won once on tour and was looking for someone to work for him at the Kemper Open in Charlotte. On Lotz's say-so, Graham hired Bruce for the week. His pay would be the standard pay for a tour caddy at the time: $15 a day plus 3 percent of any money Graham earned for the week.

"It was a good news, bad news week," Bruce remembered. "I really liked the work and I really liked David. That was the good news. The bad news was he made a late bogey on Friday and missed the cut by one."

So much for the 3 percent or working on the weekend. Graham wrote Bruce a check for $100 — $70 more than he owed him — handed it to him, and said, "Bruce, you're too nice a kid to be living this life. You should go home and go to college."

Bruce took the extra money but not the advice. Lotz had already lined up another bag for him the following week in Philadelphia with Bob Shaw, another Australian, although not a player with Graham's skills or pedigree. That didn't matter to Bruce. He was traveling and working and he had $100 in his pocket, more than enough to pay for a ticket to Philadelphia. When he arrived at Whitemarsh Valley Country Club and checked the Thursday-Friday pairings, his eyes went wide. Shaw was paired with none other than Jack Nicklaus. That was when he sent his first postcards home — to Crandall and Leahey.

"Paired with Nicklaus this week," he wrote. "Plenty of work out here. When are you coming?"

Leahey, who had just finished his sophomore year of college, was already making his plans to get out there. Crandall was impressed, maybe a tad jealous, but not quite ready to make the commitment. When Bruce called home that week to tell his parents he was okay and paired with Nicklaus, even Jay had to admit that was pretty cool.

Bruce still remembers the two days with Nicklaus. He remembers how deliberate he was and how competitive he was and how far he hit the ball. Nicklaus was at his zenith at the time. He had won the Masters and the U.S. Open the previous year en route to winning seven tournaments. That year, he had already won three times and would win the PGA Championship before summer's end. Being that close to the world's greatest golfer was an awe-inspiring experience. The only downer was that Shaw missed the cut. Like Graham, Shaw wrote Bruce a check for $100. Unlike Graham, he didn't tell Bruce to go home and go to college. Instead he told him to meet him in Milwaukee in three weeks, after the U.S. Open and the Western Open, both tournaments where tour caddies were not allowed.

Bruce could have gone home for a few days, seen his family, and taken things easy before heading to Milwaukee. But he didn't want his parents to think he was homesick, and he was afraid his father would reopen the whole college issue. So he went straight to Milwaukee and encountered his first welcome-to-the-road experience when he got off the bus. There was an older man standing in the waiting area when Bruce and his friend Tom Lovett arrived early on a Sunday morning.

"Look at you," the man said to Bruce. "You're so pretty you should be in Hollywood."

"I thought, 'Oh boy, here we go,'" Bruce said, years later.

The man was persistent. Where did they need to go? he asked. When Bruce told him the name of the motel where they were staying, he told them it was a good twenty miles away, a long, expensive cab ride or a tough hitchhike. He would give them a ride. Bruce and Lovett figured at worst it was two against one. They accepted the offer. When they got to the car, they found that their new friend had a friend of his own. Now it was two-on-two. Still, they were young, athletic, and, if necessary, fast.

"We get to the motel and we start to get out and the guy says, 'Why don't you come and go sailing with us on Lake Michigan?'" Bruce said. "I knew it was time to cut this cord, so I just said, 'Listen, thanks a lot for the ride, but this is it, we're leaving.' He never actually offered us money or anything, but it was pretty clear that's where it was going, so we got out of there. It was kinda scary, but it never got really bad. We probably should have just hitched. It wasn't as if we had anything to do that day."

Of course if Jay and Natalie had heard the story, they probably would have flown to Milwaukee to bring Bruce home that day. He did not include it in his report the next time he called home.

Bruce then made the second mistake of his caddying career. When he had parted company with Shaw in Philadelphia, Shaw had said something about calling him prior to Milwaukee. Bruce had assumed Shaw meant he should call if there was any problem, otherwise he would see him there. Shaw had meant the opposite: Call to confirm that you can work for me. "In those days he probably figured there was a chance a kid like me would just go home and not show up again," Bruce said. "But I got it confused and didn't call."

As a result, not having heard from Bruce, Shaw showed up on Tuesday with another caddy. Bruce was upset. Shaw, who felt bad, told him of another player, Ron Cerrudo, who was looking for a caddy. "That's what was so different in those days," Bruce said. "There were so few full-time caddies that you could almost always show up at a place and get a bag. Now, because there's so much more money to be made and there are so many more caddies, it's much, much harder."

This was 1973 — $15 a day and 3 percent of purses that averaged about $150,000 (total) per week, as opposed to 2003, when most full-time caddies work on an annual salary and get 5 percent when their player makes a cut, 7 percent when he top-tens, and 10 percent for a win. That's on a tour where the average weekly purse is now $4 million. Back then losing a bag was both common and hardly upsetting. Bruce found Cerrudo and worked for him that week. They missed the cut, making Bruce three-for-three. Cerrudo was as generous as Bruce's first two employers, paying him $100 and telling him he could work for him the following week when the tour went to Robinson, Illinois, for the Robinson Shriners' Classic.

He still hadn't caddied on a weekend, but Bruce was proud of the fact that all three players he had worked for had paid him far more than they had to and that two of them had asked him to work again. He was having fun and Leahey had now joined him, having worked in Milwaukee for a local pro who had missed the cut. The two of them headed for Robinson, Bruce with a bag for the week, Bill without one.

Three weeks and $300 into his caddying career, Bruce figured he was doing okay.

3

"We'll Try It for a Week"

WHEN ONE LOOKS AT THE PGA Tour and what it has evolved into today, it is sometimes hard to imagine what it was like only thirty years ago. Purses were one-thirtieth of what they are now week in and week out. Most players traveled from event to event by car, flying only when the drive would take more than a day and buying the cheapest airline ticket available whenever that occurred. Caddies also drove, often driving a player's car when he chose to fly. If the trip took more than a day, sleeping was usually done by taking turns in the car or pulling over to a rest stop and finding a comfortable patch of grass to curl up on.

The tour back then played a lot of small and midsized towns, more often than not avoiding the big cities because there was too much competition from the mainstream sports there. Towns like Greensboro, North Carolina; Jacksonville and Tallahassee, Florida; Columbus, Georgia; and Hartford were as likely to host tour events as New York, Chicago, and Los Angeles, more likely to host them than places like Atlanta, Washington, and San Francisco, to name three major cities that didn't have tour stops. Robinson, in southern Illinois, was one of the smaller towns on the circuit, the home of the annual Robinson Shriners' Classic, which tells you who put the tournament on. In those days there were almost no corporate title sponsors and only a handful of tournaments were seen on live TV.

Robinson followed Milwaukee on the calendar in 1973, the tour taking a midsummer swing through the Midwest, with St. Louis on the schedule after Robinson. Bruce Edwards and Bill Leahey, having both missed the cut in Milwaukee, headed down the road to Robinson and began looking for a place to stay. In most towns on tour, caddies would usually split a room four ways, breaking down the beds in a double room so that two guys could split a mattress and a box spring between them.

"We never went into a place if the room cost more than twelve dollars a night," Bruce remembered. "We'd get into a room and the first thing we'd say was, 'Break 'em down,' and we'd take the beds apart. Sometimes when we were in a big city where the room might cost more, we'd have six guys in a room."

Some of the smaller towns on the circuit offered the caddies housing with local families. It was common in those days for players to stay with families, because few of them were wealthy enough to afford a luxurious hotel room for an entire week. It wasn't that difficult to find families willing to put up a golf pro, but in most places people didn't exactly line up to house caddies.

"Caddying was a relatively new profession at the time," Bruce said. "Most people thought of caddies as drunks or people who were down and out or people you couldn't trust or long-haired kids like me who you probably didn't want hanging around your house for a week."

There hadn't really been caddies on the PGA Tour before the 1960s. The first group of professional caddies to work on tour came from Augusta, caddies who got to know the pros during the Masters and then made their way to tour stops to find work once Augusta National Golf Club closed for the summer each May. Some players brought friends on tour with them on occasion, but for the most part, players used caddies from the clubs — like Bruce and his friends at Wethersfield. When a small cadre of full-time caddies began to work the tour — notably Angelo Argea, who worked for

Jack Nicklaus, and Creamy Carolan, who worked for Arnold Palmer — many clubs wouldn't allow them to work at their events.

"One year at Wethersfield Nicklaus was coming to play and wanted to bring Angelo," Bill Leahey remembered. "We didn't want to set the precedent of letting the tour caddies work, so we 'protested' against the tour caddies. Nicklaus finally agreed to use one of our guys. Little did we know we'd be on the other end of that argument a few years later."

By the time Bruce and Leahey headed for the tour, there were about forty full-time caddies, which meant there was a bag for everyone every week. Most of the full-time caddies at the time were black, some of them from Augusta, others friends of the Augusta caddies who had gotten involved because they heard it was a decent way to make money. The base pay wasn't much — $15 a day and 3 percent of prize money — but the potential to make serious money was there if you could hook on with the right guy. Even though a win only paid 5 percent (it is 10 percent today), first prize most weeks was $30,000, and 5 percent of that sounded like a fortune. Bruce and Leahey arrived as part of the first wave of younger, white caddies who came out on tour, although they came with different agendas. Leahey was there because he was looking for something to do during the summertime and because his buddy Bruce said it would be fun. Bruce was mentally committed to spending a year on tour. At least.

"I knew two things when I first went out," he said. "I didn't want to go to college and I did want to travel. This was a way to travel, try to make some money, and get that rush I had felt caddying in tournaments when I was still a kid. I told people it was for a year, and in my mind that's what it was. But it wasn't as if I had done any planning beyond that."

Robinson was one of those rare tour stops that offered the caddies free housing with a family. When Bruce and Bill arrived in town, they were directed to the home of Kenneth and Donna Freed. They were not the only caddies sent to the Freed house. In fact a total of nineteen caddies spent the week at the Freeds', most of them sharing space in the basement, which was just fine with them, because the cots they slept on were, for the most part, more comfortable than the beds they broke down in motels and the price was right. The local paper ran a story that week on the Freeds and included photos of the nineteen caddies. It was Bruce's first brush with publicity.

One of the caddies bunking at the Freeds' that week was a college kid from Philadelphia named Neil Oxman. Like Leahey, Oxman was on summer break, having just finished his junior year at Villanova. Like the Wethersfield guys, he had caddied as a kid and had met some good amateur players who had invited him to work for them at top-drawer amateur events around the state. He had enjoyed the experience and the previous year had spent the summer on the circuit after a pro named Jimmy Hardy had offered him the chance to work for him at the Cleveland Open. Hardy had played a local event in Philadelphia, Oxman worked for him, and the two hit it off.

Much like Bruce, Oxman found the air inside the ropes intoxicating. "I tell friends of mine today that if you are a sports fan and you ever caddy at a PGA Tour event it will change your life forever," Oxman said. "There is absolutely no other way to be that close to a sport without actually playing it. You can't go on the field at a baseball game. You can't chat with Mike Schmidt" — Oxman is a Philly guy, so when he thinks baseball he first thinks of Schmidt — "just before he goes up to hit and ask him what kind of pitch he's looking for. When you caddy you are on the field. You are part of the rules of the game, in fact. Which means you can screw up quite easily. But it is an amazing feeling to be there."

Oxman is now fifty, a wildly successful Democratic political consultant in Philadelphia with a staff of twenty-five. He still finds caddying intoxicating and sneaks out onto the Senior Tour three or four times a year to caddy for old friends. In 1973 he had just been elected president of the senior class at Villanova and was planning on going to law school and then to follow his passion for politics. He had first worked in politics at the age of fourteen, when he stuffed envelopes at Bobby Kennedy's campaign headquarters in

Philadelphia. He had grown up in the southwest portion of the city, and politics had been his first passion. His parents were both immigrants, his father from Russia, his mother from Poland, and the family — Oxman has a younger brother — often sat around the dinner table intensely discussing the political issues of the day. "I remember it was a great thrill, when I was first old enough to drive, to take the family car on Saturday night, drive down to Thirtieth Street Station, and pick up the bulldog [early] edition of the Sunday *New York Times* and read it cover to cover before I went to bed," he said.

When Oxman was seventeen his father died of cancer, leaving a hole in his heart and in his life. He filled the life part of the hole by being a campus activist when he got to college, by helping his mother take care of his brother, and by spending his free time caddying. He was an old tour hand, working for a pro named Mike Reasor, when he and Leahey first met in Milwaukee. He was outgoing and friendly and quickly hit it off with Bruce and Leahey, especially that week in Robinson, when they spent a lot of time together at the Freeds' house. "It isn't like there are a lot of places to go out and party in Robinson, Illinois," Oxman remembered.

It was Leahey who caught the first real break of the summer. Standing outside the clubhouse on Monday, he saw Lou Graham approaching, bag on his shoulder. Leahey recognized Graham because at the time, Graham was part of the Select 60. The current tour rules, which make the top 125 players and tournament winners from the previous two years fully exempt — meaning they can enter any tournament they want — didn't go into effect until 1982. Prior to that only the top 60 players on the money list (and tournament winners) had exempt status. Everyone else had to play in Monday qualifiers to get into that week's field. Players outside the top 60 were known as "rabbits," because they were constantly hopping from place to place trying to get into tournaments. If a rabbit made the cut in a given week, he was automatically in the field the following week.

The bag of a top-60 player such as Graham was a major get for a caddy. Leahey knew that and was fairly certain Graham had a caddy. But seeing Graham carrying his bag, he figured he had nothing to lose by asking. As luck would have it, Graham's caddy had just quit to take a job in California as an assistant pro and Graham *was* looking for a caddy. Leahey asked, Graham said fine, and Leahey suddenly found himself hooked up with a top player. "Second week out and I luck into that," he said. "I was thrilled."

Bruce already had a bag for the week — Ron Cerrudo. Cerrudo wasn't a top-60 player and he had missed the cut the previous week, but he had been given a sponsor's exemption, one of several spots typically allocated to a tournament director to use as he pleased. Cerrudo was a young player with potential, and the Shriners were pleased to have him in their field.

Nowadays caddying is quite sophisticated. When a caddy arrives at a tournament site today, the first thing he does is buy an orange yardage book that is put together by a man named Gorgeous George Lucas. Lucas travels the country in advance of the tour, checking yardages from almost every conceivable spot on a golf course, looking for hidden hazards while using lasers to get his distances exactly right. He also includes funny comments and asides. When he points out a hazard that is way off line or gives the yardage from a far-flung spot on the golf course, he will often include the notation ICYFU: In Case You Fuck Up. The book costs $15 and tells the caddy almost everything he could possibly need to know about the golf course. Most caddies will double-check distances during practice rounds and will make note of all the pin placements in their yardage books, then pull the book out the following year so they'll have an idea where they think the pins might go.

It wasn't like that in 1973. There were no yardage books, and most of the time the players paced off their own yardages. (Many still do today, at least double-checking at key moments.) Caddies would arrive at the golf course early each morning to walk the course and learn where the pins were and would mark their location on the greens on their scorecards so they could tell the players where the holes were as the round proceeded. Bruce tried to leave nothing to chance, walking the course by himself — or with Leahey or another caddy — early in the week to check yardage markers (usually on sprinkler heads) to make sure they were accurate and to look for hidden hazards. He was one of the first caddies to do what is now standard procedure for caddies — walking the golf course without player or bag early in the week.

"The only problem was, I had to make all my notes on the score-card so everything was in one place when we played," he said. "Sometimes it was hard to read my own writing because I had so much stuff written down."

The other problem was the rather arcane rule which said that cad-dies could not actually walk on the greens. The rule existed in part to keep greens pristine for play, but also because walking on the greens was, in a sense, testing them — for firmness, for break around the flagstick — almost as if the caddy were out practicing on behalf of his player. "We would have one guy walk on the green to check around the pin for ridges or slopes you couldn't see," Bruce said. "Everyone else would fan out and keep an eye out for a rules official. If you saw a cart coming, you would scream, 'Rules!' and the guy would run off the green. We weren't trying to cheat, we just wanted to know what was around the hole, and you couldn't see it from the fringe."

Once, out walking by himself, Bruce got caught. The rules official put him in a cart, drove him from the seventh green back to the first tee, lectured him there on not walking on greens, and then made him walk back to where he had initially been found. "That was my punishment for being a bad boy," Bruce said.

His not always legible scorecard scribbling became a problem for the first time on Friday at the Robinson. Cerrudo was lingering around the cut line when he got to the 17th hole. This was before electronic scoreboards, so most players made educated guesses at what the cut would be. "You always knew it to within a stroke, two at most," Bruce said. "We were right on it."

As Bruce remembers it, Cerrudo hit his tee shot in the fairway and had 140 yards to the front of the green, which was elevated just enough to make it impossible to actually see exactly where the pin was located. Looking at the scribblings on his scorecard, Bruce thought he had written down that the pin was in the back of the green, 22 paces (or yards) from the front. So he told Cerrudo the total yardage was 162 yards. Cerrudo nodded, took out a six-iron, and "he hit it exactly 162 yards," Bruce said. "Perfect shot."

Perfect shot if the pin had been 22 paces from the front. As it turned out, the pin was 12 paces from the front — a difference of 30 feet. Instead of a short birdie putt, Cerrudo found himself putting from 35 feet — downhill. "I was sick to my stomach when I saw it," Bruce said. "There was nothing I could say to him except that I had misread my notes." It didn't help that Cerrudo three-putted for bogey. It helped even less when he ended up missing the cut by one shot.

"The amazing thing is he didn't fire me," Bruce said. "It was certainly a firing offense. But he didn't. He just said, 'I'll see you Monday in St. Louis.'"

Having missed the cut in Robinson and without an exemption the next week, Cerrudo would have to play in the Monday qualifier. Bruce told him he would be there. He and Leahey made it to St. Louis late Sunday night and Bruce went to the golf course where the qualifier was being held first thing the next morning, since he didn't know what time Cerrudo would be teeing off. He went straight to the locker room to check the tee times and couldn't find Cerrudo's name. He double-checked the list, then went into the pro shop to see if there had been a mistake. No mistake, he was told, Cerrudo had called over the weekend and withdrawn. It was only later, when he saw Cerrudo again, that he found out that Cerrudo had called to ask how many golfers would make it from the qualifier into the St. Louis field. When he was told there were only six spots available, he decided to take the week off. But he didn't have any kind of contact number for Bruce — imagine *that* happening today — so there was no way to let him know he was withdrawing.

Disappointed, Bruce hunted around and found a bag that day with a local pro who failed to make it into the field. He went to bed that night a bit unnerved. For the first time in his five-week career as a caddy, he was starting a week without a bag. He decided to head for the tournament site, the Norwood Hills Country Club, next morning and hope he could find a job. "I wasn't that nervous about it," he said. "I figured I would find someone. But even though I hadn't made a cut yet, the guys I had worked with had all been legitimate players, guys who were all on tour. I really didn't want to spend the week working for someone who had no chance to make the cut. But I figured I would just show up and see what happened."

July in St. Louis is always hot — except when it is blazing hot. Everyone who was there that week says the temperature never once dipped into double digits during the daytime. "It was about a million degrees," Bruce always says when retelling the story.

"More like nine million," Oxman insists.

Tuesday morning, July 17, 1973, was as blazing as one might imagine, the temperature hovering between one million and nine million degrees. Oxman and Leahey arrived at Norwood Hills Country Club knowing they had work for the week. Leahey had survived his trial the week before with Graham and was pretty confident he had the bag for the rest of the summer. Oxman's guy, Mike Reasor, had missed the cut in Robinson and, like Cerrudo, had been consigned to the Monday qualifier. He failed to qualify, leaving Oxman to search for a bag for the week. By nightfall he had run into Labron Harris, whom he had met the previous summer, and asked him if he had a caddy for the week. Harris said he didn't, so Oxman got the job.

There's a big oak tree outside the clubhouse at Norwood Hills, and that was the lingering place for caddies during the week. In those days caddies were never allowed in the clubhouse — some pro shops would put up signs during tournament weeks which said PUBLIC WELCOME, NO CADDIES ALLOWED — so everyone looked for shade when they weren't actually working.

Late that morning Bruce thought he had caught a break. He spotted Dale Douglass, bag on his shoulder, walking into the clubhouse. Bruce knew Douglass because of his friendship with Dick Lotz. He ran over to Douglass and asked him if he could work for him that week. Douglass's face fell. "I just told a guy a few minutes ago he could work for me," he said. "I'd love to have you do it. If you can find him and convince him to get someone else, I'll hire you in a second."

Bruce soon learned that the guy Douglass had hired was Mike Boyce, another young caddy whom Bruce had become friends with. "There was no way I was going to ask him to give up the bag," he said. "He had talked to Dale first, he got the job. That was it."

Douglass would have seemed like the perfect guy for Bruce. It certainly helped that he knew him, but beyond that Douglass was established as a top-60 player and as one of the solid players on tour. He was thirty-seven, had won three times on tour, and had been a member of the Ryder Cup team in 1969. Plus he had a reputation as one of the truly nice people in golf.

But Bruce had missed out by about fifteen minutes. He returned to the tree, sitting with Oxman and Leahey, who were waiting for their players to arrive for their practice rounds. Bruce was getting just a little bit nervous. He had missed his best chance, he thought, for a good bag for the week with Douglass. Morning became early afternoon, and Bruce was beginning to think he might not work at all that week.

Suddenly Oxman was on his feet. "Hey Bruce," he said. "Look over there."

Bruce saw a young pro with reddish-brown hair walking toward the clubhouse. He had a green McGregor golf bag slung over his shoulder and there was no caddy in sight. Bruce had no idea who the pro was. He had never seen him before. Oxman knew exactly who it was.

"That's Tom Watson," he said to Bruce. "He's going to be a real good player someday. Go ask him."

Bruce recognized the name immediately. He remembered watching the Hawaiian Open on TV on a Saturday afternoon that winter. Watson was in the lead, and he remembered seeing him make a bunch of putts from everywhere. "Three bombs in a row that I remember," Bruce said. "I remember thinking, 'Who in the world is this guy? He can really putt.' "

The guy who could really putt was twenty-four years old and had just returned to the tour after a two-week break. He had married Linda Rubin, his childhood sweetheart, in June and had been on his honeymoon at Lake Tahoe. Watson had graduated from Stanford in 1971 with a degree in psychology, and even though he wasn't certain he was good enough, he had decided to give the PGA Tour a try. In all likelihood, if the tour hadn't panned out, he would have followed in his father's footsteps and gone into the insurance business.

He had made it through Qualifying School in December of 1971, one of twenty-three pros awarded their playing cards after six rounds of golf at PGA National, in Palm Beach. The winner of the Q-School that year was Bob Zender. Watson finished fifth. Among those who also finished behind Zender were Lanny Wadkins, David Graham, John Mahaffey, Bruce Fleisher, and Steve Melnyk.

Watson's rookie year on tour had been respectable. He had finished 78th on the money list, making $30,413 for the year. His goal had been to make the top 60 and become fully exempt, but he fell short of that. He had started 1973 well, finishing fourth at Hawaii, and appeared to be in good position to make the top 60 halfway through the year when he took the break to get married.

He had never employed any caddy for very long during his eighteen months on tour, mostly because that was just the way caddying worked. Even now he can't remember the names of any of the men who worked for him prior to that day. As Watson walked in the direction of the clubhouse, Bruce froze for an instant. He had never yet had to approach a complete stranger about working for him. Seeing Bruce hesitate, Oxman grabbed him by the shoulders.

"Go ask him," he repeated. "Come on. Go do it. Now."

Bruce walked over to Watson and introduced himself. As he remembers it, he was talking fast, trying to give Watson a quick verbal résumé.

"My name's Bruce Edwards," he said. "I just finished high school in Wethersfield, Connecticut, and I'm going to spend a year on the tour caddying. If you don't have a caddy right now, I'd like to work for you."

Watson didn't hear that much of what Bruce said beyond his first name and the plan to spend a year on the tour. He had the impression that Bruce was asking if he could work for him for that year. Bruce isn't sure what he was asking. "If he'd have offered it to me, I'd have probably taken it," he says now.

Watson wasn't prepared to offer that. To him, Bruce looked like most caddies: long brown hair, an easy loping stride. "I saw a long-haired kid in jeans asking me to caddy," he said. "He was polite, I remember that. So I said, 'Okay, we'll try it for a week and see what happens.'"

He handed the bag over to Bruce and told him he was going to go inside to change his shoes. Then they were going to the range to hit balls. Bruce figured Watson would warm up and then go play a few holes. Walking to the range, Watson was relaxed and friendly. He asked Bruce where he'd grown up and how long he had been out on tour. Bruce liked him instantly. He had an outgoing manner and a ready smile that revealed a slight gap in his front teeth. With the reddish hair and freckles, he could easily have passed for Huck Finn.

When they arrived at the range, Watson gave Bruce some money and told him to buy a couple of buckets of balls. Nowadays when a pro walks onto the range at a tour event, someone asks him what brand of ball he plays. Whatever the answer, he is handed a free supply of as many of those balls — brand-new of course — as he wants. In the 1970s, pros were only just beginning to be able to buy range balls, the beat-up kind most people are familiar with, on-site. Most carried a shag bag with them in their trunk, and when they hit balls, their caddies were expected to stand on the range and shag the balls.

Which could occasionally be dangerous. Oxman remembers standing on the range one day shagging balls when he saw Homero Blancas, a longtime pro, completely mishit a driver. "He absolutely thinned it," Oxman said, and it screamed on a low line drive toward where he was standing, no more than 150 yards away, since his player, Mike Reasor, was hitting mid- to short-range irons. "I saw it come off the club and just ducked instinctively," Oxman said. "I heard this scream of pain next to me. The ball had nailed the guy standing there right in the chest. He pitched forward like he'd been shot and didn't move for a few seconds. It was scary."

As it turned out, the victim only had the wind knocked out of him — and a nice-sized bruise.

Bruce didn't have to shag balls that day. But he did spend the next four hours on the range as Watson hit bucket after bucket of balls. "All he would say is, 'I need more balls and some water,'" Bruce said. "I can't begin to tell you how many balls he hit that day. Could have been four hundred, five hundred, more. I don't know. But we spent four hours out there, and the temperature was a million degrees."

"Nine million," Oxman repeats.

"I'm pretty sure I hadn't touched a golf club in two weeks," Watson said. "I needed to practice. I've never been bothered by weather. I grew up practicing and playing most of the winter in Kansas City, and I played there in the heat of the summer all my life. So a hot day or a cold day or a windy day or a rainy day isn't going to stop me from whatever it is I need to do."

In fact Watson would go on to become one of the great "weather" players of all time. One of the reasons for his remarkable success in the British Open — five titles — is that the wind and the rain and the cold never bothered him. He enjoyed seeing that kind of weather, because he knew other players would be bothered by it far more than he would.

Neither Watson nor Bruce knew any of this on that steamy afternoon. But by the end of the day, Bruce had a sense that he was with a different breed of player than those he had worked for in the past. "I thought to myself, 'This guy will do anything to get better.' To me, that was half the battle right there."

They played a practice round the next day and became better acquainted walking the golf course. Watson was impressed when he learned that Bruce was the son of a dentist, that he had an older sister at Bucknell, and that his parents were counting on him to come home in a year and go to college. "You could tell he had been raised the right way," he remembered. "He was polite, he had manners, and he was well spoken. The more we talked, the more it became clear to me that this was a bright young man."

Which would become an issue between the two of them later on.

But not in St. Louis. It didn't hurt that Watson had an excellent week. Bruce finally made his first cut since his days with Dick Lotz at the GHO, and Watson played well on the weekend, especially Sunday, when he shot 67 to move up the leader board into a tie for sixth place. That was worth $6,500 to Watson. This was before caddies were paid more for a top-ten finish than for a non-top-ten (most caddies get 7 percent these days for a top-ten), but 3 percent of $6,500 was $195. Add in $15 a day for the six days he had worked and Bruce found himself being handed a $300 check for the week by Linda Watson. She had rounded up from the $285 he was actually owed.

Almost as good as the check was what Watson handed him soon after that: the keys to his Buick Cutlass. "I'll see you in Montreal Tuesday morning at nine a.m.," he said.

He had the job. He also had 1,200 miles to drive in a little more than thirty-six hours. He wasn't about to complain or point out how far he would have to drive in such a short period of time. He felt certain his life had just changed, and he felt richer than he had ever felt in his life.

"That three hundred dollars might just as well have been three thousand or thirty thousand," he said. "I mean, I was rich."

Leahey and Oxman had also had good weeks — in different ways. Lou Graham had made the cut and finished twenty-fifth, providing Leahey with his first weekend check. Labron Harris had missed the cut but had provided one of the funnier scenes Oxman had ever seen. Harris had been paired at the start of the week with Jim Colbert and Bob Dickson. By the time he reached the 10th tee Friday, both men had dropped out of the tournament. Colbert had withdrawn after the round Thursday, feeling sick. Dickson managed nine holes Friday before the heat got to him.

"It wasn't one of those deals where he was playing bad and quit," Oxman said. "He was really sick."

Rather than play nine holes in a single, Harris decided to catch up to the threesome in front of him and play in as a foursome. He hit his tee shot on number 10 down the right side of the fairway. As he walked to the ball, several marshals asked him where his playing partners were. "Way left," Harris said. "They hit their balls way, way left. They need help."

The marshals, ever polite, scrambled to the left to help look for the golf balls. Harris hit his second shot and walked to the green. As he did, he turned and waved the marshals even further left. "When we last saw them," Oxman said, "they were disappearing over the hill."

Bruce had a job. Leahey did too, and he had made a cut. Oxman hadn't made a cut yet that summer, but he had helped Bruce get a job and he'd had some laughs.

The carnival moved on. Next stop, Montreal.

As it turned out, Bruce's trip to Montreal was a lot easier than Tom and Linda's. They flew through a nasty thunderstorm en route. Bruce and Leahey simply kept driving, one sleeping while the other drove. They made great time and pulled into the parking lot at the Richelieu Valley Golf and Country Club, the site of that year's Canadian Open, shortly before dusk on Monday. Watson was on the range — of course — finishing up a relatively brief session. Bruce proudly handed him the keys and told him he had parked the car in the players' lot.

"Go home and get some sleep," Watson said, knowing how long the drive had been. "I'll see you here in the morning."

Bruce did just that. Watson hit a few more balls, went back to the locker room, and then walked out to the parking lot. There was the car, looking none the worse for wear after the long trip. Watson got in, turned the key, and . . . nothing. The car was completely dead. Watson had to call a tow truck. When the rig arrived, the driver looked under the hood and told Watson the problem was simple — the car was bone dry, not an ounce of water in it. He put water in it, and an hour later than planned, Watson drove back to the hotel to meet Linda.

There were a lot of pros on the tour back then who would have fired a caddy one week into a relationship for leaving them with a dead, waterless car. Watson never flinched. "It was my fault for not checking the water before a long trip like that," he said. "It wasn't a big deal."

When Watson mentioned it to Bruce the next morning, he was momentarily terrified. When he saw Watson smiling as he described turning the key and finding the car dead, he breathed a sigh of relief. "For a split second I thought I'd blown it, lost the job," he said. "But he was great about it, took the blame himself. That was one of the things I noticed about him right away during that first week, he wasn't a whiner. A lot of players never hit a bad shot. It's always someone else's fault, and a lot of time it's the caddy's fault. It could be a wind gust, a bad golf course, a terrible lie. On the green a guy misses a putt, there was a spike mark. Tom never does that, I mean *never* does it, even sometimes when there is a legitimate excuse. He hits it and finds it and hits it again. And in those days, a lot of the time finding it wasn't all that easy."

During that first week Bruce had been struck by how hard Watson hit the ball every single time he swung. "You never knew which direction it was going," he said. "It could go straight, dead left, dead right. But it was always solid, right on the club face. And he could really putt. I remember thinking, 'This guy is going to make a lot of money, because he makes putts from everywhere.'"

Watson had noticed several things about his new caddy too. "He walked fast," he said. "That's important to me, because I've always been a fast walker and I need a caddy who can keep up with me without huffing and puffing. He did that from the start. Still does it today. He was clearly smart, had a quick wit, which I enjoyed right away. And he wasn't a whiner at all. He never complained about how long we were on the range or how long the day might be. When I handed him the keys and said get the car to Montreal by Tuesday morning, he didn't roll his eyes, didn't talk about how far it was. He just said, 'I'll see you there.'"

Watson smiled at the retelling. "He got there in plenty of time. Of course, he never did promise the car would actually start when he got it there."

4

The Boss

IN MORE WAYS THAN ONE might imagine, the backgrounds that landed Tom Watson and Bruce Edwards together were similar.

Bruce had grown up in an upper-middle-class family, the second of four children, all of whom were expected to go to college. He had lived in a comfortable suburb and had spent a good deal of time during his teenage years around a country club. Watson's background was more upper class. He was the son of a very successful Kansas City insurance broker named Raymond Watson, the second of three sons born to Raymond and Sarah Watson. He is five years older than Bruce, born on September 4, 1949. The Watson brothers were also expected to go to college. Specifically, they were expected to go to Stanford. That was where Raymond Watson had gone, and eventually all three Watson brothers went there too.

Raymond Watson was a member of Kansas City Country Club and was an outstanding amateur player. He won a number of important junior tournaments, including the Western Junior Open when he was seventeen, and once had Frank Stranahan, one of the great amateur players of the 1940s and '50s, three down in a quarterfinal at the U.S. Amateur before losing to him one down. "He was still upset about that years later," Watson said. Everyone who ever met him, including his middle son, described Ray Watson as an intense competitor. As a boy Tom first competed against his brother Ridge, three years his senior, working constantly to be better than Ridge in anything, but especially in golf. "For years he beat me at everything," he said. "I was, I guess, the typical little brother, always scrambling to keep up with my big brother. When I was thirteen, I started beating him in golf. But I still couldn't beat my father."

When Tom was fourteen, he and his father faced each other in the finals of the club championship at Walloon Lake Country Club (which was near their summer home in northern Michigan). Tom had Ray two down with three to play, but his father rallied to even the match on the 18th hole and then won it on the second hole of sudden death. Undeterred, Tom came back a year later, when both again reached the final, and won two-and-one. "That was a big deal, to beat my dad," he said. "The funny thing is, I think he was more upset when I beat him than I had been when he beat me. I think the only thing that might have upset him more was when his sister beat him one day. He shot eighty or something like that and she shot seventy-seven. He didn't take that well at all. He was that kind of competitor. Very tough. Never gave an inch, never asked for one."

Ray Watson wasn't just competitive when it came to golf. He genuinely loved the game. Years after he had become the world's best player, Tom told people that the most fun he had playing was still when he went out at Kansas City Country Club with his father and Stan Thirsk, his longtime teacher. Tom was a very good junior player but not a spectacular one. The same could be said for his career at Stanford. He was a good college player, good enough to qualify for the Masters in 1970 by finishing fifth at the U.S. Amateur (in those days it was stroke play and the top eight qualified for Augusta), but he wasn't a dominant college player. And the same could be said of him as a student. He drifted through majors, from communications to economics, before finally settling on psychology.

It was a class experiment in a psych class that convinced him to settle there. The professor gave each student in the class a sealed packet which, he said, contained an analysis of each of them done by the school based on their records and class work. The students were supposed to read the analysis and then write a paper on why they agreed or disagreed with what their report said. "Almost ninety percent of us agreed," Watson said. "It was only then that the professor told us that the analysis given to each one of us was exactly the same."

Stanford changed Watson in many ways. Being his father's son, he arrived with what would best be described as typical midwestern Republican values. Like his father, he favored the Vietnam War and thought those who protested it were wrong. He wrote a paper for a freshman English class criticizing those who had protested the war on campus, which led to a spirited discussion with the professor about the war and the antiwar protests. "I had come from a very closed and structured environment growing up in Kansas City," he said. "Stanford opened my eyes up to a lot of things."

By the time he graduated, Watson had taken part in antiwar protests himself. A year after graduating he voted for George McGovern for president. When he told his father that he had voted for McGovern, Ray Watson said simply, "You are an idiot." Watson laughs now when he retells the story and says, "Of course he was right." A voracious reader, Watson often quotes from the books and writings of famous men. One that he mentions often is Winston Churchill's oft-quoted line on liberals and conservatives. There are many different versions of the quote. Watson's is: "If you are not a liberal at eighteen, you have no heart. If you are not a conservative at thirty-five, you have no brain."

At eighteen, Tom Watson clearly had a heart.

But he had very little idea of what he wanted to do with his brain when he graduated from Stanford. Insurance was there, he knew, but Watson didn't have any great passion for it, nor did he have great grades — about a 2.5 GPA. "I also knew," he said, "that clinical psychology was not in my future." He knew that he liked golf, liked it a lot. Frequently he would wake up before dawn, get in his car, and make the two-hour drive down the coast from Stanford to the Monterey Peninsula and be the first player to tee off at Pebble Beach.

"I'd stop at a little place right near the golf course and pick up a dozen miniature glazed donuts," he said. "That was my breakfast. The starter, Ray Parga, would get me out first, I'd play eighteen holes, get in the car, and be back at school by lunchtime. But I wasn't all that good, certainly not good enough to think that a successful pro career was a sure thing."

It was during the fall of his senior year that he finally had the epiphany that told him what he wanted to do. He was playing by himself one evening on the Stanford golf course, not even playing all that well, when he walked onto the 11th green and noticed something.

It was dark. He could see stars, but that was about all he could see. The golf course was completely empty. It occurred to Watson that a college senior who found himself all alone on a golf course after the sun had gone down might want to seriously consider the notion of trying to play the game for a living. He went home for Thanksgiving break and, sitting in the car coming home from a hunting trip, told his father he was thinking about turning pro when he graduated in the spring.

"That's the right thing to do," Ray Watson said. "Because if you don't try it, you'll regret it the rest of your life."

By then there was a second person whose approval was important to Watson: Linda Rubin. The two had met in high school when both had worked on a production of *The Pirates of Penzance* and had dated steadily since then. Linda had transferred from an eastern school to Mills College near Palo Alto as a junior and, whatever Watson's post-Stanford plans were, they clearly included her. Linda wasn't thrilled with the idea of life on the road as opposed to being the wife of a nine-to-five jacket-and-tie executive. But Watson has never been someone easily swayed once he makes his mind up, and as he put it, "I wanted to find out if I could be any good."

So psychology degree in hand, he went off to the PGA Tour's Qualifying School in the fall of 1971. There were a record 357 entrants in the Q-School that year (in 2003 there were 1,508). He made it through regional qualifying and became one of 75 finalists.

The top 20 (and ties) made it to the tour, and Watson, even with a nervous 75 on the last of the six days, finished a solid fifth, making him a member of the PGA Tour. He wasn't shocked to get his card, but certainly he was relieved. "I thought I could get through it," he said. "But I certainly wouldn't have been shocked at that stage of my career if I hadn't made it."

Qualifying School is perhaps the most difficult and intimidating event in golf. Players half-jokingly refer to it as the fifth major, because the pressure is so intense and because there is at least as much lore connected to Q-School as to any of the four majors. Many players need four or five attempts before they get through. Others get through, then end up back there — often on more than one occasion. Watson made it on his first try and never went back. At the time, Q-School was held in October and survivors were eligible to play on tour for the rest of that year. Watson played in the final six events of 1971 and made five cuts. He finished in a tie for 17th at the Azalea Classic, earning $472. Today a 17th-place finish in your run-of-the-mill $4 million tour event is worth $64,000 — more than double the money Watson earned playing in thirty-two tournaments during his first full year on tour. Seventeenth was his highest finish in '71, but his biggest check came in his first event, the Kaiser Open. There he tied for 28th and earned $1,065.

His first full year was a success. He made twenty-two cuts, had a second-place finish — at the Quad Cities Open — and made $30,413. That enabled him to pay back his father and the group of sponsors he had put together. It also landed him in 78th place on the money list for the year. These days, 78th place would have put Watson in a very comfortable spot, completely exempt for the next year, able to pick and choose what tournaments he wanted to play.

But the rules that made 125 players totally exempt for the following year didn't go into effect until ten years later. When Watson first arrived, only sixty players were fully exempt at the end of each year. The rest had to go through Monday qualifying each week — unless they had finished in the top 25 of that tournament the year before, had made the cut at the previous week's event, or were invited on a sponsor's exemption. Many young players who were out of the top 60 would write tournament directors asking for sponsor exemptions. Anything to avoid the dreaded Monday qualifiers. Watson never asked for a sponsor's exemption. It just wasn't his way.

"I think I got two without asking," he remembered. "But I never saw any reason to ask for one. If you were playing well and making cuts, you didn't have to worry about Mondays. That's the way I approached it."

If you spend enough time with professional golfers, you will hear about a million different reasons why they aren't playing well. It can be bad luck, bad karma, a bad teacher, a bad caddy, a bad sports psychologist, bad golf courses, or bad press. No one who has ever talked to Tom Watson about his golf has ever heard him make an excuse. He is a clear-eyed realist on most topics, but especially on his game. Most people who followed the tour in the early 1970s saw him as a rising star. Watson saw glimmers of potential, but not much more.

"The one thing I knew was that I wanted to get better," he said. "I knew my game wasn't anywhere close to a point where I could beat the best players on a regular basis, and that's what I wanted to do. I was willing to work as hard as was necessary to get there." Tour players today talk in awestruck tones about the work ethic of Vijay Singh, his willingness to take up residence at the end of a range and pound balls until darkness. Watson was doing that twenty years before Singh set foot on the tour. Bruce's caddying buddies grew accustomed to telling Bruce where to meet them for dinner, because they knew that more often than not, Bruce was going to be on the range with Watson until dark — at least.

"I wanted to get good," Watson explains simply.

He continued in that direction in 1973. By the time he took his break in June to get married and go on his honeymoon, he was solidly inside the top 60. His sixth-place finish in St. Louis was his fifth top ten of the year. He had finished fourth in Hawaii during that week when Bruce noticed him making bombs from all over on Saturday — when he had the lead. That was the way he played in those days. If nothing else, watching Watson play was always exciting. As

Bruce noticed right away, he had a hard, fast swing that propelled the golf ball long distances — in many different directions. Even as he worked to become more consistent with his ball-striking, Watson was rarely deterred by an off-line shot. He was an absolute genius at figuring his way out of trouble, especially around the greens. Years later, if a player hit a ball from woods to water to bunker to green and somehow made par, tour players came to call such an escape a "Watson par." It almost seemed as if he had invented that kind of escape from disaster.

He was also a remarkable putter, especially from long distance. He was so confident that he could make any putt of any length that he never lagged the ball on long putts. He fired at the hole. "I always took the approach with any putt of any distance that I was trying to make it," he said. "I think I can honestly say that I've broken a lot of hearts out here through the years with some of the long putts I've made." His face lights up at the memory of those heartbreakers, and it is apparent he has enjoyed every one.

"You better believe I did," he says in confirmation.

If Watson wasn't convinced he was on his way to stardom in 1973, his new caddy was. There was nothing about his game Bruce didn't like. Even the wildness didn't bother him, because he saw it as part of the aggressive style that he quickly became convinced was going to make his player a star. "He played the game the way I liked to see it played," Bruce said. "He played fast, he played aggressive, and he never complained when he hit a bad shot. If he made a mistake, he didn't sulk about it." Even Watson admits that has been one of his strengths. "I've always been good about coming back from a double bogey to make a birdie," he said. "I mean that both in the sense of going from one hole to the next but also one tournament to the next. I don't brood. I move on."

If Bruce had any doubts about Watson's ability, they were dispelled forever that fall at what was then known as the World Open Golf Classic. The tournament was played over eight rounds — four rounds, a two-day break, then four more rounds. "Actually, to show you how different the tour was then, we all decided we didn't want a two-day break, we just wanted a one-day break," Watson said. "It was mid-November, it was the end of the year, we all just wanted to get out of there. So we just took one day and then kept playing. Can you imagine trying to do something like that today, with the way everything is now controlled by TV? Back then it was no big deal. We all wanted to play, so we played."

In the final round before the break, Watson shot 62. He and Bruce both talk about that round to this day as a key step forward in his career. "It wasn't just the fact that he shot such a low number," Bruce says. "It was the way he shot it. He was just firing at flags all the way. On eighteen, he hit a three-iron — after driving the ball into the left rough — that just bored right through the wind to about ten feet and he made the putt for birdie. A lot of guys, they get five, six under for the day, they start protecting. All they want to do is make pars and get in without messing up. Tom just wasn't built that way. He felt good and he just kept on firing. I knew that day for certain I was working with someone really special."

Watson is generally reluctant to pick out rounds as special. But he agrees with Bruce that the 62 was important. "It told me I was going in the right direction," he said. "The work I was doing was starting to pay off, that maybe I had the game to be pretty good." He didn't win that week, backing up the last couple of days to finish fourth, but that check more than wrapped up the top 60 for him for the year. He ended the year with $73,692 in earnings, which put him 35th on the money list. His days in the Monday qualifiers were done with forever.

He was now, at the age of twenty-four, a married man, an established young star on the PGA Tour, and a player with a regular caddy. He and Bruce had clicked as a team from the start. "We just seemed to fit together," Bruce said. "Our personalities worked well. We're both very opinionated, but Tom's always been someone you could argue with and disagree with and it never became a big deal. I noticed that about him right away, he seemed to me to have an open mind about things — whether it was politics or sports or anything else. I think we enjoyed working together as a result of those things."

Just as Watson was the kind of player Bruce was comfortable with, Bruce was the kind of caddy Watson had been hoping to find. In addition to being a fast walker, Watson said, "he had a good sense of humor, a quick wit. He knew when to say things that could loosen me up, he knew when to encourage me, and he knew when to yell at me. That's important too."

Of course not all players want to be yelled at. Encouraged, yes. Told that they're right, told that a bad shot wasn't their fault, probably. But yelled at? Not usually. Watson had no problem with the idea that there were times when Bruce would disagree with him or, as Bruce put it, "kick him in the butt." Caddies on the PGA Tour grow used to the notion that poor play by their player is likely to lead to their getting fired. The old caddy saying is, "They have to fire someone and most would rather fire their caddy than their wife." So caddies are routinely blamed when things go wrong. Fred Couples, who is a lot like Watson in that he rarely blames Joe LaCava, his longtime caddy, for mistakes, does look at LaCava at times when he's in a bunker or a bad lie and say, "Jeez Joey, look what you've done to me now." He's kidding . . . sort of. Other players actually *believe* it's the caddy's fault. The best recent example of that phenomenon came at Augusta in 2003 when Tiger Woods pointedly mentioned that Steve Williams, who has caddied for him in seven of his eight major victories, had suggested he hit driver on the third hole Sunday, a decision — ultimately made by Woods — that led to a disastrous double-bogey six.

Watson has never taken that approach. "Look, a caddy is important, and a good caddy can be a big help to a player," he says. "Bruce has certainly helped me throughout the years, without a doubt. We've been a very good team in the best sense of the word. But Lee Trevino" — a close Watson friend — "always likes to say that if the caddy was that good, he'd be out there playing against you. In the end, you listen to your caddy, consider his opinion, and *you* make the decision on what club to hit. Then *you* hit the shot. The only time I've ever given Bruce a hard time out there is if he gives me the wrong yardage, and in twenty-seven years that hasn't happened very often. If he suggests five iron and I think it's six and I end up hitting five and the ball goes in the bunker, it was *my* decision to hit the five.

"As a player, you have to understand that neither you nor the caddy is always going to be right. If I go against what Bruce is saying and make the wrong decision, it was my decision. If I go along with what he's saying and it's wrong, it was still my decision. If we agree and we're right, I'm still the one who has to hit the shot. Same thing if we disagree. Caddies don't get credit for winning golf tournaments, so they shouldn't get blame for losing them."

Bruce realized early on that Watson felt that way, which allowed him to be bold with opinions and with his thoughts on how a round was going or on Watson's attitude. "Tom always let me make mistakes," he says. "That made me a better caddy. A lot of guys out here become 'yes-caddies' because they know if they disagree and it doesn't work out, they're going to get blamed. I never got blamed, and that allowed me to tell him what I thought with confidence, which made me a better caddy and helped make him a better player."

The classic Bruce-Tom story along those lines took place years later, during the AT&T Pebble Beach National Pro-Am, which is played on three courses along the Monterey Peninsula, most notably Pebble Beach. Because the tournament is played on three different golf courses the first three days — everyone plays Pebble the last day — the cut comes at 54 holes. On the third day, Watson wasn't playing very well and was lingering around the cut line coming down the stretch. He was playing at Spyglass Hill, and having teed off on the back nine that day, came to the seventh hole — a par-five with a risky second shot over water if a player wants to go for the green — feeling generally lousy about his game and his shotmaking. He finally hit a decent drive, getting into the fairway in position where he could try to carry the water, get the ball on the green, and give himself a chance to make a birdie that might ensure that he made the cut.

When player and caddy arrived at the ball, Watson turned to Bruce and asked him what the yardage was from there to the water.

The reason for the question was obvious: He wanted to hit a safe layup shot, then play a wedge with his third shot and hope he could get the ball close enough with his wedge to make birdie.

Bruce heard the question but acted as if he hadn't. "You've got two thirty-five to the front of the green, plus twelve to the flag," he said. "The total's two forty-seven."

"I didn't ask you that," Watson said. "I asked you the distance from here to the water."

Now Bruce turned to his boss and faced him. "I heard you," he said. "You don't need to lay up. You can take a three-wood and hit this ball on the green from here."

Watson didn't think so. He didn't think he was hitting the ball well enough to try that shot on a windy day. Plus he was unhappy with his game and didn't want to gamble — very out of character. He just wanted to hit a safe layup and if he could make birdie, fine. If not, well, that was probably fine too.

So he again asked Bruce what the distance was to the water, his tone making it clear that was the shot he intended to play. Bruce told him the yardage — neither man can remember exactly what it was — but then got angry.

"He called me a chicken-blank mother-blank," Watson says, laughing in the retelling.

"I did," Bruce says. "Then I took out a three-wood and a six-iron, threw them on the ground, and said, 'You do what you want to do, but it's two forty-seven to the flag, and you've got that shot unless you want to *prove* that you're a chicken-blank mother-blank.'"

With that he stalked up the fairway as if he didn't even want to be seen with Watson at that moment. Sandy Tatum, the ex–U.S. Golf Association president, who is always Watson's amateur partner in the AT&T event, was standing off to the side up the fairway from Watson when Bruce walked up to him. "You've got a lot of guts," Tatum told him, having seen Bruce toss the two clubs onto the ground.

Bruce didn't see it that way. He knew, regardless of what happened, that Watson wasn't going to fire him. He was trying to get his player pumped up, breathe some confidence and fire back into him at a time when he was lagging. He knew perfectly well that whichever club Watson picked up, it would be Watson's decision and he would take responsibility for the outcome. He wasn't 100 percent correct in this case.

"He embarrassed me into it," Watson said. "That hasn't happened very often in my career, but that time it did. I figured if he was angry enough with me to call me those names, maybe I should think about what he was saying."

Watson picked up the three-wood — "I did hold my breath a little bit while the ball was in the air," Bruce now says, laughing — and cleared the water and hit the ball just to the right of the green.

"I *still* didn't make birdie," Watson said. "I took three to get down and made par."

It is not surprising that Watson would remember that. But he knows, just as Bruce knows, that isn't the point of the story.

Of course that incident occurred after the two had been partners for years. During that first year, the two men were still feeling each other out, growing to know each other as their comfort level increased.

"You have to remember that back then, caddying was different," Bruce said. "I would go out and check yardages, but Tom, like all the players, had his own yardages. I never read putts back then. He was so good at it, there was no reason for him to ask me to do it anyway. But most caddies didn't read putts in those days. Most players just wanted someone who would show up on time, keep the clubs clean, and carry the bag."

In fact, Bruce and his contemporaries are seen now as the group that changed caddying, not only in the way they did their job, but in the way they were viewed by players and by the public. There were other very good caddies who came along at about the same time as Bruce did, but because he was caddying for Tom Watson, he became the public face of those changes. Once Watson exploded and became the world's number one player, Bruce's face and walk and smile were as familiar to the golfing public as most players not named Watson or Nicklaus or Palmer. Because he did walk fast and never lingered behind, it often seemed as if he and Watson were walking down the fairways in lockstep, Watson with the gap-tooth smile, Bruce with the red-and-white Ram bag appearing to sit lightly on his shoulder. He had a way of carrying the forty-pound bag that made it look as if it wasn't the least bit heavy.

"That was probably," he said, "because I always enjoyed being out there carrying it."

Bruce was the best-known of that first generation of — for lack of a better word — professional caddies, the ones who helped make it a true profession. He is seen by today's caddies as a crucial figure in the evolution of caddying. "To me, he's our Arnold Palmer," said Jim Mackay, who has caddied for Phil Mickelson since Mickelson turned pro in 1992. In many ways, Mackay is symbolic of today's PGA Tour caddy. He is a college graduate, a very bright, well-read man who clearly could have opted for graduate school or a career in business. But, like Bruce thirty years ago, he enjoys the travel, the competition, and the camaraderie of being part of the PGA Tour. And because purses have soared and the way caddies are paid has changed so much since the 1970s, Mackay, like any caddy who works for a successful player, makes an annual income well into six figures.

"Palmer changed the way people looked at golfers," Mackay continued. "Bruce changed the way people looked at caddies. He was the person a lot of us looked at in the '80s and said, 'Now that would be a cool thing to do.' I can remember when I was a kid and I had done some caddying, going out to the Bay Hill Invitational every bit as much to see Bruce caddy as to see Tom Watson play golf. And the best thing, I think, for a lot of us when we came on tour, was that the guy we had all looked at and thought was so cool was the first guy to make you feel welcome, the first guy to want to help you out and show you the ropes. Palmer was always that way with young players. Bruce has always been that way with young caddies."

In 1973 Bruce had no thoughts about becoming an iconic figure in his profession. All he knew was that he had somehow hooked on with a very good young player. He was making good money, he was having a good time, and any thoughts he might have had early on about his time on tour not working out were long gone. Visions of returning home and going to college were starting to fade too, but he didn't say anything to his parents along those lines. No reason to start that battle again.

Back home in Wethersfield, the Edwards family was extremely happy to see Bruce having success. Jay and Natalie were relieved that he was making enough money to survive and seemed to be working for someone who was not only a good player but, based on Bruce's description of him, a good man. They became very big Tom Watson fans. "As in, whenever Watson was in contention, we would set up trays in the family room, eat our dinner in front of the TV set, and watch every single shot," Gwyn remembered. "A lot of our Sundays were built around Tom Watson's golf game."

And every time they turned on the TV with Watson on the leader board, there was Bruce, stride for stride with Watson, looking healthy and happy. Brian was just amazed that he was seeing his older brother on TV. Gwyn, who had just turned eleven, thought it was thrilling and of course cool because Bruce had always been cool. Jay and Natalie were still waiting for Bruce to come home and go to college. But, perhaps grudgingly at first, they had to admit that they weren't just relieved, they were . . . proud. "He knew exactly what he wanted to do," Jay says now, the perspective of thirty years making his vision clearer. "And he went out and did it."

Watson and Bruce finished 1973 at the modestly named Walt Disney World Open Invitational. It had been launched in 1971, soon after Disney World opened, and was played on the two golf courses that had been built inside the park. Jack Nicklaus had won the tournament in '71 and again in '72, and he would win it a third straight year in '73. Perhaps to add some suspense to the proceedings, Disney turned the tournament into a team event for the next eight years. Watson ended up missing the cut, only his second missed cut in the twelve tournaments Bruce had worked for him since July. On Friday, November 29, Linda wrote Bruce one last check and Watson and Bruce agreed that he would get a raise at the start of 1974 — to $25 a day and 4 percent of winnings. There was no discussion about what Bruce might get for a win because Watson hadn't won yet.

They shook hands in the parking lot and Watson said, "I'll see you at Pebble."

That would be the first event of 1974. There was now no doubt that Bruce and the Watsons were a team.

"I had my dream job," Bruce said. "I had gone on tour not even thinking about who I wanted to work for. I just wanted to work. But once I started working for Tom, I knew I was doing exactly what I wanted to do every single week. There was no thought in my mind of doing anything different."

Bruce didn't go home during his break. He knew that even with the success he had had, his parents would ask questions about filling out college applications for the following fall. He didn't want to deal with that. Not only that, he now had some money, real money. He decided to go to Hawaii for the holidays. He was nineteen years old, he was single, he had some cash, and he had no problem meeting people and making new friends.

His life was pretty close to perfect.

5

Rocket Man

LOOKING BACK NOW, Jay and Natalie Edwards agree that they were probably living on Fantasy Island for ever thinking that Bruce was going to go to college. Jay, who fought the good fight for years and years, now shakes his head when the subject comes up and says simply: "Bruce knew what he was doing. It just took *us* a long time to figure that out."

Once he hooked up with Watson, there was little chance that Bruce was going to give any serious thought to quitting the tour and going to school. He was making good money. He was traveling with people he liked. He was young and single and meeting people — male and female — everywhere he went. He liked his boss. He was living his boyhood dream. And he was proving to his parents that he could succeed doing it his way, not theirs.

"I've always thought that at least part of the reason Bruce never gave serious thought to college was that doing so would mean giving in to his father," Bill Leahey said. "Bruce has a stubborn streak, and there isn't much doubt where it comes from — Jay. But it was more than that. Listen, we were leading a great life on tour. It was a simpler time, guys driving from stop to stop; there was much more camaraderie among the caddies than there is now, because it wasn't as competitive. Now you hear stories about guys trying to steal bags from one another because there's so much money at stake if you get the right player. That just never happened back then. Never. Bruce was the life of the party wherever we went. And we went to a lot of parties."

When 1974 started, Bruce hadn't yet ruled out college. He was still telling people that the plan was to stay out for a year and then make a decision about what to do next. But he certainly wasn't filling out college admissions forms in Pebble Beach, Tucson, or Phoenix, as the tour made its way through the annual West Coast swing that starts the golf season. His parents weren't around to bug him about applications, and they were smart enough not to bring it up on the phone — at least not very often. But now, Bruce had someone else pushing him toward college: his boss.

"I'm probably no different than Bruce's parents in that I believe in a college education," Watson said, years later. "I know I benefitted from it, I think most people do. Bruce is a bright guy and I thought college would be good for him. I loved having him work for me as my caddy, but there were times when I would say to him, 'You know, Bruce, this isn't what you want to be doing for the rest of your life.'" Watson smiled as he said this. "Turns out I was wrong."

He clearly had the heart of a gypsy during the 1970s. Leahey had gone back to college at the end of the summer of 1973 and so had Oxman. But Gary Crandall had finally given in to Bruce's badgering and come out at the end of the summer. "I had balked at going to college because my father kept telling me it was the right thing to do and we were in all sorts of conflict because he and my mother were divorcing," Crandall said. "I was in a dead-end job" — working in a local drugstore in Wethersfield — "going noplace and trying to figure out what to do next with my life. Bruce kept writing me and calling me to tell me how great it was out there. One week I get a postcard from Philadelphia: 'Hey, we were paired with Nicklaus yesterday. It was amazing. When you coming out?' Eventually he wore me down with stuff like that and I decided to try it."

One of Crandall's first tournaments that summer was a homecoming for him and for Bruce and for Leahey: the Greater Hartford Open. Steve Hulka, a friend of Bruce and Crandall, had been caddying that summer for Bruce's old friend David Graham. Since Graham wasn't planning on playing Hartford, Hulka had arranged to work for a tour rookie named Andy North. At the last minute, Graham entered Hartford and Hulka had two bags. Since Crandall didn't have a bag yet, Hulka offered him North. That turned out to be the beginning of a six-year relationship that climaxed in 1978 when North won the U.S. Open.

"We missed the first two cuts and then finished fifth the third week," Crandall said. "I had never seen a guy putt like that in my life. Plus we got along right away, even if he did talk obsessively about his [Wisconsin] Badgers."

So Crandall was on tour making good money with a regular bag and so was Bruce. As it turned out, Watson and North ended up becoming close friends, so the two caddies often found themselves together during practice rounds. They traveled together and in 1976 they were joined by Greg Rita, who had grown up one town over from Wethersfield in Glastonbury. Like Bruce, Greg Rita had been sent away to prep school by his parents because he struggled academically. Like Bruce, Rita was the only person in his high school class who did not go to college. And, like Bruce, Rita is now convinced that he had ADD and was never diagnosed. Bruce was a veteran caddy — three years — by the time Rita arrived on tour and he quickly took him under his wing. For a while, until Crandall decided to give up the tour and go back to school and eventually into the business world, Bruce, Crandall, and Rita were the three musketeers. Leahey took a year off after college to join the group, and Oxman kept popping up throughout his three years at Duquesne law school.

"I probably spent more time on tour than I actually spent at law school," he said. "I did just enough to get through, and I mean just enough. I remember being at a tournament in the spring of '76 after my first year. My mother called to say my grades had come in. I knew I needed a 2.0 to move on. I told her to open the envelope. She said I had three C-pluses and a C. I remember running out to the range to tell everyone I had somehow made it. They all looked at me like I was nuts."

There were other caddies Bruce became close to: Hulka was one. Another was Dennis Tunning, also a Wethersfield caddy. Mike Boyce, the caddy who beat Bruce to Dale Douglass that fateful day in St. Louis and who, like Bruce, has stayed on the tour for most of the last thirty years (he now works on the Champions Tour for Gil Morgan) was another close friend. So was Drew Micelli.

"We were a traveling circus," Leahey said, remembering his year as a full-time caddy. "I think we basically looked at ourselves as the luckiest guys alive to be leading the lives we were leading. I never looked at it as a forever thing, though. Obviously neither did Ox or, eventually, Gary. But Bruce did. And since he was with Watson, why would he think any differently? He was attached to a rocket ship and he would have to have been crazy to want to get off."

Bruce now says that if he had any doubt at all about the direction his life was headed in, it was dispelled when Watson won his first PGA Tour event, the Western Open, in the summer of 1974. Two weeks earlier, Watson had led the U.S. Open for three rounds only to collapse during the final round at Winged Foot Golf Club, in Mamaroneck, New York, and shoot 79. Bruce was walking outside the ropes that day — tour caddies were not allowed to work the Open at the time — and he remembers feeling completely helpless because there was nothing he could do. "It was an awful feeling," he said. "I'm not saying he would have done any better had I been there, but I would have at least felt as if I had the chance to try and help him."

That day at the Open, painful as it was, proved to be a turning point in Watson's life. It was on that day that he first talked about golf with Byron Nelson. A month earlier, when Watson had played in the tournament named for Nelson, Bruce's life had also come to a crossroads. There was one difference: When Nelson and Watson had their post-Open talk, Watson had a feeling that something important had just happened to him, because one of the sport's icons had shown an interest in him. Bruce had no idea what had happened to him. In fact he really didn't understand it until almost thirty years later.

The PGA Tour first came to Dallas in 1944 for what was then called the Texas Victory Open — soon to become known as the Dallas Open. The winner that year was Byron Nelson, hardly a surprise, since Nelson won eight tournaments that year and *eighteen* the next year, including his untouchable streak of eleven straight tournament victories. Nelson, a gentle, soft-spoken man who had grown up — along with Ben Hogan — in Fort Worth, would go on to win fifty-two PGA Tour events in all, including five majors. He almost certainly would have won more majors if not for the fact that World War II shut down the British Open for six years, the U.S. Open for four years, the Masters for three years, and the PGA Championship for one year. That meant Nelson missed out on fourteen opportunities during the years when he was golf's dominant player.

If that mattered to Byron Nelson, he didn't show much evidence of it. He retired from golf at a young age and went back to his cattle ranch in Texas. He came back to golf in 1966, when ABC hired him to be the network's lead commentator soon after it had acquired the rights to the U.S. Open.

The first three winners of the Dallas Open were Nelson, Sam Snead, and Ben Hogan. That's a little bit like saying when you decided to start up a baseball team, your outfielders were Babe Ruth, Willie Mays, and Henry Aaron. Nevertheless the tournament wasn't played for nine years, from 1947 to 1955. It returned in 1956 but still couldn't seem to find firm ground on the tour's schedule. In both 1963 and 1965, there was no Dallas Open. After Bert Yancey won the event in 1967, the tournament organizers came up with an idea that they thought would give it an extra level of prestige: Name it for Byron Nelson. They moved it from Oak Cliff Country Club to Preston Trail, a highly regarded old men's club in Dallas, and renamed it the Byron Nelson Golf Classic.

The new golf course and the new name helped attract better fields and higher TV ratings. In 1970 and 1971 Jack Nicklaus won, and the following year Chi Chi Rodriguez beat Billy Casper by a stroke to win. In 1973 the champion was twenty-three-year-old rising star Lanny Wadkins. Watson and Bruce arrived at the '74 Byron Nelson feeling good about the way their year was going. Watson was in the top 20 on the money list, rapidly closing in on earnings of $100,000 with the year less than half over. By now he and Bruce had been together for almost a year and each could almost read the other's thoughts on the golf course.

Even though he doesn't remember it, there's little doubt that Watson knew what Bruce was thinking early in the week when he spotted sixteen-year-old Ruthann Cox standing by the putting green. Ruthann Cox was a Nelsonette, one of a group of teenage girls and young women who volunteered at the tournament during the week. The Nelsonettes all wore the same outfit: white cowboy hat, blue denim blouse, very short blue denim skirt, and white boots. All of them wore a sash across their chest à la Miss America which said NELSONETTES. They were not selected based on SAT scores or the quality of their golf swings. Ruthann Cox was a Nelsonette that year because her older sister, Kay Barton, a flight attendant for Braniff at the time and a Nelsonette, had recommended both Ruthann and her best friend, seventeen-year-old Marsha Cummins, to the committee that selected the Nelsonettes.

Bruce took one look at Ruthann Cox and decided she was someone he needed to know better. He began chatting her up, and soon after, he was introduced to Kay, who was ten years older than he was. "Kay took one look at me and decided she better do a background check," Bruce said, laughing. "I think she talked to Linda Watson and maybe a couple of the other wives. But I must have passed."

Having passed the Kay background check, Bruce was invited to her house. It was there — he thinks — that he first met Marsha. "All I remember is that I thought he was really cute," Marsha says now. "But he was with my best friend. I had to behave, even though I didn't want to."

Neither Bruce nor Ruthann took their new "relationship" all that seriously. Ruthann was, after all, a high school junior. Bruce was a nineteen-year-old gypsy who wasn't likely to spend a lot of time in one place anytime in the future. The closest friend Bruce made that week turned out to be his background checker, Kay Barton. She told him that whenever he needed a place to stay in Dallas, he was welcome to stay in the extra room she and her husband had in their house. Bruce took her up on it on several occasions and still saw Ruthann from time to time. In 1975 he came back for a full week during the Nelson. Marsha had retired as a Nelsonette by then, but she was around for the tournament.

"I was still nervous because of Ruthann," Marsha said. "But then one night he kissed me and all sorts of bells went off. Maybe I should have felt guilty, but at that point I was way beyond worrying about guilt."

She was eighteen, he was twenty. She went off to college — at Houston Baptist University — and, after Watson won the tournament that year, Bruce went back to the road. Even though he ended up setting up headquarters in Dallas for several years, first at Kay's, then on his own, their paths rarely crossed during the next nine years. "It was a wonderful memory," Marsha said. "But that's what it was. I had enough on my hands dealing with my own life by then."

Bruce was blissfully unaware at the time that the pretty blonde Nelsonette he had met in 1974 and had a brief fling with in 1975 would eventually hold the central place in his heart. He was far too busy in the mid-'70s riding the Tom Watson rocket. The collapse at Winged Foot on the final day of the 1974 Open was devastating for Watson. Every kid who grows up playing golf in the United States is either an Open guy or a Masters guy. In other words, when he is alone on the putting green trying to make his last putt of the day he will say to himself either, "This is to win the U.S. Open," or, "This is to win the Masters." Depending on where he grows up, or how he grows up, it's one or the other.

Watson was an Open kid because Ray Watson was an Open guy. In fact Ray Watson could name every single U.S. Open champion dating back to 1895 and, in most cases, give you details on how he won and why he won. Ray and Tom often played a game they called "Name the Open Champion." When they first played the game, it was extremely one-sided. The father knew every answer; the son only a few. By the time Tom was a teenager, he could just about match his father. If there was one thing he wanted to do above all things in golf, it was win the national championship of his country. To lead the Open on a golf course like Winged Foot at the age of twenty-four was pretty close to a dream come true. But the dream was shattered on Sunday, when he shot that 79 and ended up tied for fifth place, five shots behind winner Hale Irwin.

Bitter as it was at the time, the day turned out to be an important one for Watson. "You learn from things like that," he said. "It isn't pleasant, but you learn. You learn what it feels like to lead, to be in the last group, to feel that kind of pressure, which is different from the pressure you feel on the last day of a nonmajor." The significance of the day went well beyond that of a hard lesson learned. After he had finished talking to the media, Watson returned to the locker room and found a familiar figure waiting near his locker: Byron Nelson.

Nelson had just finished working on the ABC tower behind the 18th green and had come straight to the locker room to look for Watson as soon as ABC was off the air.

In a scene straight out of a commercial, Nelson offered Watson a Coke and sat down with him. He spent the next several minutes telling him how much he thought of his game and his approach to the game. He knew Tom was disappointed, but he was convinced there would be other days and other chances. He volunteered to help Watson out any way he could. Anytime Watson wanted to fly down to Texas and talk about golf or the golf swing, he would be delighted to have him visit.

Watson was flattered and delighted that one of the game's greatest names would say such things about him, especially at the end of a day when he felt as if his game had fallen apart under pressure. He and Nelson spent several minutes talking before Watson remembered that Linda was waiting outside and it had been raining when the round ended. The two men promised to talk again soon.

A friendship was born.

Two weeks later Watson won for the first time on the PGA Tour, at the Western Open, then played at Butler National Golf Club, proving his ability to recover quickly from a setback, even a devastating one.

The victory put him over $100,000 in earnings for the year. It also came very close to marking the one-year anniversary of Bruce's arrival on tour. His parents had naturally been asking if he was planning to come home when that year was over. If Bruce had any lingering doubts about what he was going to do, they were completely dispelled by Watson's victory at the Western. "I had been pretty convinced that he was destined to be a great player," he said. "But until then he hadn't won, so you couldn't be sure. When he came back right after that loss at the Open and won his first tournament, I pretty much said to myself, 'That's it, this guy is going places very few players have gone.' I really believed that. And there was no way I was giving up the bag at that point."

His parents were disappointed, but they also understood. "We knew by then that he had a good thing going," Jay Edwards said. "We knew Watson was doing well and Bruce was happy working for him. Plus Tom was so clearly a class guy, how could you not feel good about your son working for him." He smiled. "We figured he'd stay out another year or two, see how it played out, and then go to college. There was plenty of time."

Watson finished the year with $131,537 in earnings, placing him 10th on the money list. In three years he had gone from 74th to 35th to 10th. He had now won a tournament. And he had just turned twenty-five. He and Ben Crenshaw and Lanny Wadkins were viewed by most people as the coming stars on the PGA Tour. Bruce's pay had continued to go up, although not always as fast as he would have liked.

"In the early years, Tom never made it easy," he said, smiling. "I think he was like my dad, thinking I needed to go to college, and if he made it *too* easy for me I wouldn't ever think about going. Whenever I'd ask, he'd say, 'I have to talk to Linda.' Eventually, though, I'd get the raise."

Watson was growing as a player in leaps and bounds now, and Bruce was right there along for the ride. Back home, Brian was getting ready to graduate from high school and was telling his parents that he wanted to caddy on tour too, just like Bruce. Of course it wasn't likely that he was going to be able to do it just like Bruce, because he probably wasn't going to hook up with one of the hot young players in the game after a month out. Still, he wanted to try it. Chris had graduated from Bucknell, spent a year in France, and had returned home not sure what to do with her life. She finally settled on the Navy — one of the first women commissioned as an officer — and went off to Newport, Rhode Island, for basic training. After wanting to quit the first few weeks — everyone wants to quit the first few weeks — she stayed with it and ended up becoming very successful during her twenty-two-year career as an officer. Gwyn was still just a kid, only thirteen, but as proud of her big brother as a little sister could be.

"Hey, he was on television all the time," she said. "And all my friends knew who Tom Watson was by then. It was great."

Even Jay and Natalie were coming around. Jay started taping all the tournaments Watson contended in, building a library of tapes that he would later turn over to Bruce.

In May of 1975, Watson and Bruce won their first tournament together. The Western was still an event that didn't allow tour caddies (in fact it was the last event on the PGA Tour to finally give in and allow them, doing so in the late 1980s), so Bruce had not worked there when Watson won. But he was on the bag — and dating Marsha for the first time — at the Byron Nelson when Watson won, beating Bob E. Smith by two shots. That victory was worth $40,000 to Watson and $2,400 to Bruce (Watson had upped his pay to 6 percent for a win), the biggest check either of them had ever cashed.

There was another disappointment a few weeks later, when Watson led the U.S. Open at Medinah for thirty-six holes and again couldn't close the deal, finishing in a tie for ninth. He had now won a couple of times on tour, was making good money for himself and for his caddy, and was a respected player. But after the Open, there were whispers that he couldn't finish when the pressure was greatest. There were even some people who invoked the C-word — as in choke. Clearly those people didn't know Watson very well.

It wasn't until 1960, when Arnold Palmer, having won both the Masters and the U.S. Open, decided to go to the British Open for the first time, that most American pros began to think seriously about making the trip across the Atlantic Ocean to play. Crossing the Atlantic by plane wasn't exactly a picnic, but it had come a long way from the early days, when Americans made the trip by ship or, starting in the 1950s, occasionally by airplane.

It wasn't as if American golfers never went to the British Open, they just didn't go very often or in great numbers. Bobby Jones had won it three times in five years, beginning in 1926. The last time was in 1930, en route to his Grand Slam, which back then consisted of the U.S. and British Opens and the U.S. and British Amateurs. Gene Sarazen had won it in 1932 and Sam Snead had won at St. Andrews in 1946. Ben Hogan had only played in one British Open — his famous victory at Carnoustie in 1953.

Palmer's decision to go and play at St. Andrews that year had a lot to do with the venue and a lot to do with the fact that he had won the Masters and the U.S. Open. No one had ever really talked about a modern slam before then, but Palmer figured if he won at St. Andrews and then won the PGA, he would have something that amounted to a Grand Slam. As much talk as there is nowadays about the Slam — especially in any year when Tiger Woods wins the Masters — it had hardly been discussed before then. In fact when Hogan won the Masters, the U.S. Open, and the British Open in 1953, he had no chance to win the PGA because it began before the

British Open ended. By 1960 the PGA had gone from match play to stroke play. Still, to most Americans the two titles that really mattered were the Masters and the U.S. Open.

Palmer changed all that. He didn't win at St. Andrews, finishing a shot behind Kel Nagle, but he drew huge crowds and brought a lot of attention to the championship in the United States, a big difference from most years in the past. Most Americans on the tour didn't play the event at the time, in part because of the travel, in part because the prize money was tiny, and in part because any money they did win didn't count on the official money list. In fact a victory in the British Open didn't even count as an official PGA Tour victory until 2001, when the tour got around to making all British Open wins (dating back to 1860) official victories. Palmer didn't need official money or official victories. He loved playing the Old Course, loved the crowds and the links style of golf. A year later, he went back and won at Royal Birkdale. The following year, at Royal Troon, he beat Nagle by six shots for his second straight British Open win.

If Palmer hadn't lost a playoff to a chubby twenty-two-year-old tour rookie named Jack Nicklaus at Oakmont Country Club in the U.S. Open a month earlier, he would have been three-fourths of the way to a Grand Slam at that point. Nicklaus, fresh off his U.S. Open victory, followed Palmer to Troon and finished twenty-third. That was the first of thirty-six straight British Opens he played in.

When Watson first came on tour, the top Americans were regularly going to the British Open. Lee Trevino had won it back-to-back in 1971 and 1972, and Tom Weiskopf had beaten Johnny Miller in 1973 for what proved to be his only major title. But those players were stars. They could afford to take a week off from the tour, spend the money for the trip, and know that they were almost certainly going to miss out on playing the following week too. For the journeyman player trying to keep his playing card or a rising young player trying to prove himself, the British Open just wasn't worth the hassle.

By 1975, though, Watson was a star. He was making a lot of money, he had won tournaments in consecutive years, and he wanted to follow the other top Americans who had gone over and played. So he decided to play at Carnoustie, arguably the toughest golf course on the British Open rota, if not in the world. He told Bruce he was planning to make the trip to Scotland and Bruce was welcome to come along and caddy if he liked.

In those days, a caddy who traveled overseas with a player had to pay his own way. Nowadays, players pay for their caddies and often take them along on their private jets. Watson was flying coach himself, and if Bruce wanted to come, he would have to come up with the money. Bruce had the money and he wanted to go, but he didn't want to make the trip alone. So he talked Bill Leahey into going with him. Leahey had just graduated from college and was taking a year off to work on the tour before deciding what he wanted to do next with his life. He didn't have a player going over to play, but he figured he would certainly be able to get a bag once he and Bruce reached Scotland. So he agreed to go.

Then problems cropped up. Neither one of them had given any thought to the fact that they needed passports. A few days before they were scheduled to fly over, they didn't have passports and getting them in time was becoming a major hassle. They had no idea where they were going to stay. Neither of them had been overseas before.

"We finally decided it was too much of a hassle," Bruce said. "We agreed we'd pass on it this year but try to go the next year."

That turned out to be a crucial decision in Bruce's life. Watson went without him, hired a local caddy for the week named Alfie Fyles, and, in his first British Open, won. This time there were no late collapses. Watson finished the final round tied for first place with Australian Jack Newton. This was still the era of 18-hole playoffs at all the majors (only the U.S. Open retains that outmoded format today), so Watson and Newton had to come back and deal with the howling winds of Carnoustie the following day. Watson shot 71; Newton 72. In his first attempt, Watson had become the British Open champion.

It was a remarkable breakthrough for a golfer still only twenty-five years old. It put the choke talk to bed and it put Watson into a different category of player. Every player is viewed differently when he wins his first major, but when a young player who has flashed big-time potential does it, golf people pay serious attention. Watson was thrilled with the win but still viewed himself as a work in progress.

"It was big because it was the British Open," he said. "It showed me that I had potential. But I never thought for a second that there wasn't a lot of work still to do. I honestly believed I still wasn't nearly as good a player as I could be or wanted to be."

The British Open wasn't on live TV in those days, so Bruce had to keep checking radio reports to see how Watson was progressing. He was thrilled when Watson won but angry with himself for not having figured out a way to get over there and work.

"Next year," he told Leahey. "Next year, we're definitely going."

With that, he went out and got himself a passport.

6

Joy Ride

NOW THAT HE WAS WORKING for the winner of a major championship, Bruce wasn't even thinking about giving up caddying to go to college. The winner of the major championship, however, was thinking about it more and more often.

"I wasn't trying to tell him you have to go right now," Watson said. "I knew he was having fun. So was I. And I liked having him around — a lot. Our relationship was evolving at that point to something that went beyond caddy and player. We were becoming friends."

It wasn't as if the two men socialized very often away from the golf course. Watson was married, and Linda traveled with him most of the time. Bruce was single and spent most of his time away from the golf course hanging out with other single caddies. But when you are with someone all day, every day, six days a week for twenty-five to thirty weeks a year, you either make each other crazy or you become close. There's no in between.

From the beginning, Watson and Bruce got along. They argued frequently. Watson was an ardent fan of the Kansas City Royals, Bruce a fan of the Philadelphia Phillies. Bruce loved the Eagles, Watson the Chiefs. They made an annual $100 bet on the NCAA basketball tournament, each of them picking teams once the field was chosen, then adding up who had the most wins when it was all over. They also argued about politics: Watson, the midwesterner who had grown up hunting with his dad, was very anti–gun control. Bruce, the easterner who had never touched a gun in his life, argued for gun control.

"I think I've brought him around on the issue of the Second Amendment," Watson would say years after they first debated the subject.

"No he hasn't," Bruce insisted.

Most of all, they had fun together. It certainly didn't hurt that Watson was as successful as he was. "I've often wondered if I would have stayed out there if I hadn't gotten lucky and gotten Tom when I did," Bruce said. "I mean, who knows? I was spoiled early. I got used to being with someone who played well most weeks and guaranteed me a good income. Maybe if I'd had to jump from player to player or had to work with guys I didn't like as much, I would have gotten to a point where I would have said, 'Okay, I've had enough of this.' But it didn't turn out that way."

Brian Edwards thinks it might well have been different if his brother hadn't worked for Watson. When he finished high school, he followed Bruce onto the tour. He spent the next year working for two pretty good players: Tom Purtzer and Jack Renner. He even won a tournament with Renner — the 1977 Pleasant Valley Classic — but realized after a year that this was not the life he wanted to lead. "I just didn't like the idea that my success rode on someone else's success or ability," he said. "You can be the greatest caddy in the world, and if you don't have a good player or if you have a good player who is playing poorly, it doesn't matter. I know there are times when you can help; you can say the right thing, read a putt well, talk a guy into the right club. But long term, like Watson says, the player has to hit the shots. He does well, you do well. He does poorly, you do poorly — regardless of your performance. I didn't like the way that felt week in and week out.

"If you work for Tom Watson, I think it feels different because you know success is going to be there. He might go through a stretch of holes, days, or even weeks where he doesn't play that well. But sooner or later, he's too good a player — too *great* a player — to not play well. Bruce always knew that if he did his job well, he was going to see positive results at some point. Most caddies aren't that lucky. Don't get me wrong, Bruce is a great caddy, I know that. But I think he's the kind of person who if he reached the point where he felt his input made no difference one way or the other, he'd walk."

Watson and Bruce got their first whiff of frustration in 1976. Watson had finished 1975 in seventh place on the money list with $153,796 and two victories, one of them a major. He had accomplished a rare feat, finishing in the top ten at all four majors: a tie for eighth at the Masters, tie for ninth at the U.S. Open, the win at the British, and ninth at the PGA. Finishing in the top ten in all four majors is one of the more difficult things to achieve in golf. Watson did it one other time in his career, in 1982. Jack Nicklaus, the greatest major championship player in history, managed to do it five times. Tiger Woods has done it once.

Even though Watson still thought of himself as merely a player with potential, most in the golf world thought he was about to explode into major stardom. It didn't happen that next year. Watson didn't win a tournament, finishing second twice and third once. His earnings went down by about $15,000 and he dropped to 12th on the money list. Not a bad year for most players but a mediocre year for someone who appeared ready to become one of the game's dominant players.

The low point, for both Watson and Bruce, came when Watson returned to Great Britain to defend his British Open title. True to his word, Bruce had planned the trip well in advance and was standing on the first tee at Royal Birkdale with Watson when he teed it up on the first day. Fifteen minutes later, he was wondering why he had bothered. Watson began the championship with a triple bogey and never recovered. He ended up missing the 54-hole cut by one shot, a frustrating week for him and for his caddy.

"I remember being so excited going over there," Bruce said. "I knew how much it had meant to Tom to win there the year before, and I thought, 'Now I'm going to be part of it.' Well, I wasn't part of it for very long."

In those days, the British Open cut the field twice — once after 36 holes, the second time after 54. Watson barely made the 36-hole cut and had little chance to stay alive for the final day. The wind was blowing at Birkdale on that third day and, on the 10th hole, a dogleg left where Watson had hit three-iron, nine-iron in the opening round, he had to hit three-wood, three-wood just to reach the bunker next to the green. Coming out of the bunker, he cut the ball, so he took it out of play. Golf balls cut far more easily in those days than they do now, and players frequently declared them unplayable.

By the time Watson reached 18 that day, it was clear he wasn't going to make the cut. The 18th at Birkdale is what caddies call a forecaddy hole. Instead of walking back to the tee from the 17th green, they give their player the driver and walk ahead to the 18th fairway. It saves about 200 yards of walking. Bruce was forecaddying for Watson when he saw him sail his drive out of bounds. That meant Watson needed to re-tee, but he didn't have a ball. Bruce grabbed a ball out of the bag, raced back toward the tee, and when he got within throwing distance, stopped and threw "a perfect strike on a hop" to Watson. "I'd like to see [Yankee centerfielder] Bernie Williams make a throw that accurate," he said proudly years later. Watson grabbed the ball, teed it up, and hit it down the middle.

When he reached Bruce he had a smile on his face. "Do you know what ball you just threw me?" he said.

Bruce thought about the question for a second, then groaned. "The one we took out of play at ten?"

"Yup."

The rules of golf state that if you take a ball out of play before completing a hole, you may not put that ball back into play again during the round. "If he hadn't been so far over the cut line, it would have been a disaster," Bruce said. "Fortunately, two more shots didn't make much difference at that point. But I was thoroughly embarrassed. It was the perfect end to a perfect week: Start with a triple bogey, finish with a two-shot penalty because I brain-locked.

"I spent more than a thousand dollars to make that trip, which was a lot of money in those days, and got almost nothing for it. I came home saying, 'Well, that's a mistake I won't make again.' "

The rest of the year felt like a long run through wet sand for both Watson and Bruce. Both were frustrated. For the first time, Bruce had some understanding of what Brian and other caddies felt when their players weren't doing well. "But it's all relative," he said. "He was still twelfth on the money list and I was still making good money. Plus I knew it would come back. He was just too good and too determined for it not to come back."

Watson was certainly determined. "I just played lousy all year," he says now, looking back. "I wasn't swinging very well, I wasn't hitting the ball well, and I didn't make enough putts. I wasn't a good player, simple as that. I was searching."

Like most great players, Watson is almost always searching for a swing key that will allow him to feel that he can repeat the same swing and make solid contact every single time. He's a feel player, someone who will tinker constantly — on the golf course, on the driving range, in the locker room, alone in a hotel room at night making phantom swings in front of a mirror. Nothing he tried during 1976 seemed to work.

"That doesn't mean you can't play well," he said. "There are ways to get around the golf course and play well even when you aren't that comfortable with your swing. But it's a lot more fun if you feel like you know what you're doing."

In the fall of that year Watson did two things. First he went to Texas to spend some time with Byron Nelson, taking him up on the offer first made at Winged Foot. The two men spent several days talking about the golf swing and the game, about how to succeed under pressure, and about life. Watson felt completely comfortable with Nelson, no doubt because Nelson is one of those men who is so comfortable with himself that he makes others feel that way about themselves.

"Byron has such a simple approach to things — in golf and in life," Watson said. "He's very direct. In that way he's like my father, who had a simple and direct approach to things. You never had any doubt talking to them how they felt or why they felt it."

Then, armed with new good feelings about his game, Watson went to Japan to play in a late fall tournament. On the 18th hole of the pro-am on Wednesday, he had a nine-iron shot from a sidehill lie and he tried a swing that he'd been fooling around with on the range, trying to keep his shoulders more parallel as he brought the club downward. As soon as he swung the club, Watson knew he had found his swing key. It wasn't just the flight of the ball — which was perfect — it was the way the swing felt. "Right then I knew I had something," he said. "I had found something that I was convinced was going to make me hit the golf ball better and more consistently than I had in the past."

Which was why he began 1977 feeling better about his golf than he ever had before, in spite of his relatively poor 1976. He arrived at the Monterey Peninsula, site of what was then called the Bing Crosby National Pro-Am, brimming with confidence. He ended up in a battle down the stretch with Tony Jacklin, a past U.S. and British Open champion, and held him off to win by one shot.

"That just opened the floodgates," Bruce remembered. "He was so confident from that point on. I don't think there was a week when we didn't start off thinking we could win."

By April, Watson had doubled his career win total. But he had done far more than that: He had gone head-to-head with Jack Nicklaus coming down the stretch in a major championship — and won.

Watson had followed the victory at the Crosby with a win in San Diego. He arrived at the Masters leading the money list and hoping for a better year in the majors than he'd had in '76, when he had top-tenned only at the U.S. Open (seventh). After 54 holes, he was tied for the lead with twenty-five-year-old Ben Crenshaw. Rik Massengale was one shot back and Nicklaus three shots behind. Even though Watson had already won a major, there were many in the media who still vividly remembered Winged Foot in '74, Medinah in '75, and a couple of other tournaments in which Watson had led on Sunday and not won. The issue of his ability to cope with Sunday pressure at Augusta was raised. A lot of players will bridle at such a question, especially a player who has already won a major. Watson had no trouble with having the issue come up.

"I know," he said, "that the thing I have to overcome the most out there tomorrow is me."

The final day turned into a two-way duel between Watson and Jack Nicklaus, who at the time had already won fourteen majors, including the Masters five times. The outcome may have turned on what Nicklaus later insisted was a misunderstanding. Playing one group ahead of Watson, Nicklaus holed a long birdie putt on the 13th hole to tie Watson for the lead. Standing in the fairway, Watson thought he saw Nicklaus turn his way and wave a hand in his direction after picking the ball out of the cup, as if to say, "Match that." Nicklaus told Watson that he did no such thing, that he was responding to the crowd and would never think to make a gesture like that to Watson or any other player.

Today Nicklaus and Watson are close friends. Back then they were just getting to know each other. Bruce wasn't on the bag — it wasn't until 1983 that Augusta let players bring their own caddies to the Masters — but he was walking outside the ropes and saw the look on Watson's face after Nicklaus made his putt and his gesture. "At that moment, he was convinced Nicklaus was gesturing at him," Bruce said. "And it really fueled the fire. Later he talked to Nicklaus about it and Nicklaus told him that wasn't what he was doing. But right then and there, he thought he was."

Watson matched Nicklaus's birdie at 13, then bogeyed 14 and birdied 15. Nicklaus also birdied 15, so the two men were tied, with Watson on 17 and Nicklaus on 18. Nicklaus had hit his drive down the middle on 18 and was standing over a six-iron when he heard a huge roar behind him. Watson had rolled in a 20-footer for birdie at 17 to take a one-shot lead. Knowing that was what the roar was for, Nicklaus backed off his shot. "It changed my strategy," he said later. "I was thinking if we both parred in there would be a playoff. Now I needed a birdie." Firing at the flag tucked behind the left front bunker, Nicklaus did something completely out of character, hitting a fat six-iron that plunked down in the bunker. From there he made bogey. Leading by two, Watson calmly parred the 18th for a two-shot victory and a place in golf's pantheon. He had now won two majors, including the Masters, and he had beaten the game's greatest player head-to-head down the stretch on a golf course where Nicklaus had already won five times. If there had been a scintilla of doubt left about Watson's ability to play under pressure, it was gone forever after the performance at Augusta.

The victory also cemented Watson's status as Nicklaus's prime challenger. In the '60s, Nicklaus had dueled with Arnold Palmer and Gary Player. In the early and mid-'70s, it had been Lee Trevino. At thirty-seven Nicklaus was still considered the number one player in the world. Now Watson, ten years younger, became the player most likely to succeed him. Exactly when that torch was passed is impossible to say, but many people point to that year's British Open. The championship was played that summer for the first time at Turnberry, located on Scotland's west coast, the most scenic of the Scottish links courses.

Watson arrived feeling great about his game. He had just won his second Western Open, giving him four victories for the year and putting him comfortably ahead of the field in the money race. Unfortunately he arrived without Bruce, who, after the disaster the previous year, had decided it wasn't worth the money or the effort to make the trip. In that sense Bruce was like a lot of American golfers, who were put off by the cost and inconvenience when a week off in midsummer was extremely enticing.

"Remember too that back then the money at the British wasn't very good," Watson said. "When I won at Carnoustie in '75 I made seventy-five hundred pounds, which was about twelve thousand dollars. A lot of American players weren't going to spend the kind of money it took to get there for the chance to win twelve thousand dollars in a best-case scenario. And from Bruce's point of view, about the only way for him to break even on the trip was for us to win."

So Bruce was in Ocean City, New Jersey, visiting friends — and kicking himself — when Watson and Nicklaus became engaged in what many people still believe was the greatest two-man duel in the history of golf. "My luck," he said laughing. "I stay home and miss him winning the playoff at Carnoustie, make it over there to miss the cut, and then stay home and miss one of the most dramatic moments in golf history. I'm surprised Tom ever let me caddy for him in any major after that."

The 36-hole leader that year at Turnberry was Roger Maltbie, with Watson and Nicklaus tied two shots back at two-under-par 138. The conditions the first two days were typical of a Scottish links, windy and difficult. But Friday morning (the British was played Wednesday to Saturday prior to 1980) dawned bright, clear, dry, and windless. Most links golf courses — so called because they are built on slices of land that link the land to the sea — are dependent on the wind if they are to remain difficult. Because they are so old, most of them aren't very long; the greens are never fast, and as those who have seen them know, they rarely have anything resembling trees. The wind — or rain or hail or sleet or snow — is what protects them from low scoring by great players. There is a wind that sweeps in off the Firth of Clyde some days that locals simply call the Giant because its gusts are so huge they can make standing up on the golf course almost impossible.

The Giant was sleeping that weekend. The Scots like to say, "If it's nae wind and nae rain, it's nae golf." For at least two days, Watson and Nicklaus proved them wrong. They both shot 65 on Friday and left the rest of the field in their wake. They went to bed that night tied for the lead, five shots ahead of everyone else. For the mortals, Turnberry that day, even windless, wasn't that easy. On the final day, Nicklaus took a three-shot lead on the front nine. Nicklaus in front on the last day of a major was a little bit like Secretariat coming down the stretch. He wasn't likely to be caught.

But Watson kept grinding. He was even after seven holes and trailed by one on the 14th tee. Both players were now at 10 under par for the championship, and 90 percent of the fans on the golf course — or so it seemed — were following them. At that moment Watson had no idea if he was going to win or lose. But he was keenly aware of the fact that he was smack in the middle of something truly special. Standing on the 14th tee, he turned to Nicklaus and said quietly, "This is what it's all about isn't it?"

Nicklaus, who understood too, smiled and nodded his head. It was only later, when Watson became familiar with Theodore Roosevelt's famous "Man in the Arena" speech, that he felt he fully comprehended what that day meant to him. "Jack had been through it a lot more times than I had," he said. "I was aware that something very special was going on, regardless of the outcome. It was the last round of the British Open and I was paired with Jack Nicklaus and playing against him for the title. For me, that was a wonderful thing whether I won or lost, just to be *there*. To be in the arena."

"It is not the critic who counts," Roosevelt said in 1910,

> not the man who points out how the strong man stumbles, or how the doer of deeds might have done them better. The credit belongs to the man who is actually in the arena, whose face is marred by dust and sweat and blood; who strives valiantly; who errs, and comes short again and again; who knows the great enthusiasms, the great devotions, who spends himself in a worthy cause . . . and who . . . if he fails, at least fails while daring greatly, so that his place shall never be with those cold and timid souls who know neither victory nor defeat.

It wasn't until years later that Watson became aware of those words. He first read them in a letter sent home by one of his children's teachers. He was so taken by them that he taped the speech to the mirror in his bathroom. In 1993, when he captained the U.S. Ryder Cup team to its only victory on European soil since 1981, he read the speech during the closing ceremony to explain how he felt about the Ryder Cup. On that day at Turnberry, Watson was unaware of the speech but knew that he and Nicklaus were experiencing something only a handful of elite athletes ever get to experience: the notion that you are facing the best when he is at his best in a setting that guarantees that the outcome will be a part of your sport's history. Watson knew Nicklaus wouldn't back down in the closing holes, and Nicklaus, especially after what had happened at Augusta in April, knew Watson wouldn't back down either.

So they went shot for shot right to the finish. Watson got even again by making a 55-foot birdie putt from off the green at 16, and then took his first lead of the day with a birdie on the par-five 17th. He went to the 18th tee and hit a perfect drive around the dogleg. Nicklaus, knowing he had to make birdie to have any chance, flamed his tee shot to the right into the rough. Any other player would have been lucky to make par from the thick gorse over there; in fact finding the ball wasn't all that easy. Nicklaus found it and somehow gouged it out of the rough and onto the green, 32 feet from the flag. That left him a very long birdie putt. But Watson knew exactly who he was playing against, and he wasn't taking anything for granted. He fired his second shot — a seven-iron from 175 yards — at the flag. It took a couple of hops and stopped no more than two feet away.

Walking onto the greens to cheers that could no doubt be heard all over Scotland, Watson did not think for a second that he had already won. "When you're in match play, which at that point we were, you always think your opponent is going to make a long putt — especially if your opponent is Jack Nicklaus. You have to be mentally prepared for him to make it. If he doesn't and you can two-putt to win, fine. But you have to stand there figuring you'll need to make yours."

Sure enough Nicklaus, being Nicklaus, made his birdie putt — about as remarkable a three as anyone had ever seen, given where his drive had landed. Watson, always a fast player anyway, wasted little time over his putt. "I think I wanted to get up there and hit it and have it be over," he said. "I certainly didn't want to stand around and think about it."

The two-foot putt went right in the hole and Watson had won one of golf's epic duels. Nicklaus had shot 65–66 the final two days. Watson had shot 65–65. The third-place finisher, Hubert Green, was 10 shots behind Watson. They had lapped and relapped the field.

A couple of hours later, after the awards ceremony and the press conferences and the TV interviews that are all part of winning a major championship, Watson and Linda had returned to their hotel room to get ready for dinner. The Turnberry Hotel is a massive building that sits on top of a hill looking right down at the golf course. Coming inward on the back nine, it is the one landmark visible from almost every hole. It was closing in on ten o'clock at night, but the sun was still shining brightly since it doesn't set until close to eleven during that time of summer in Scotland. As he was getting dressed, Watson heard a lone bagpiper playing outside the open window.

At that moment, the enormity of what had just happened overwhelmed him. He had won the British Open on a great Scottish golf course, beating the best player of all time in an extraordinary finish. He and Linda both started to cry, overcome by the emotions of the day, the beauty of the setting, and the joy in what Tom had just accomplished. In 1986, just before the British Open returned to Turnberry, the great Frank Deford wrote a lengthy piece in *Sports Illustrated* re-creating the incomparable duel. He ended by retelling the story of Tom and Linda hearing the lone piper.

Nine years later, recounting that moment to Deford, Tom Watson cried again.

If winning the Masters didn't make Watson a genuine star, Turnberry certainly did. Even though the British Open wasn't carried on live TV in the United States in those days, golf fans had watched on tape and had read about what had taken place. Many people now believed that Watson had supplanted Nicklaus as the world's number one player. Watson wasn't really interested in that. But he now realized that he had become more than a player with potential. "I think it's fair to say that starting in 1977, I was on a run," he said. "Bruce and I were partners on that run. I know it was disappointing for him to not be on the bag for those majors, but he was an important part of what I was becoming as a player."

It is, as players and caddies will point out, very difficult for those outside the ropes — or as Watson might put it, outside the arena —

to understand the relationship between a player and a caddy, especially a successful, long-term relationship. Not only do they spend all those hours together, but many of those hours are fraught with tension, frustration, and emotional twists and turns. That's why most player-caddy relationships don't last that long. Most players who have lengthy careers on the PGA Tour will go through multiple caddies during that time. And longtime caddies will experience several changes of employer. Greg Rita, generally considered one of the best caddies of the last twenty-five years, has had five different full-time bosses since he came on tour.

"You have to understand that in the case of Tom and Bruce, they're not as close as brothers; they're closer than that," Neil Oxman said. "Tom has two brothers, Bruce has a brother. I have no doubt they all love and care about one another. But they haven't been through the sorts of things together that Tom and Bruce have been through. Remember, these two guys have gone out and worked together in tournaments more than six hundred times. That's mind-boggling when you think about it. And in spite of all that, you ask them about the fights they've had and they can't come up with anything."

The closest thing either can remember to a fight took place in Hawaii years ago. Watson had hit his tee shot on the 13th hole at Waialae Country Club so far to the right that it landed in a patch of mud and red clay. He walked across the clay and mud, dug his heels in as best he could, and punched the ball out, splattering himself from head to toe with the mud and the clay. Seeing the ball land in a spot where there were no yardage markers, Bruce hustled ahead to get Watson a yardage. Standing there with mud and clay all over his shoes, pants, and shirt, Watson wasn't thrilled to see Bruce bolting ahead of him.

"Hey, where do you think you're going?" Watson yelled. "Get back here and give me some help!"

Bruce turned around, saw Watson covered in mud and clay, and couldn't help but laugh. Watson was not amused. "Get over here and give me a towel!" he yelled, probably as close to being angry as he had ever been with Bruce on the golf course.

Bruce ran over, gave Watson the towel, and soon after all was well.

"We were both a little angry for a little while," Bruce remembered. "I wasn't used to having him yell at me, because it just wasn't his way. Of course later I realized he was reacting to having mud all over him and seeing me running away."

Remarkably, that is the only story either man can remember in which there was any anger directed at one by the other. They had disagreements — some loud, some profane — over golf decisions, but no *real* fights. "I don't think that's remarkable," Watson said. "We've always had a good working relationship, and we respect one another."

Perhaps so. But to work with someone for twenty-seven years and only have one exchange like that is something most people do find remarkable.

"I can't remember ever having a bad day on the golf course with Tom," Bruce said. "We've had disappointing days and days when it went badly and days when we thought we were going to win and didn't. That's part of competition. But I've never had a day out there where I wished I was someplace else. I was always exactly where I wanted to be when I was out there walking with him."

"You have to understand the two personalities," Oxman said. "Tom is the ideal player for a caddy because he's considerate, will always treat him with respect, and, unlike so many players, doesn't blame the caddy for his mistakes or failures. Bruce is the ideal caddy for any player because he works hard, he's never late, he knows what to say and what not to say. I've always said there's a big difference between a bag-toter and a caddy. I'm a pretty good bag-toter. Bruce is a great caddy, and he's fortunate to have spent most of his career working for someone who recognizes that."

If you ask other caddies what made Bruce so good, they will talk a lot about his work ethic and his loyalty. But they all come back to one thing all the time: attitude. "You never see the bag slump on Bruce's shoulder," said Bob Low, who has worked the tour for fifteen years and now caddies for Joe Durant. "A lot of times you can look at a guy and tell his man is having a bad day from the look on his face, from the way he's walking, from the way he's carrying the bag. Some guys have it practically dragging on the ground.

"That never happens with Bruce. He looks like he's having a good day no matter what, and I know that has to help Tom."

Low paused, because like almost all the caddies on tour these days, he was becoming emotional trying to talk about Bruce. "Throughout my career out here, no matter who I've worked for, there have always been days when things aren't going so well and I'll get down and maybe start to slog a little bit. When that happens, a lot of times I'll just say to myself, 'What would Bruce do?'" He smiled. "Maybe we should all wear bracelets that say WWBD. When I do that, I can see him in my mind's eye, always step for step with Tom, carrying the bag easily, either smiling or looking determined, but never down. And I will literally say to myself, 'Okay Bob, come on, that's the way you want to look.'

"Bruce has been a role model for caddies for a lot of years out here. Caddying is like any other profession, there's a pecking order. You come out as a rookie and you know who the big guys are. Bruce had been one of the big guys for a long time when I first came out, but he was the first one to make a point to try to help me — give me advice on hotels and restaurants, point out do's and don'ts around the golf course. I've seen him do it for years with the new guys. That's just his nature."

If you ask Watson if there's one sentence to sum up his friend, his answer comes back quickly. "Bruce Edwards," he will say, "hasn't got a mean bone in his entire body."

Watson didn't win again in 1977. It was almost as if the British Open had drained him of so much emotion and energy that he just couldn't get back to that level again. He played well at the PGA, finishing tied for sixth, but there just wasn't much he could do for an encore after Turnberry. He finished the year with five victories and $310,653 in earnings, making him the fourth player in the history of the PGA Tour to win more than $300,000 in a year. This may not sound like a lot when you consider that first prize for one weekly $4 million tournament these days is $720,000. Still, 310 grand was a lot of money at the time, and Bruce's cut was about $35,000, including salary, percentages, and work he did for Watson at some nontour events.

He was living in Dallas by then, first in an extra room that Kay Barton and her husband had and then in an apartment with a friend. Watson was still bugging him to go to college. In fact he told Bruce that if he went to college he would buy him a car. "Within reason," Watson said, smiling. "I told him I'd buy him a nice car within reason. Not something crazy. I just felt as if he had accomplished a lot as a caddy and maybe it was time for him to go on to the next thing. I was like his parents. I thought the next thing was college."

Bruce had given it some thought. At one point he had established residency in Colorado because Hale Irwin's mother worked in admissions at the University of Colorado and he thought perhaps he might apply there. But he never got around to it. He did enroll briefly at North Texas State, spent a semester there, and then decided he had seen enough of the halls of academia. "Never did get the car," he said. "I guess one semester wasn't enough."

After 1977 it wasn't likely that Bruce was going to give up his place next to Watson. He was enjoying himself too much. "We were on a roll," he said. "You don't get off a great ride in the middle of the ride. You stay with it." In truth, he was probably making more money than most twenty-three-year-old college graduates were at that point. And the gypsy life was as appealing then as it had been four years earlier; perhaps more appealing, because it had become easier with money. He was still driving to tournaments with other caddies, but more often than not he either had his own room or just one roommate. No more breaking down beds.

He began 1978 working for the world's number one player and was generally considered among his peers and those who followed golf to be the world's number one caddy. "I still felt as if every day I was on the golf course with Tom, I was exactly where I wanted to be," he said. "There was nothing about my life at that point that I would have changed."

7

"I'm Gonna Make It"

THE NEXT FOUR YEARS were not all that different from 1977. In 1978, 1979, and 1980, Watson was the tour's leading money winner. Purses were now climbing steadily, and in 1980 Watson became the first player in tour history to win more than $500,000 ($530,808) in a single season. In September of 1979, the Watsons had their first child, Meg. Some of Bruce's closest friends gave up caddying. After spending a year on the tour after college, Bill Leahey got a job in Boston working for an industrial sales company. Neil Oxman graduated from law school in 1977 and went to work as a Democratic political consultant. In 1980 Gary Crandall got married, moved to Texas, and went back to school, learning to be a computer scientist.

Bruce missed having them on tour, but by then he had a host of new friends. He and Greg Rita had become travel partners and close friends. Like Bruce, Rita had come to caddying because of his father's membership in a golf club — Glastonbury Hills — and because of the Greater Hartford Open. Richard Rita had been general chairman of the GHO when Greg was very young, and he always played in the GHO's pro-am. Going over to watch that tournament was Greg's first exposure to the PGA Tour, and while growing up as a caddy at Glastonbury Hills, he often thought it would be fun to be inside the ropes someday. "By the time I was in high school, I would go over to the GHO and talk to some of the caddies," he said. "The way they described their life sounded like fun: traveling the country, meeting new people every week, being a part of the competition, and getting close to great players."

Like Bruce, Greg struggled in school and landed in a prep school. Unlike his ninety-four classmates, he never gave any thought to going to college. When he decided to give caddying a try in 1976, Bruce was one of the first people he met. "By then Bruce was a star in the caddying world because he was working for one of the best players in the world," Rita said. "I noticed two things about him right away: his willingness to help new guys like me and his closeness to Tom. It wasn't your typical caddy-player relationship. It wasn't as if they went out together every night, they didn't. But they enjoyed each other's company, on the golf course, on the range, on the putting green. It wasn't just boss and employee. They were friends."

Rita has gone on to have great success as a caddy. He began working for Gil Morgan early in his career and has caddied regularly since then for players like Curtis Strange, John Daly, and, most recently, Mark O'Meara. He's been on the bag for three major championship wins: two Opens with Strange and the 1995 British Open with Daly. He and Bruce made perfect traveling companions: same age, similar temperaments — although Bruce is more outgoing than Rita by nature — and remarkably similar backgrounds. "The only complaint I ever had with Bruce was having to listen to him talk about the Eagles — in May," Rita said. "Every spring he would start telling me why this was going to be the Eagles' year."

Rita paused for a moment. "He's always been the eternal optimist. That's part of the reason why he's such a great caddy."

The only disappointment for Watson and Bruce in 1978 and 1979 was Watson's inability to add another major to his résumé. He tied for second both years at the Masters, falling victim to Gary Player's stunning Sunday 64 in '78, then losing in a three-way playoff with Fuzzy Zoeller and Ed Sneed in '79. Sneed bogeyed the last three holes to create the playoff, then it was Zoeller who took advantage, birdieing the second playoff hole for the victory. The real crusher came at the '78 PGA, when Watson led by four with nine holes to play at Oakmont only to lose in another three-way playoff (Jerry Pate was the third player) to John Mahaffey. That was a tough one on Bruce, who thought he was about to win *his* first major, only to watch it disappear on the back nine on Sunday.

"Disappointment is part of the game, that's one thing Tom taught me," he said. "He's always been good at handling defeat and moving on to the next thing. I had to learn how to do that. That one was especially disappointing, because it really looked as if we had won the golf tournament."

Even with those losses, Watson was still the world's dominant player. He won five times in '78 and five times in '79. Then in 1980 he won *seven* times and did add another major when he won his third British Open — again without Bruce — beating his good friend Lee Trevino by four shots at Muirfield.

"When you're playing major championships, all you can really hope for is that your game is there that week," Watson said. "What you've done in the past doesn't mean anything. It's how you are playing right at that moment. During that period, my game was consistent enough that more often than not, I was in a position to contend on the last day. Then all sorts of things come into play: nerves, luck, another guy getting hot. You aren't going to win every time you contend, but the more times you are in position to contend, the more your odds of winning go up."

The one major where Watson seemed to have trouble putting himself into contention on a consistent basis was the major he wanted to win the most: the U.S. Open. After the '74 meltdown at Winged Foot, he had top-tenned the next four years but hadn't been in serious contention on Sunday. Bruce came out of the '78 Open at Cherry Hills Country Club outside Denver with all kinds of mixed emotions: once again Watson hadn't been able to win the event he wanted most. Bruce was still waiting for the day when he would be inside the ropes when Watson won a major. And now his buddy Gary Crandall had been on the bag for the winning player at a major:

Andy North won the Open while Watson finished tied for sixth, but nowhere near the Sunday lead.

"At that point it really wasn't that bad," Bruce said. "There were times when I thought about nicknaming myself the Black Cat, but Tom wasn't even thirty yet and I knew he was going to win more majors. The only problem was, we still couldn't work at Augusta then, and Tom had pretty much decided after '77 that Alfie [Fyles] should work for him at the British. I couldn't blame him for that. Alfie knew the golf courses over there better than I did and he had two wins to show, and all I had to show was a cut. When Andy and Gary won, I was thrilled for them, but I'd be lying if I said I wasn't just a little bit envious. I wanted to know that feeling myself."

Years later Linda Watson told Bruce that it was her idea to stick with Alfie Fyles at the British. "She said it was more about superstition than anything else," he said. "Again, how could I blame her for feeling that way?"

Buoyed by his third win at the British (1980), Watson won another memorable Masters in 1981, holding off Nicklaus and Johnny Miller on the last day for a two-stroke victory. Once again Bruce was outside the ropes watching. "Given my track record in majors, I'm surprised he even gave me a ticket at that point," he joked. "But I kept on believing my time was going to come. He was still the best player in the world. It was only a matter of time."

That year's U.S. Open was held at Merion Golf Club, outside Philadelphia, one of golf's most famous venues. It was at Merion in 1950 that Ben Hogan hit his famous one-iron shot on the 18th hole on Saturday (the last two rounds were played on Saturday then) to get himself into a playoff with Lloyd Mangrum and George Fazio, which he won by four shots over Mangrum the next day. Watson's sense of the game's history combined with his desire to win the tournament he had grown up dreaming about made that Open an ideal place for him to finally win, as he often calls it, "the national championship."

He was in the process of putting himself into position to do just that, closing on the leaders on Saturday afternoon, when he stepped up on the 15th tee and duck-hooked a three-wood out of bounds. At that moment he was in sixth place and trailed the leader, George Burns, by five shots with all of Sunday still ahead of him and Burns starting to struggle. He trailed no one else by more than two shots. When he walked off the green with a triple-bogey seven, he trailed by eight and had allowed a dozen players in the pack to go past him. By the time he holed out on 18 that afternoon — three-putting the 18th green — it was raining and it was apparent that another year was going to go by without a U.S. Open title. Frustrated, Watson signed his scorecard and, instead of taking the crowded path back to the locker room, walked around to the front of the 18th green, taking a route off-limits to most of the public to await a shuttle that would take him to the driving range. He politely turned down a couple of autograph seekers, saying, "I have to get right to the range now." He said the same thing to two reporters when they approached.

Unfortunately for Watson, the van sitting at the shuttle stop wasn't going to the range. Forced to wait, he was too polite to say no to a little girl who asked for an autograph or to the two reporters who were still there. "I just didn't play very well," he said quietly. "The last five holes are really the only hard part of this golf course, especially on a day like this, and I couldn't do the job on them."

Someone asked if he was going to the range to pound out his frustrations. "No," he insisted. "There's something I want to work on."

The range van mercifully arrived and Watson escaped. He ended up tied for 23rd the next day. Perhaps it was coincidence, but the rest of the year was a virtual washout for Watson. He finished tied for 23rd in defense of his British Open title and missed the cut at the PGA. In fact he didn't finish higher than 20th in a single tournament the rest of the year. For the first time since 1976, he wasn't the leading money winner on the tour. He still finished third, thanks to his three victories prior to the Open, but his earnings dropped by almost $200,000 from the previous year. He also wasn't the player of the year for the first time in five years. British Open champion Bill Rogers was. Watson was again searching for a swing key, trying to find something to get him back to where he had been prior to Merion.

For Bruce, watching Watson struggle was difficult. It wasn't just that not being in the hunt on Sunday was no fun and less rewarding financially. It hurt him to see Watson so frustrated. By then Watson was giving Bruce more responsibility. Always a very confident reader of greens, he had started to check with Bruce at times for his thoughts on some putts. When the two would work on the range, if Watson was trying something he would often say, "How's that look?" knowing that Bruce's response, while not that of a trained teacher, would be honest.

It started to come back early in 1982 — slowly. Watson won in Los Angeles. He finished tied for fifth at Augusta. He won again at the Heritage. But the swing still wasn't where he wanted it to be. "I'm getting by right now because my strength is still getting the ball in the hole," he said that spring. "The swing's not there yet, but it's coming. I really believe it's coming."

The Open that year was to be played at Pebble Beach, the place where Watson had so often started his mornings while at Stanford. Frequently he would stand on the 15th tee there and tell himself, "Okay, you have to play these four holes in one under to beat Nicklaus and win the Open."

"Of course then I'd play them in two over," he said. "I had a long way to go back then."

He had come a long way since. Now there were some in golf who wondered if he would ever win an Open if he couldn't win at Pebble, a place he loved and was familiar with. Of course Pebble in January or February when the AT&T is played is a lot different than Pebble in June after the USGA has gotten through setting up the golf course. Familiarity would help, but perhaps not as much as some people might have thought.

Watson visited Byron Nelson in May to spend time working on his mind and his golf swing. Soon afterward, Nelson told a reporter: "The only thing on his mind right now is winning at Pebble. Every shot he hit when he was here was designed to work on some hole there. If I know Tom Watson, he will be hard to beat there."

Watson would have laughed if that statement had been repeated to him on the night before the championship began. "I knew I had no chance to win," he said, "because I was hitting the ball sideways. I don't mean sideways, I mean *sideways*. The only thing I had going for me was that I was so far off-line on a lot of shots that the ball was landing outside the ropes where the gallery had walked and I was getting decent lies."

In many ways Watson's genius comes out on those days — and during those weeks — when he is struggling to find his swing. With Bruce murmuring in his ear constantly that it wasn't as far away as he thought it was, Watson somehow sneaked around the first two days in 72–72 — even par — and was only four shots out of the lead. "I'm really not sure how I did that," he said. "But I managed to finish strong both days. I played the last four holes in a total of five under: two under the first day; three under the second. That got me to even par and left me still, somehow, in the golf tournament."

Amazed to be in contention and still searching, Watson and Bruce headed for the range after Friday's round. Watson tried one move, then another. Something in one swing told him that he was lifting his arms too quickly on his backswing. He tried cutting down on his shoulder movement in order to turn his shoulders more quickly as he took the club away. One shot flew straight and true. Then another. A few more. Watson turned to Bruce and said quietly, "I've got it."

This has become a ritual between the two men. When Watson is searching for something in his swing, he and Bruce may spend hours on the range together. Watson rarely consults with a teacher, especially when he is at a tournament. He will keep trying different things until something clicks. He may go weeks without anything clicking, but when it does, he can usually tell with a few swings that he's found something. Only then will he turn and deliver what may be Bruce's three favorite words: "I've got it."

"There is no question," Watson will say with a laugh, "that he enjoys hearing those words."

As soon as Bruce heard Watson deliver the three words on that Friday afternoon, he began thinking the tournament could be won. Four shots back with 36 holes to play? That was nothing. Especially when Watson "had it." The two men walked onto the tee on Saturday afternoon brimming with confidence.

"And I went out that day and absolutely striped it," Watson said. "Hit the ball about as well as I can hit it."

The result was a four-under-par 68 and a tie for the lead with Bill Rogers. A number of players were close behind, notably Nicklaus, who was three shots back and would play three groups in front of the leaders on the final day.

Watson and Bruce went to bed that night excited but nervous. Watson had slept on the 54-hole lead at the U.S. Open before, but that had been eight years earlier, when he was a tour novice, someone who had never won a PGA Tour event. Now he was the winner of five majors and thirty tournaments overall. He was the world's best player. And, he says, he was every bit as nervous as he had been in 1974.

"What you've done in the past doesn't matter one bit on the last day of a major," he said. "It's all about how you're playing that day. I felt good about my swing, but I didn't have any cush [cushion] for any sort of mistakes. I knew Sunday would be a long, tough day."

The best thing for the leaders about playing a major on the West Coast is that there's a lot less waiting on Sunday. In those days, ABC wanted the last ball in the hole by 7 p.m. East Coast time. That meant that Watson and Rogers, playing in the final group, would tee off at 11:40 a.m. West Coast time. Even with the shorter wait, Watson was tight walking onto the first tee. So was Bruce.

"You have to remember," he said, "Tom was going for his sixth major. I was going for my first."

Watson hit his opening tee shot in the fairway, then turned to Bruce as they walked off the tee.

"You nervous?" he asked.

"Real nervous," Bruce answered.

"Good," Watson answered. "Because I'm real nervous too."

It was almost as if acknowledging the nerves helped calm them both down. Watson birdied the par-five second hole but bogeyed the fourth, and he was still four under for the championship as he stood on the tee of the tiny, scenic par-three seventh. Even though he was playing steadily, Watson was hearing huge roars from up ahead, and he knew they could only be for one person: Nicklaus.

"It didn't really surprise me," he said. "The first seven holes at Pebble Beach aren't that hard. You can make a move there."

Nicklaus had done just that. After a poor start — bogey at the first, par at the second — he had reeled off five straight birdies from number three through number seven. That got him to five under for the tournament, meaning he had taken the lead. Watson had not been able to take advantage of the early holes at Pebble. He had birdied the two par-fives but also had two bogeys. When he reached the seventh tee, he trailed Nicklaus by one shot.

Being mano a mano with Nicklaus didn't seem likely to spook Watson. After all, he had come out of their two head-to-head confrontations on the last day of majors in 1977 just fine. He floated a perfect pitching wedge to within two feet of the flag at number seven, giving him a tap-in birdie that would give him a share of the lead.

Except that he missed the putt.

His second shot at the difficult par-four eighth hole came up short of the green. From there he putted to eight feet but made the par-saving putt, beginning a string of tough putts he would make. Fortunately Nicklaus had bogeyed the hole, so the two men were now tied for the lead. Watson took the lead outright with a birdie at the ninth hole and then made a classic "Watson par" at the 10th. He hit his second shot over an embankment, halfway down a hill that led to the beach and Carmel Bay. After hacking out of the weeds there, Watson was 24 feet from the hole on the fringe a couple of steps from the green. He rolled the putt into the heart of the hole.

"That really got me going," Bruce remembered. "It was Tom being Tom under pressure. When we walked off the green, I said to him, 'Let's go, he's made his big run. This is ours.' The look in his eyes told me he was really into it. Which was what I wanted to see."

Naturally Bruce didn't have to specify who "he" was. Everyone on the property at that moment knew this was another two-man duel: Watson vs. Nicklaus. Pumped by the save at 10, Watson made another bomb at 11 — this one from 22 feet for birdie. Nicklaus had bogeyed the hole a few minutes earlier, so Watson suddenly had a two-shot lead. Maybe Bruce was right, maybe Nicklaus had made his run.

Not quite. Nicklaus was forty-two, but still just about as good at responding to a challenge as anyone. He birdied the 12th to cut the lead to one and then birdied 15 while Watson was walking off 12 to tie the game up again. Watson's turn. At 14, he was on the fringe, 35 feet from the flag, and holed yet another over-hill-and-dale putt. "From the eighth hole on," he remembered, "I putted just about as well the rest of the way as I possibly could."

Again he led by one. Bruce's major concern at that moment was that the thousands of fans following Watson and Rogers could hear his heart pounding.

"I get tight sometimes out there, that's part of it when you're inside the ropes," he said. "But that day, coming down the stretch, my mouth was dry and I could feel my heart about to come through my chest. I knew how bad Tom wanted this one. And I wanted it just as bad."

At 16 Watson made his only real mistake off the tee of the day, landing his drive in a fairway bunker. In January, during the Crosby, he probably would have had a shot from there. But the USGA had lowered the level of the sand and had built a new, higher lip on the bunker for the Open. Bob Rosburg, ABC's longtime "on the ground" reporter, was the first person to get to the ball. "Jim," he said to Jim McKay on the tower at 18, "that one is absolutely dead."

"That one is dead" has been Rosburg's trademark for most of thirty years. He's right a lot more often than he's wrong, although there are instances in which players have pulled off miracles to come back from the dead.

Not this time.

Watson took one look at the ball, the lie, and the lip and knew his only option was to play out sideways. "Rossi was never more accurate than he was with that comment," he said. "At that point, I was happy to get off the hole with a bogey."

He had to two-putt from 50 feet with a 10-foot right-to-left break to get that bogey, but he did so and walked onto the 17th tee tied for the lead with Nicklaus at four under par. Nicklaus was already in the scorer's tent, watching on a monitor, feeling pretty good about the situation. "Seventeen is always a hard hole," he said. "And birdieing the 18th hole to win a U.S. Open is a pretty tall order for anyone. I was thinking there was a good chance we would be playing [in an 18-hole playoff] on Monday."

In fact at that moment, no one in history had ever birdied the 18th hole on Sunday to break a tie and win the U.S. Open. And the 17th at Pebble Beach is one of the most daunting holes in golf.

It is a long par-three — playing 209 yards on that day — to a double green with weeds and water on the left, weeds on the right, and more water (and the tiny 18th tee) behind it. Since it sits on a corner of land with water on two sides, the wind is almost always blowing hard there, especially later in the day. Ten years earlier, the first time the Open had been played at Pebble Beach, Nicklaus had wrapped up the title by hitting the flag with a magnificent one-iron shot.

"What you have to do at that hole is fairly simple," Watson said. "You take a long iron and try to hit into about a twenty-foot by twenty-foot area of green with the wind almost always blowing. There's really no margin for error."

Watson and Bruce were between two-iron and three-iron as they stood on the tee. Looking back, Bruce now says if he had it to do over again, he would have pushed harder for a three-iron, because Watson tends to be more accurate with a hard swing as opposed to an easy one. They agreed, however, on the two, wanting to take the front bunker out of play.

"The wind was blowing right to left," Watson said. "I wanted to aim for the middle of the green and let the wind blow it left toward the pin. But I overcooked the shot [hooked it], and then the wind started to take it."

The ball started out more left than Watson wanted it and, as he said, the wind kept carrying it left. It took one hop and disappeared into the weeds to the left of the green. Both men's hearts sank. "There just isn't a good spot over there," Watson said. "Not one."

Walking off the tee, a little bit disgusted with himself, Watson flipped the two-iron to Bruce and became Bob Rosburg: "That one's dead," he said.

At that moment, something Ben Hogan once said flashed through Bruce's mind. "Golf is a game of missed shots," the great man said. "It's what you do afterward that matters."

"Hey," he said in response to Watson, "let's see what kind of lie we have. We can still get it up and down."

He wasn't feeling terribly optimistic himself at that moment, but he knew Watson needed bolstering. He had just bogeyed 16 to give up the lead and was now looking at another bogey. The last thing he wanted to do was go to 18 needing a birdie to tie Nicklaus. Sitting in the scorer's tent, Nicklaus went from thinking playoff to thinking he might be accepting the trophy for a fifth time within the next half hour.

Walking ahead of Watson, Bruce thought he saw a glimmer of hope as he approached the ball. "I could see it," he said. "That meant it wasn't buried completely. Which gave us at least a fighting chance."

Watson saw the same thing Bruce did and, like Bruce, went from thinking "dead" to "life support."

"It was still far from an ideal shot," he said. "It was a hanging lie, the ball was below my feet, and the lie was still pretty gnarly. But at least I could get my club on the ball. There were places over there where I might not have been able to do that."

The other problem was that he was only 18 feet from the flagstick. He had, as the players say, "short-sided" himself, meaning he had almost no green to work with. The ball would come out of the high grass hot (moving fast), and getting it to stop quickly once it hit the green would be almost impossible. "The one thing I had going for me was that I'd practiced shots like that all week in the practice rounds," he said. "You know you're going to have shots like that at Pebble Beach, that's the way the golf course sets up. So I'd practiced quite a few shots from spots like that."

The other thing he had going for him was genius. It may well be that there has never been a player in golf history with a better short game than Watson at his peak. His ability to get the ball up and down from seemingly impossible spots is something other players still discuss in awed tones. "What always amazed me," Ben Crenshaw said, "was his unbelievable confidence. The thought that he couldn't do something around the green almost never crossed his mind."

That may have been the key to what happened next. As Watson looked the shot over and took a couple of practice swings, opening the face of his wedge as far as he possibly could, Bruce, ever upbeat at critical moments, said, "Come on, Tom, get it close."

Close would be near miraculous. And yet Watson's answer was direct and firm: "Close?" he said. "Hell, I'm gonna knock it in."

It was part bravado, part self–pep talk, and, remarkably, part logic. "I knew that my only real chance to get the ball anyplace close to the hole was to hit the flagstick," Watson said. "No matter how soft I landed it, if it didn't hit the stick, it was going to pick up speed and go at least ten or fifteen feet, maybe more, past the hole. I had to aim for the stick, try to hit it, and hope that if it didn't go in, it would stop close enough to the hole that I could make the putt. But when I stood over the ball, I was absolutely trying to make it. It was my best chance."

Always a fast player, Watson wasted little time once he was over the ball. He gently dropped the club underneath the ball, hitting it about as softly as was humanly possible while still actually moving it. The ball popped up into the air, landed just on the green, and began rolling — picking up speed as Watson had predicted — right at the flagstick. Halfway there, Watson thought it had a chance. Three-quarters of the way there, he was convinced he had holed the shot.

He began running in the direction of the ball while Bruce, frozen to the spot with fear, anticipation, and hope, stood staring at the ball, afraid that if he thought it had a chance it would roll past.

The ball hit the flagstick, paused for a split second, and then dropped into the hole. Watson was in full flight by now, sprinting in a circle around the hole. When he turned back in Bruce's direction, he pointed his finger at him and yelled, "I told you! I told you I was gonna make it!"

In the scorer's tent, Nicklaus stared at the TV monitor in disbelief. The late John Morris, then the USGA's director of communications, was sitting there with Nicklaus, preparing to guide Nicklaus and Watson through their postround media paces, when the ball went into the hole. "You could tell everyone in the tent wanted to throw their arms in the air because it was such an amazing shot," he said years later. "It wasn't a matter of rooting for Jack or for Tom, it was just such a stunning shot. I think a few people may have said, 'Oh my God!' in disbelief. But then we all looked at Jack and got ahold of ourselves."

As Morris remembered it, Nicklaus looked around at the other people in the tent, somehow produced a smile, and said, "Just another tap-in for Tom."

Watson had never in his life celebrated a shot like that when there was still golf to play. Always in control of his emotions on the golf course, he never let loose before the 18th green. This time, though, he did. "It was just instinct," he said. "It was a miraculous shot and it gave me a one-shot lead with one hole to play in the Open. So I celebrated more than I normally do."

Bruce was already thinking about the 18th hole, the long par-five with Carmel Bay all the way down the left side. Back then, before equipment changed the game, no one tried to reach the green in two. All Bruce wanted was for Watson to get his tee shot in the fairway, hit a safe layup, and leave himself an easy third shot to the green. "It wasn't over, because that's a tough driving hole," he said. "But he'd hit the ball well off the tee all day, except for the one at sixteen. So I knew he would stand up there and feel confident."

He did. His three-wood split the middle. Then the layup. Wanting to be absolutely certain he didn't chunk a wedge into the front bunker, Watson played an easy nine-iron to the green. He caught it a little bit thin and it landed about 20 feet behind the hole. Which was fine with Watson. As he handed the club to Bruce, he thought about something Byron Nelson always said to him.

"Byron always says, 'Hit it thin to win,'" he said. In other words, if you hit a shot a bit thin it is far less likely to get into trouble than catching a shot fat.

Just shy of nine years after they first met, Watson and Bruce did what they had always dreamed of doing: They walked onto the 18th green together at a major championship with victory close at hand.

"This is exactly where I want to be," Watson said to Bruce as the crowd engulfed them in cheers.

"Above the hole?"

"No, walking onto the eighteenth green with two putts to win the U.S. Open."

As it turned out, Watson only needed one of those two putts. After Bruce pulled the pin, his birdie putt curled down the hill, picking up speed as it broke left to right. For a brief moment, both Watson and Bruce had a panicked thought.

"That ball's really moving," Bruce thought as he stood holding the flag.

Watson went a step further. "It's moving," he thought, "too fast."

At that stage of his career, Watson didn't know *how* to lag a putt. He charged every putt he looked at, believing he was going to make them all, but just as convinced that if he did miss, he would make the putt coming back, regardless of the distance. Pumped up by the moment, he put too much speed on the putt. "If it had missed the hole," he said, "I would have had some serious concerns about the one coming back. It could have been tricky."

As it turned out, there was no need for concern. Watson's read of the putt and his aim were perfect. It was moving fast when it hit the hole, but that's what it did, dropping dead center.

Bruce's arms were in the air and he was sprinting at Watson for the hug he had fantasized about while watching from the sidelines during those other major victories. When Bruce got to Watson, they wrapped their arms around each other and Watson said simply: "We did it."

Bruce was shouting and crying all at once. "Damn right," he said. "We *did* do it."

It was one of the most extraordinary finishes in the history of the U.S. Open. Watson had finished birdie-birdie on two of the most difficult closing holes in championship golf to beat the greatest player of all time.

Nicklaus was one of the first people to greet Watson after he and Bruce untangled and shook hands with Bill Rogers and his caddy, John Griffin.

"You did it to me again, you little son of a bitch," Nicklaus said, a huge smile on his face, an arm around Watson's shoulder, his voice filled with admiration. "I'm really proud of you."

Watson remembered Nicklaus adding one more sentence. "If it takes me the rest of my life, I'm gonna get you one of these times."

At that point neither Watson nor Bruce really cared if Nicklaus did get them one of those times. Both men felt completely fulfilled by this victory.

"I missed the others," Bruce said years later. "But the one I got made up for the rest. Because it was so *hard* and it meant so much to both of us. I mean, come on, Pebble Beach, the Open, Nicklaus, the chip-in, what more could you possibly ask for?"

Not a thing.

Since that day, few people play Pebble Beach for the first time without pausing at the 17th green, dropping a ball or two to the left of the green, and chipping it in the direction of the spot where the flagstick was that day. Most who follow golf can point to almost the exact spot where the ball was and to the spot where the pin was too, especially since that moment has been replayed thousands and thousands of times through the years, always punctuated by Watson pointing at Bruce and saying, "I told you . . ."

Very few people chip it anywhere close to the spot where the flag was that afternoon.

Years later Watson and a group of friends were having dinner at Club 19, which is on the Pebble Beach property. They were celebrating the work they had just completed on a new golf course for The Inn at Spanish Bay, which adjoins Pebble Beach. A good deal of champagne had been passed around the table and the subject of The Chip came up.

On that June day in 1982, Bill Rogers had declared the shot one in a hundred. Nicklaus had said it was more like one in a thousand. When reporters asked Watson about those odds, he smiled and suggested he wouldn't mind going back out to 17 to see if he could make the shot more than one time in a thousand. "It was an impossible shot," he said in a rare moment of immodesty, "for most mortals."

Now when his friends asked what the chances were of ever getting the ball close to that spot again, Watson shrugged and said, "Why don't we go find out?"

He went up to his room, pulled a wedge and some golf balls from his bag, and the group walked down the 18th fairway to the 17th green. There, with the moon providing the only light and waves crashing behind them off Carmel Bay, they all took a few swipes. No one — including Watson — came close.

"It was the champagne," Watson insisted, laughing as he told the story.

Perhaps. Or maybe he simply made a once-in-a-lifetime shot.

The beginning. Bruce and Dick Lotz at the Greater Hartford Open. *(Photo courtesy of the Edwards family)*

The first win.
Bruce and Tom
celebrate at the
Byron Nelson
Classic in 1975,
their first of many
wins together.
(*John Mazziotta*)

Partners. Bruce and Tom during their victory at the Tradition in
August 2003. (*Stephen Szurlej/The Golf Digest Company*)

The perfectionist. Bruce did his homework before every tournament. Here he refers to the caddy's bible, Gorgeous George's yardage book. (*J. D. Cuban / The Golf Digest Company*)

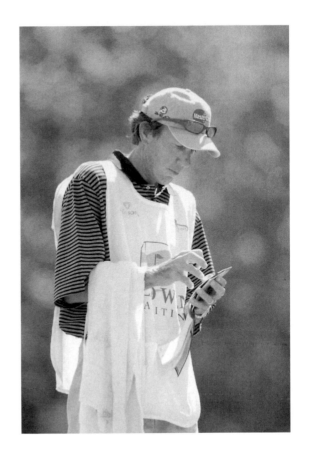

Bruce with the cart he was obliged to use in the summer of 2003. (*J. D. Cuban / The Golf Digest Company*)

The caddy and his Nelsonette finally connect. Bruce and Marsha at the Caves Valley Fundraiser in May 2003. (*Photo courtesy of the Edwards family*)

A new skill for Bruce. He tips his cap to the crowd after Watson's remarkable 65 at Olympia Fields in the 2003 U.S. Open. (*J. D. Cuban/The Golf Digest Company*)

Bruce reads a putt for Watson during 2003's Open. "He has remarkable eyes," Watson says. (*J. D. Cuban/The Golf Digest Company*)

Bruce's new family. Avery, Marsha, Bruce, and Brice.
(*Photo courtesy of the Edwards family*)

Jay and Natalie Edwards with their children at the reunion in fall 2003. Front row: Gwyn, Jay, and Natalie. Back row: Bruce, Brian, and Chris. (*Photo courtesy of the Edwards family*)

At the JELD-WEN Tradition. The last senior "major" of 2003. (*J. D. Cuban/The Golf Digest Company*)

"Closer than brothers." (*J. D. Cuban/The Golf Digest Company*)

8

Tough Times

THE OPEN VICTORY in 1982 took Watson to yet another level of stardom. He had now won three of the four major championships, and three of his six major victories had come in head-to-head stretch duels with Jack Nicklaus. Two of them had produced endings that would go down in golf history as among the most dramatic of all time. Buoyed by that victory — and aided by a late Sunday collapse by then twenty-five-year-old Nick Price — Watson won his fourth British Open a month after Pebble Beach. By this time ABC was televising the British Open live on Sunday (the last day had been moved to Sunday in 1980, when Watson won at Muirfield), and Bruce was parked in front of a TV set watching Watson watch Price as he stumbled through the final holes. This time, though, it wasn't so hard to be at home, because when he got up from the couch and walked into his den, the flag from the 18th green at Pebble Beach was hanging on the wall.

It is an old caddies' tradition to take the flag home from the final hole after a victory, and Bruce had made certain to hang on to the flag at Pebble in the aftermath of the win there. "Looking at that, thinking back to everything that happened that day, it was impossible not to have a smile on my face," he said. "I still hoped the day would come when I'd get to work the British again, but having that Open really made up for feeling as if I'd missed anything."

Watson also finished tied for ninth at the PGA, marking the second time in his career (he had tied for fifth at the Masters in April) that he had top-tenned in all four majors. After the disappointing way 1981 had ended, 1982 was quite a bounceback year: four wins, two in majors, and the knowledge that — finally — when a father and son played "Name the Open Champion" in the future, the correct answer for 1982 would be "Tom Watson." And then the father could fill in the remarkable details if he so desired.

Michael Barrett Watson was born on December 15 of that year, climaxing a near perfect year. Watson was still only thirty-three years old and, with seven majors in the bank, appeared almost certain to become only the third professional in history (Nicklaus and Walter Hagen were the other two) to reach double digits in professional major victories. The following year wasn't all that different, except that this time Watson was the victim of a remarkable shot at the U.S. Open rather than the perpetrator. Playing at Oakmont, the site of his nearest PGA miss, in 1978, Watson had come from behind on Sunday to take the lead from Seve Ballesteros (the one and only time Ballesteros seriously challenged at the Open) and looked to be on his way to a second straight victory when Larry Nelson, playing several groups ahead, started making birdies. Rain came late and the players had to return Monday morning to finish. Soon after play resumed, Nelson faced an 83-foot birdie putt at the 16th hole. He would have been delighted, if offered, to accept two putts and a par and proceed to the 17th tee. Instead he holed the putt, took the lead, and went on to beat Watson by one shot.

Watson bounced back from that disappointment to win yet another British Open — his third in four years and fifth in all — this time aided by Hale Irwin whiffing on a two-inch tap-in that allowed Watson to win by one shot. That was Watson's eighth victory in a major. He had no way of knowing — nor did Bruce — that it would be his last. Exactly what happened to his game over the next few years is difficult to pinpoint, even for Watson and Bruce. It wasn't as if he simply stopped playing well or got old all at once or completely lost his putting touch. His putting woes would come later.

It was all so gradual that it was almost impossible to see. In fact there was little sign of it in 1984. Watson won three times. He finished second at the Masters and looked on his way to a sixth British Open title before Ballesteros charged late at St. Andrews and Watson bogeyed the 17th, the Road Hole, to lose any chance of catching Ballesteros. Watson still won the money title for the year — for the fifth time — and Bruce was still making an excellent living. It was also in 1984 that Bruce again dated Marsha Cummins, the former Nelsonette he'd dated briefly in Dallas in 1975.

After graduating from high school in 1976, Marsha Cummins had gone to Houston Baptist University, where she technically majored in nursing but actually majored in partying for a year and a half. Then she dropped out when she fell in love — or at least thought she had fallen in love. The relationship lasted five years and produced a daughter, Brittany, born in 1979. It was just about the time that she got pregnant that Marsha decided she was with the wrong guy.

"I left him and went to work for a real estate agency," she said. "I was very pregnant and very confused. My parents were losing it. I mean, I'd never married the guy, now I was pregnant and about to try to raise the baby on my own."

That never happened because she met someone else while working in real estate. "I was like the girl everyone felt sorry for because I was single and pregnant," she said. "We started out as friends, because he was just very sweet and helpful. After Brittany was born we ended up moving in together."

And they ended up having a baby together, Taylor, born in 1982. Almost like déjà vu, Marsha decided the relationship wasn't working soon after finding out she was pregnant with Taylor. Confused and upset, she took her two children and moved back to Dallas so her mother could help with their care. "Then I decided I needed some space and moved to Fort Worth," she said. "I was living there in 1984, struggling to figure out what to do with my life when I looked up in May and realized that the Colonial was coming to town."

The Colonial is one of the great traditional stops on the PGA Tour. Colonial Country Club is known as Hogan's Alley because Ben Hogan won four of the first seven tournaments played there and five in all. The club also became his headquarters, the place where he spent most of his time in his later years. Marsha called her old friend Kay Barton and asked if she would mind contacting Bruce to see if Bruce could get her a pass for the Colonial. Bruce not only got her the pass, he showed up at her front doorstep to deliver it.

"I thought, 'Uh-oh, something's going on here,'" Marsha said. "Next thing I know, it's 1975 all over again."

Bruce either had a girlfriend at the time or didn't — depending on whose version you believe — but he spent that week with Marsha. "I had already broken up with her," he now says of the girlfriend.

"Which would explain why there were women's clothes all over your place," Marsha responds. "All I know is, whenever we went over there, I was very, very nervous that she was going to show up."

"We were just friends," Bruce says, grinning.

"I know, that's what worried me," Marsha answers, "that she was going to show up and find us being friends."

That week's friendship soon faded just as 1975 had faded.

Bruce turned thirty that November and perhaps for the first time wondered how much longer he wanted to caddy. "I still loved it, loved being out there," he said. "But I did start to think a little about having a family and maybe someday settling down. Seeing how much Tom's children meant to him and seeing how much the kids of other friends of mine meant to them, did make me think about it every once in a while."

Still, there was no concrete plan, no notion that there was something else he might do as an alternative. A few years earlier, Bill Leahey had forced him to sit down and start to get his finances in something resembling order. By then Leahey was working for the investment firm Smith Barney, a job he had landed in 1981 because of his willingness to step in and help Bruce in the midst of a tragedy.

Leahey and his wife, Karen, had just rented a house in the town of Shrewsbury in the Jersey Shore area. Karen was from there and Bill liked the idea of living there. He was ready to move on from the job he had held for five years at the Norton Company, a Boston-based industrial manufacturer, and had decided this was the time to take a gamble and see what was out there. He was planning to work at the U.S. Open in June for John Mahaffey, his old tour boss, and then see if he could find work near the Jersey Shore.

The night after signing the paperwork for the house, Leahey was in Philadelphia, where he was based at the time, when he got a frantic call from Bruce. The father of the woman he was dating at the time had committed suicide. She was very close to him and desperately wanted Bruce to fly to Chicago for the funeral. Bruce was in Washington, where Watson was about to play in the Kemper Open, which was being played at Congressional Country Club, in Bethesda, Maryland. He needed someone he could trust to caddy for Watson while he flew to Chicago.

"It was about ten-thirty on Tuesday night when he called," Leahey remembered. "I took a shower, packed, and drove to Washington. I picked Bruce up and drove him to some early-morning flight and then went straight to the golf course, because Tom had a morning tee time in the pro-am. I had no idea what I was doing. I had never seen the golf course, had no yardages, nothing. Tom understood, though, and was very patient."

Most pro-ams are the same. Local businessmen ante up large amounts of money — these days the going rate is anywhere from $3,500 to $6,000 per player — for the right to play 18 holes, usually in a fivesome, with one of the pros in that week's field. In 1981 Watson was as big a name as there was in any field, so the four players he was paired with came from big companies who had paid a good deal in sponsorship money for the week.

One of those companies was Smith Barney. Among the players in the group was a man named Jeffrey Kahn, who was Smith Barney's senior vice president for sales on the East Coast. "That was the week they had launched those John Houseman 'We make money the old-fashioned way, we earn it' commercials," Leahey said. "We started talking about the commercials and ended up becoming quite friendly by the end of the round. At one point Kahn asked Leahey why he — and not Bruce — was caddying for Watson. Leahey explained the story. Perhaps it struck a chord with Kahn, or maybe he just liked Leahey. In any event, he told him to give him a call, he might be able to help him find a new job sometime in the near future.

"I followed up," Leahey said. "I didn't know if he was being polite or not, but I had fooled around with stocks and bonds a little and the market interested me. So I called him. He told me to come see him at his office in New York. I did. He said they were looking for someone to work in one of their New Jersey offices, specifically the one in Tinton Falls. The office where he sent me was literally an eighth of a mile from the house we had just rented. Talk about karma."

Leahey spent the next twenty-one years working there, eventually ran the office, moved it to a large building in Red Bank, and then decided at the age of forty-nine that he'd had enough and retired. Long before that, though, he had sat Bruce down to talk about taking better care of his money. Bruce, being Bruce, simply turned his portfolio over to Leahey. "Which was probably one of the few smart things I ever did in my life," he said. "Who knows where my money would be today if Billy hadn't handled it for me."

Bruce didn't know it when they started dating again in 1984, but Marsha probably would have jumped at the proposition of marriage at the time if he had been ready. But he wasn't. Even though the thought of changing his lifestyle crossed his mind, he never really acted on it. He was sharing an apartment in Dallas with a nongolf friend and still enjoying life on the road. It had changed considerably by then. More often than not, he now flew to tournaments and, more often than not, he had his own room. Occasionally, for old times' sake, he might bunk in with Rita or one of his pals, but usually he had a single. His parents would occasionally wonder if he thought the end of his caddying days might be near, but there wasn't any stridency to it.

"I think by then we did it out of force of habit," Jay Edwards said.

"It was pretty clear that Bruce had put together a very good life for himself by then."

Bruce's sister Chris was married by that time, having met John Cutcher while both were stationed in Italy. When Chris announced that she was marrying John, that had sent Jay and Natalie spinning just a bit, because John was divorced and had children from his previous marriage who were thirteen and eleven. "Instant family," Chris said. "I knew there would be challenges with it, but to me it was clearly the right thing to do. I know Mom and Dad weren't real happy at first, but I had to do what was right for me, and I figured once they got to know John they'd get over it."

They did. Jay and Natalie now readily admit that the one time they thought their perfect daughter was making an imperfect move, it turned out to be just as correct as all the other things she had done with her life. And ironically it was John, perhaps the least athletically inclined member of the family, who was at Pebble Beach on the day of Watson's chip-in. "I was out there for a meeting," he said. "Bruce got me a ticket. I wasn't even sure I understood exactly what I was seeing, but my God it was thrilling."

The rest of the family had watched on TV that day. "By that time our hearts were in our throats whenever Tom was in contention," Gwyn said. "But that one was the worst — and then the best. We all knew how much it meant to Bruce to finally be there for a major. And to do it that way . . . wow."

Gwyn had graduated from Lafayette in 1983 and had gone into public relations work. Brian, after deciding the caddying life wasn't for him, had gone back to school to take the courses he needed to go to dental school. He went to dental school, then decided to become an endodontist. "I think he spent eleven years in college, counting graduate school," Bruce likes to say. "Then he worked for eight years and retired."

Brian insists Bruce is exaggerating — slightly. He did go to school for nine years and, after starting his own business in Charlotte, sold it and decided to take some time off before figuring out what to do next. By then he had met Laurie during a charity run and they had gotten married. A year after selling the business, Brian and Laurie moved to Colorado and Brian opened an office — where he and Laurie both work three days a week.

"The funny thing is, when Chris retired from the Navy in 1997 and Brian retired and then Gwyn quit her job to have kids, I was the only kid in the family with a steady job," Bruce jokes. "None of us could get over how ironic and funny that was, me being the only gainfully employed member of the family."

That came later. In '84 Bruce was still happily riding the Watson Express. But the train began to slow in 1985. For the first time since 1976, Watson failed to win a tournament. He dropped to 18th on the money list, the lowest he had been since 1973, Bruce's first year on the bag. Even though he top-tenned twice, he didn't seriously contend in any of the majors. He wasn't happy with his golf swing or his game, and that made life less fun for him and for Bruce. The one relief for Bruce was that Watson never blamed him for his troubles.

That was not Watson's way, and even if it had been on any level, he and Bruce were too close by then for the thought of blaming Bruce to cross his mind. Nineteen eighty-six wasn't much different. This time there was only one top ten at a major (sixth at the Masters while Nicklaus was winning his sixth Masters at the age of forty-six), and there were no wins and no seconds. Watson was 20th on the money list. For most players, a solid year. For him, a genuine slump.

"I just couldn't find a swing I was comfortable with for a long time," he said. "I tried different things and they didn't work. I was still trying as hard as I ever did on the golf course, but I was getting frustrated. The game's not as much fun when you can't play it the way you think you should, and I wasn't enjoying it as much."

What's more, his children were now school age, which meant they couldn't travel on tour as often as they had as infants. Any week at a tournament was a week away from the children, and as with any parent, that too became a distraction and a frustration. Watson began talking about cutting back on his schedule. He wasn't enjoying playing as much, he certainly wasn't enjoying the travel. He told Bruce that if there were weeks when he wanted to work for other players, that was fine with him. Watson had played thirty-one times on tour in 1973 and twenty-nine times the next year. After the kids were born, he started going home for most of the fall events. By 1986 he had cut his schedule back to no more than nineteen or twenty events a year. Bruce was still making good money working for Watson — his pay was up to $1,000 a week and 5 percent for a made cut, 7 percent for a top ten, and 10 percent for a win — but he didn't want to sit home for half the tour season. He began putting out the word that on weeks Watson didn't play, there would be times when he would be willing to work. He was careful about how he went about doing this, because he didn't want players with regular caddies giving them weeks off in order to pick him up. By then he was so highly thought of among the players that there were players who might have been willing to do that. Bruce wasn't.

"I didn't really want to work for anyone who had someone," he said. "But if a guy didn't have someone or if he was in the process of changing guys, I might work for him a little. It was just to have something to do when Tom started playing less."

The respect Bruce had gained through the years from the players came about for several reasons. Certainly working for Watson helped, but it went beyond that. Players paired with Watson couldn't help but notice how much the world's best player relied on him; they noticed his work ethic, how he never seemed caught without an answer when Watson asked a question about distance or wind or where a hidden hazard might be. Beyond that, they liked him.

"One of the fun things about being paired with Tom has always been being around Bruce," said Jay Haas, who has been on the tour for twenty-five years. "A lot of caddies are so buried in what they're doing with their player, they hardly notice the other guys. Bruce not only noticed you, he made a point of being friendly, of bringing something up that had to do with you. If Wake Forest" — Haas's alma mater — "won a big ball game, his opening comment would be something like, 'You must be fired up today about your Deacons.' He made a day on the golf course more fun even if he wasn't working for you."

Mike Hulbert, another longtime tour player, remembers Bruce grabbing him one day after he had been paired with Watson. "I was kind of struggling, and he came over to me on the putting green after we'd played and said something like, 'Hubby, I watched you today and I don't think you're that far away. Your swing looks good to me, you just have to trust it a little more.' First, that meant a lot because I respected his knowledge of the game. Second, it meant a lot more that he would take the time to come over and try and encourage me, knowing I was kind of in a down period."

Because Bruce was so well thought of, players essentially lined up to ask him to caddy when he was available. Among them were Fred Couples, Payne Stewart, Jeff Sluman, John Cook, Scott Hoch, David Frost, Peter Jacobsen, Denis Watson (no relation), Jack Renner (Brian's old boss), Andy Bean, his old friend David Graham, and the tour's resident iconoclast and gadfly, Mac O'Grady. "I think I was one of the few caddies he actually liked," Bruce remembered.

Bruce had a good deal of success on other bags. Denis Watson won in Las Vegas with Bruce working for him; Bean won at Kapalua; and Renner appeared to have won in Hawaii in 1983 until Isao Aoki holed a 128-yard wedge shot on the final hole for an eagle to beat him by a shot. Bruce enjoyed working for other players when Watson wasn't playing, and the fact that so many good players sought him out was gratifying. Stewart, who won three major titles before his death in 1999, once said that having Bruce on the bag made a bad day not such a bad day. "He's always had the best attitude and approach to golf and life I think I ever saw," Stewart said during the 1999 Ryder Cup, which Bruce worked as an assistant captain to Ben Crenshaw. "If you're with Bruce on a golf course and you don't get pumped up, then you can't get pumped up."

It was during this period that Bruce first became friendly with Greg Norman. Like everyone else in golf, he was impressed with the young Australian player who was given the nickname the Great White Shark early in his career in the United States. When Watson was paired with Norman, Bruce enjoyed his presence, his charisma and humor, and the fact that Watson and Norman together always drew an excited crowd regardless of the tournament. Norman's caddy early in his career was Steve Williams, the New Zealander who has become quite wealthy the past few years working for Tiger Woods. Norman is not one of those players who sheds caddies every fifteen minutes — he's only had four full-time guys in his twenty-two years on the PGA Tour — but he is a demanding boss and, as happens sooner or later in most player-caddy relationships, he had split with Williams in 1987 and then, a year later, with his successor, Pete Bender, another highly respected veteran caddy.

Soon after that, Norman walked up to Bruce one day on the range, handed him his phone number, and said, "Please give me a call whenever you can."

Curious, Bruce called and Norman came quickly to the point: "I'm looking for a caddy," he said. "Would you be interested in coming to work for me?"

Bruce was stunned. The thought of leaving Watson had never crossed his mind. They had been together for fifteen years. The last few hadn't been nearly as successful as the first eleven, but Watson had rallied in 1987. He had almost won the U.S. Open, coming up a few inches short on a birdie putt on the 72nd hole that would have forced a playoff with Scott Simpson for the championship on Monday. He had come back to win the Tour Championship (a new event that year, played at the end of the season by the top 30 on the money list), and that victory had vaulted him to number five on the money list. It was his first tour win in three years and came as a great relief to both player and caddy. Even without that win, Bruce wasn't looking to work for anyone else. He told Norman he was extremely flattered but he was committed to Watson. Norman said he understood but if Bruce ever changed his mind, the job was his.

Unfortunately the victory in the Tour Championship did not turn out to be a turning point for Watson. He had one of his worst years ever on tour in 1988, falling to 39th on the money list, the lowest he had finished on the list since his rookie year, 1972. Like all players who are struggling with their game, Watson was exasperated, perhaps more so than most because it had not been that long ago that he was the world's best player. He was not yet forty, he was in excellent shape, and his game had deserted him.

"It was a bad time," he said. "If you work very hard at something and reach a certain level and then you can't do what you do anywhere close to that level it is absolutely no fun — to put it mildly. I was like a writer with a permanent case of writer's block. Nothing I did, nothing I tried, could get me out of it. I talked to Byron, I talked to people I respected, I fiddled and tried to go back to swing thoughts that had worked in the past. Nothing."

Watson would never take his frustrations out on Bruce, but seeing his friend so frustrated and upset was tough on Bruce. Going to the golf course, which had been such a joy for him for so many years, became something he almost dreaded, "because I knew there was a good chance we weren't going to have a good day. I knew that was going to hurt Tom and that hurt me," he said. "It was a tough time for both of us."

And there was Norman, if not the number one player in the world, certainly the number one money-earner in golf, beckoning. He called Bruce again to see if perhaps he had changed his mind after having some time to think about it. Bruce was adamant. He worked for Tom Watson and would continue to work for Tom Watson until Watson told him he wasn't working for him anymore. Or quit playing — which at that point was more likely than Bruce's getting fired.

Watson said he never heard any rumors about Norman trying to entice Bruce to come work for him. But he was certainly aware of how respected Bruce was by other players, many of them top players, and knew that any number of players whom Bruce had worked for on off weeks would have loved to have him with them on a permanent basis. One night, after another frustrating day, Watson said to Bruce, "You know, if you ever get an opportunity to work for someone else in a job which can further your career, you should seriously consider it."

Bruce was stunned. He was even a little bit angry. "What about loyalty?" he said. "I've worked for you for fifteen years. Why would I work for anyone else?"

"Because," Watson answered, "at the end of the day this is a business, and you owe it to yourself if you have the chance to work for someone else who can make you more money to go and work for him. In fact, if that chance comes up I would *want* you to take it, because it would be the best thing for you. If I'm going to be loyal to you, that's the way I should feel. I'm not playing well right now, and you know I'm going to cut my schedule back more the next few years to spend more time with the kids. You have to think about your future. You have to do what's best for you, not what's best for me."

Bruce really didn't want to take Watson seriously. But he knew Watson was serious, because Watson was not the kind of person to even broach the subject without having given it a good deal of thought. "It was a father talking to a son," Watson said, years later. "It was time for him to think about leaving the nest and moving on with his life. When I looked at myself at that point, there was no reason to think that I was going to snap out of my playing funk anytime soon. I wanted what was best for him, and never for a second would I have seen his leaving as an act of disloyalty."

Bruce still wasn't ready to leave the nest. It was still quite comfortable, even with Watson's struggles. He was doing just fine financially, especially with the extra income he was making working for other players. He stuck with Watson for the rest of 1988 and began 1989 hoping that a new year would bring about a renaissance in Watson's game. But the new year was very much like the old. Watson had only played nineteen times in '88 and he wasn't planning on playing any more than that in '89. There were now missed cuts on occasion, something that had almost never occurred during the heyday. In fact, from 1977 through 1983 — seven seasons — Watson had missed a total of eight cuts in 148 starts, including not missing any in 1980. In 1988 and 1989 he missed nine cuts in a total of 37 starts.

Even when he did make the cut, he wasn't contending the way he had in past years. His highest finish in a major in 1988 was a tie for ninth at the Masters. He wasn't in the top 25 in any of the other three. What bothered Bruce most was what bothered Watson most: the notion that the condition might be permanent. "It was more about attitude than anything else," Bruce said. "I had never seen Tom not try, I had never seen him not willing to work. He had gotten where he was by outworking everyone else on tour. But I did sense a shift in priorities. He wasn't playing that well and he wanted to be home more. That has to change your approach to what you're doing on a daily basis."

The moment that finally forced Bruce to sit down and think about Norman's offer and Watson's words came at the Memorial Tournament in May. Watson's game was way off and he played the last few holes on Friday with no chance to make the cut. For one of the few times in the sixteen years he had been with him, Bruce sensed that Watson was having trouble caring. He was still trying on each shot, but he was almost listless, as if the way he was playing had simply taken the fight out of him. "It really depressed me," Bruce remembered.

When the round was over and Watson had signed his card, he told Bruce to contact him over the weekend because he was thinking of withdrawing from the Colonial, which was the following week. "I think I may need a break," he said.

Bruce knew the break wouldn't be for that long — the U.S. Open was only a few weeks off and Watson almost always played at Westchester, which was the week before the Open. But it was completely out of character for Watson to withdraw from a tournament for any reason other than illness or a family emergency. This was neither. This was just him feeling over-golfed.

Bruce spent most of the afternoon thinking about what Watson had said about making a business decision and doing what was best for him. He knew he would make a lot more money working for Norman. The idea of not working for Watson scared him, but he knew that Watson was going to be making decisions on his future based on what was best for him and had counseled Bruce to do the same. Finally he took a deep breath and went to the range, where he knew Norman was hitting balls. He pulled him aside and said quietly, "If the job is still available, I want it."

Norman was clearly surprised — it had been a year since he first approached Bruce — and asked Bruce to call him that night. When

Bruce called, Norman told him he was delighted that he had reconsidered and asked him if he could start in a week at Westchester. Bruce swallowed hard and said he'd be there.

The next morning he called Watson. "I actually thought about flying to Kansas City to tell him in person," he said. "But the way the caddy world works, I knew it would be all over the range at the Memorial by that afternoon that I was leaving Tom and guys would start calling Tom looking for the job, and I didn't want him to find out that way."

"Hey Bruce, what's up?" Watson asked when he heard his friend's voice.

For a moment Bruce couldn't even speak. Finally he said, "Tom, I think I'm gonna take an offer from another player. He's going to play more than you're playing right now and he's offered me a lot of money, so since you said you're going to cut back some more on your schedule, I think I'm going to take it."

"Who's the player?" Watson asked.

Bruce took a deep breath. "Greg Norman."

There was silence on the other end of the line. Bruce knew that Watson had to be shocked, and even if he had told Bruce this was the right thing for him to do, it was tough for him to take. To use the Watson analogy, it was as if Bruce were going off to college: Your parents know it's the right thing for you to do, but they still cry when they say goodbye. Watson wasn't crying, he was just very quiet. Bruce was the one who thought he was going to cry.

"Do you want me to find someone to work for you at Westchester?" he asked.

"No," Watson answered firmly. "I'll just show up there and find someone when I get there."

Bruce couldn't help but think, "Just like you did on that day in St. Louis sixteen years ago."

"As soon as I hung up the phone, I started to cry," Bruce said. "At that moment, that was the toughest thing I had ever done in my life. I knew Tom believed it was the right thing for me to do, but it still felt awful. I was filled with guilt."

True friends never want to feel they have let one another down in any way. Watson honestly believed at that moment in time that he had been letting Bruce down by not playing better and because his life had reached a point where he wanted to play less. That was why he had pushed him to leave. Even knowing that, Bruce still felt guilty about leaving.

"For sixteen years, he was the constant in my life," he said. "I lived in different places, met a lot of different people, made a lot of different friends. But the one person I always knew I would see sooner or later was Tom. And there was never a day I didn't want to work for him. Near the end, some of the days were tougher than others because he wasn't playing well, but I never felt as if I had a bad day with him. Frustrating maybe. But never a bad day. You couldn't have a better friend or a better boss."

Now, though, he had a new boss.

When Bruce showed up at Westchester with Norman's bag slung across his shoulder there were waves of shock among both players and caddies. On Tuesday, when Norman went out to play a practice round, he and Bruce found a small posse of reporters — most of them from Australia — waiting for them as they came off the ninth green. Bruce sprinted to the 10th tee, not wanting to talk to anyone. Norman lingered for a few minutes. When he walked on to the tee, he pulled out his driver, smiled at Bruce and said, "That was all about you, Bud."

"Great," Bruce said. "That's just what I need."

He heard all sorts of comments that week from other caddies, from players, even from fans. "They ranged from 'You'll help make Greg a real winner,' to 'You won't last working for him,' to 'Traitor.'"

That one, naturally, hurt most.

On the first day of the tournament, as he walked down the fairway with Norman, someone yelled from behind the ropes, "Hey Bruce, that bag on your shoulder doesn't look right!"

"Yeah, but it feels right!" Bruce yelled back. And then a thought crossed his mind: "For now."

9

The Norman Years

FROM DAY ONE, Life with Greg was a lot different than Life with Tom. Bruce had gone from working for a star golfer to working for a rock star. The flashiest thing Watson had ever done in his life was point at Bruce on the 17th green at Pebble Beach. Away from the golf course, he lived about as low-key a life as a celebrity could, often walking into restaurants unnoticed unless there were serious golf fans in the room. Without a golf club in his hands, Watson looked no different from most people walking down the street: 5 feet 9, reddish-brown hair, conservative clothes, and an unassuming manner.

Norman, in striking contrast, was 6 feet 2 with a mane of white-blonde hair that was impossible to miss wherever he went. Watson dressed quietly; Norman designed his own clothing line. Watson's entourage was Linda, perhaps the children, occasionally Bruce. Norman had family, friends, agents, personal assistants, golf course design consultants — a whole retinue of people everywhere he went. Watson played golf for a living, and when he wasn't playing golf he was home playing golf with friends, spending time with his kids, doing a little hunting with his dad and his pals. Norman never shut down. He was all over the world playing golf, designing courses, making appearances for sponsors, scuba diving. Private jets were the norm for him, usually with a car idling on the runway awaiting his arrival.

In the beginning, Bruce found it all very exciting. He was amazed by Norman's ability to walk between the ropes and shut out the hundreds of things going on in his life and focus on golf. He was working more than he ever had, because Norman played all over the world. Watson generally played overseas three weeks a year — the week before the British Open (sometimes), the week of the British Open, and in Japan in the fall. Norman was then a client of the International Management Group (IMG), which is, if nothing else, very aggressive about placing clients in overseas events in return for huge appearance fees. Norman was the best-known and highest-paid golfer in the world in the late 1980s and early 1990s and could command appearance fees well into six figures, especially in his native Australia. He made two trips a year there and played in Japan, Europe, and South Africa. Private jets were just starting to be the rage among top players, and Norman — along with Arnold Palmer and Jack Nicklaus — was one of the first to purchase a Gulfstream jet capable of transoceanic flights. In fact Norman has far more career victories overseas — sixty-six — than he does on the PGA Tour — twenty.

"We went everywhere, or so it seemed," Bruce said. "Everything was big-time, first class all the way. Five-star hotels, private jets, fancy cars, the best restaurants. Greg never did anything quietly, it just wasn't his way. It was fun and exciting at the start, although very, very different."

Jay and Natalie Edwards remember getting a call that first year from Bruce while he was on a trip to Australia. "He was calling from a cell phone, which was just about unheard of back then," Jay said. "And he said he was about to take his first scuba-diving lesson. We were all pretty impressed with where he had landed himself, even if we'd had concerns about him leaving Tom."

What amazed Bruce more than anything about Norman was his energy. There seemed to be no downtime in his life. "There were days when he would play eighteen holes and practice, go to a planning meeting for a golf course he was building, and then do some corporate deal at night," he said. "I know there were times when he didn't feel like doing some of those things, but he always did them. And if you watched him, you would never think he was tired or bored or had done these things a million times. He just kept on going."

For his part, Norman was thrilled with his new caddy. "I thought we meshed very quickly, although I knew it was an adjustment for Bruce," he said. "I felt comfortable with him, felt like we were friends. When we were overseas and I didn't have my family with me, we went to dinner. He was bright and interesting and we could talk about a lot of different things. It was like having a buddy traveling with you."

Less than two months after signing on with Norman, Bruce almost got to do something he had never done with Watson: win a British Open. Norman's only major victory at that stage had come in the 1986 British Open at Turnberry. On the second day, with the Giant blowing in off the Firth of Clyde and scores skyrocketing, Norman shot a mind-blowing 63 to take complete control of the tournament. Watson, who knew a thing or two about playing well in tough conditions, later told Bruce it was one of the great rounds of golf ever played.

Norman was better known, however, for the major championships he had lost than the one he had won. In 1984 he had made remarkable putts on the final three holes of the U.S. Open to force a playoff with Fuzzy Zoeller and then lost the 18-hole playoff the next day by eight shots. In 1986 he had bogeyed 18 to lose the Masters to Jack Nicklaus by one shot. Later that year he had blown a four-shot lead on the final nine holes of the PGA and lost when Bob Tway holed a bunker shot on 18 to beat him by two. A year later he had lost the Masters when Larry Mize miraculously chipped in from 140 feet to beat him on the second hole of sudden death.

Some people thought Norman got too keyed up in pressure situations, played too aggressively, and beat himself. Others thought he was more flash than substance and pointed to his record down the

stretch in majors as proof. Still others thought he had just been un-
lucky: Nicklaus had come out of nowhere with 65 on Sunday at
Augusta in '86; Tway and Mize had produced miraculous shots. Norman was just thirty-four when Bruce signed on with him, a player
very much in his prime, especially since he was perhaps the best-
conditioned player on the tour.

Bruce had heard the stories about Norman being a tough and
demanding boss. He respected both Pete Bender and Steve Williams and knew both had been fired by Norman. He was convinced
he could handle the pressures that he knew would come with the
new job.

"I told myself right from the beginning that I should never compare Greg to Tom," he said. "It was pointless and it wasn't fair. No
one was Tom and no one was Greg. They were entirely different
people. It was up to me to adapt to a new boss. People do that in life
all the time."

Norman and entourage flew in to the British, which was at Royal
Troon that year, after a two-day exhibition in Brussels. The weather
that year was completely out of character: dry and hot. It had been
that way all summer in Scotland. "I brought sweaters, raincoats, um-
brellas, rain pants, extra shoes, you name it," Bruce said. "As it
turned out, the only thing I needed was chapstick. It was amazing
looking at all the Scots. They were all completely red from the sun
because none of them had any idea what sunblock was or how to go
about getting it."

Bruce's first truly awkward moment since his job switch occurred
early that week. Bruce was carrying Norman's bag up to his room in
the Marine Hotel, which is located a few yards from the Troon clubhouse. As he began to walk up the stairs (there are only four floors in
the hotel and the elevator is tiny and slow), he bumped into Linda
Watson. After an initial cordial greeting, Linda said to him, "You
know, things have changed between us because you left to go work
for Greg."

Bruce was both surprised and hurt by the comment. He had assumed — hoped? — that Linda felt the same way Tom did about his

decision. "Nothing will change the way I feel about you and Tom," he said. "I'm really sorry if you feel hurt. I would never want you to feel that way."

"I believe that," Linda answered. "But I do."

Bruce had always felt close to Linda, felt she had gone out of her way, especially in the early days, to take care of him. It upset him to see how she felt. "All I could do," he said, "was hope that someday she would understand."

In the midst of the record heat wave, Royal Troon was playing fast and, with little wind, relatively easy. Scores were predictably low all week with no wind to protect the golf course. For three days Norman played solidly, hanging on the fringes of contention, but several shots behind the leader, Wayne Grady, a fellow Australian, who played resolute golf for 54 holes and led the championship by one shot going into the final day over, you guessed it, Tom Watson. Norman was six shots back and playing about eight holes in front of Grady and Watson in the last group.

He would have trailed Grady by only five shots if not for a bogey at the 18th hole on Saturday that left Bruce upset with his player. "He was right in the middle of the fairway, maybe a hundred and forty yards from the flag, which was cut on the right side of the green," he remembered. "It was an eight-iron and the play was left of the flag, get it on the middle of the green, and try to make a birdie putt from there."

Instead Norman drilled the shot directly at the flag and, when it drifted a little bit right, it landed in the right-hand bunker. Norman had made the classic overaggressive mistake: short-siding himself by playing at a pin instead of at a safe spot on the green.

"Absolutely dead," Bruce said. "No green to work with and it was downhill to the pin to boot. He hit a good shot from there to get it to twenty feet and make bogey."

Later, after the scorecards were signed and everyone had a chance to relax a little, Bruce, who was still feeling his way with Norman at that point said, "Why did you play that shot right at the flag on eighteen?"

"I was trying to be aggressive," Norman said.

"You can't be aggressive to that kind of pin," Bruce said. "You have to aim for an area of the green and be sure you make par."

Norman said nothing. Bruce had no way of knowing what that meant. Only later would he figure it out.

The next day was one of those remarkable rounds when Norman left people in awe of his talent. Knowing he had to make birdies all over the place to make any sort of run at the leaders, he came out firing on Troon's much easier front nine. "Now that was a situation where his aggressiveness was great," Bruce said. "There were birdies to be made, and he went after them. He could really get on a roll out there when he was hot and confident. It was something to see."

Norman birdied the first six holes. As a past Open champion, he is hugely popular in Great Britain, and the crowds came running as he charged up the leader board. Bruce found himself looking around in awe at the scene as Norman continued to close on the leaders. Norman might have shot 62 if he hadn't bogeyed Troon's most famous hole, the tiny par-three eighth hole, known as the Postage Stamp because the green is so small and difficult to hit. Eight years later, in his first British Open as a pro, Tiger Woods would make a seven on the hole, which is barely more than 100 yards in length.

Norman made one other mistake that day. After hitting a superb second shot on the par-five 16th to within 15 feet, he charged his putt for eagle five feet past the hole and then missed the birdie putt coming back. "Three putts for par," he said. "Inexcusable. I made a real mental mistake there."

Even with that mistake, Norman came to the 18th hole seven under par for the day and tied for the lead with Grady, still out on the golf course, and Mark Calcavecchia, who had also made a run to get to nine under par for the championship. Bruce had enough major championship experience by then to know the best thing Norman could do was post a number and make the players behind him on the golf course match it or beat it.

"I was convinced if we could make one more birdie we would win," he said. "Of course that's easier said than done."

The 18th at Troon is a difficult par-four even without the wind. A driver is risky for a big hitter because of a large fairway bunker on the right side that comes into play if one crushes the ball off the tee. A three-wood is a safer play, although it will almost certainly leave a long second shot to the green because the hole is almost always played into the wind, even in mild conditions. Norman absolutely killed a driver down the left side of the fairway into perfect position. Just as he and Bruce arrived at the ball, they spotted Jack Nicklaus cutting across the fairway behind them to the ABC-TV tower, which sat to the right of the 18th hole. In those days Nicklaus worked for ABC at the majors, arriving in the booth soon after he finished playing — unless of course he was in one of the final groups.

Spotting Nicklaus, Norman waved and said, "Hey Jack, you flying home tonight?"

Nicklaus, a close friend who had been a mentor to Norman early in his career, stopped for a moment and said, "Greg, why don't you just focus on birdieing this hole and winning the golf tournament, okay?"

That exchange may well sum up the difference between Norman and Nicklaus — or Watson for that matter. Norman is by nature always outgoing. He sees everything and everyone. Nicklaus is the opposite; if his own *mother* had been walking across the fairway at that moment, chances are good he never would have noticed her. If he had, he would have ignored her. There was work to be done.

Norman's second shot ran through the green and started up a little hill that led to an out-of-bounds marker. But it rolled back down the hill and stopped just off the green, about 30 feet from the hole. As Norman and Bruce walked up to the green, the huge crowd around the green was screaming. At the British Open, the 18th green is surrounded on three sides by huge grandstands, and players will tell you that on Sunday afternoon, when the stands are full and the tension is highest, walking to the 18th green is one of the great moments of their golf lives. It is a great moment for caddies too. For

Bruce, this was the first time, since his only British Open with Watson, back in 1976, had ended on the third day, when Watson missed the 54-hole cut.

"I remember looking around and thinking, 'So this is what it would have been like with Tom all those years,'" he said.

Norman had a long putt for birdie, but he had already made a 35-footer and a 60-footer that day, so anything seemed possible. Bruce tended the pin and watched the putt die a foot short, "right in the heart," he said later. Norman tapped in for 64, an amazing round under any circumstances on the final day of a major championship. Then he and Bruce waited to see what Grady and Calcavecchia would do. Calcavecchia came through with a birdie at 18 to tie Norman. Then, with a chance to win, Grady missed a birdie putt, and all three men headed back to the first tee for a playoff.

As Norman's luck would have it, this was the first year the Royal and Ancient Golf Club, which administers the British Open, had decided to abandon the 18-hole playoff format. Given the momentum he had built with his 64, Norman probably would have been tough to beat over 18 holes on Monday. He also would have been tough to beat in sudden death, since he birdied the first hole of the playoff. But the playoff wasn't sudden death either: It was played over four holes, the Royal and Ancient feeling that 18 holes were too many and one hole was not enough. So Norman's birdie — his ninth of the day — simply gave him a one-shot lead over Calcavecchia and Grady, who both made par.

"If it's sudden death, end of story," Norman said, forcing a laugh years later. "But you know the old saying, there's a reason why golf is a four-letter word."

Norman hadn't won after the first playoff hole, but he was still sizzling. He birdied the short, downwind second hole to go two under on the playoff. Calcavecchia also made birdie, though, and trailed by one; Grady was now two shots behind. The players cut across from the second green to the 17th tee to play the last two holes. Standing on the tee, Norman asked Bruce for the same four-iron he had hit in regulation. Bruce hesitated.

"I know a little bit about adrenaline," he said. "And at that point Greg was really, really pumped up. I started to say to him, 'You know, right now the play might be the five,' but I didn't. If it had been Tom, I just would have said it and then let him decide. In fact I think I can honestly say, with Tom if I had said it, he would have known exactly *why* I said it and would take the adrenaline into account before deciding what to hit. But I wasn't that comfortable with Greg and didn't know how he would react if I said something he wasn't expecting. So I decided to let him go with what he felt most comfortable with at that moment.

"It was a mistake. As soon as the ball was in the air, I could see it had too much on it."

The ball went through the green to the back fringe. When Bruce and Norman got to the ball, they could see some high grass right behind the ball. Norman would have to be careful to keep his putter from getting stuck on the grass when he drew it back. Norman tried a couple practice swings, then told Bruce to stay close because he might want his wedge. Bruce didn't like that idea either. "It was a downhill shot on a green without much grass on it," he said. "Once the ball landed, it was going to take off no matter how much he got under it."

Here again, Bruce resolved to say nothing. "I never said anything to Tom around the greens," he said. "That kind of shot is so much about feel it has to be whatever the player is feeling at that moment." He smiled. "Of course it also helped that Tom was maybe the greatest short-game player in history."

Norman's very good, but the wedge was a mistake. As Bruce had thought, the ball simply couldn't stop. It rolled 15 feet past the hole and Norman missed the par putt. Calcavecchia made par, so now he and Norman were tied with one hole to play. Grady bogeyed and was two back and out of contention.

"I really believe to this day that I cost Greg the golf tournament on the 17th tee," Bruce said. "I should have spoken up. That's where my experience should have taken over. If I said something and he ignored me, then it would be on him. But I didn't, so it's on me."

Not so, says Norman. "I pulled the club, I hit the shot," he said. "If Bruce had suggested five, I might not have listened. Who knows? That's typical of Bruce, though. I don't agree with him, but I'm not surprised he said it."

Back to the 18th tee. Calcavecchia's tee shot flared way right, so far right that he was outside the ropes in the trampled-down area where the gallery walked, meaning he would have a decent lie. Norman again took driver. Up in the ABC tower, Nicklaus immediately questioned the play. "I don't understand it," he said. "He's all pumped up, a three-wood is plenty to get into good position. All he does with driver is bring that bunker down the right side into play."

Bruce didn't think so. Neither did Norman. The bunker was 330 yards away. Even on a dry golf course it would take a huge shot and a bad bounce for the ball to end up there. Which, of course, is exactly what happened. Norman crushed the shot down the middle, it took one long bounce to the right — and caught the corner of the bunker. "The results say I was wrong," Bruce said. "But I don't second-guess that one."

Norman does . . . a little. "Bruce is right, the result says we got it wrong," he said. "But I'd driven the ball great all week, and I'm sure that was our mindset. Why mess with success at that point?"

While Norman and Bruce watched from the bunker, Calcavecchia hit a superb second shot from the rough to about 12 feet from the hole.

"How close is he?" Norman asked, because from the fairway it was impossible to tell exactly how close the ball was, and the crowd's going nuts didn't really mean anything at that point.

"I think it's close," Bruce said. "Can't tell exactly how close."

It was close enough that Norman felt he had to try to get the ball on the green. If Calcavecchia made birdie, laying up and making par would be worthless. Nicklaus, who had the advantage of knowing exactly how far from the hole Calcavecchia was, again first-guessed the play. "With the lip on that bunker, there's almost no way to get the ball up fast enough to hit it far enough to get it to the green," he said.

Right again. The ball caught the lip, flew high in the air, and landed in the bunker in front of the green. Now Norman and Bruce could see where Calcavecchia's ball was in relation to the flag. Norman had to get his bunker shot close, hope to make par, and hope Calcavecchia missed. Forced to try the spectacular shot, Norman didn't take enough sand and the ball flew over the green, over the out-of-bounds marker, and stopped on a little path next to the clubhouse.

That was the end of the dream. As if to twist the knife, a Royal and Ancient official standing near the bunker said to Norman as he came out, "You're still away."

Norman and Bruce looked at each other in disbelief. Norman remained remarkably calm. "I'm hitting five," he said. "Let Mark putt, and if there's any need, I'll play my next shot when that time comes."

Calcavecchia quickly put Norman out of his misery by making his birdie putt. Twenty brilliant holes had gone for naught, undone by two adrenaline-pumped shots that brought disaster. "It was an awful feeling," Bruce remembered. "Because I think we were both convinced until eighteen that he was going to win."

"Never should have been a playoff," Norman said. "If I don't make that mistake with the three-putt at sixteen in regulation, we win it without playing off. But golf is all about ifs and buts."

Norman did recover from Troon to win twice on tour that summer and won another tournament overseas. None, of course, were majors, but Bruce was making more money than he had ever made in his life. The most money he had made in any full year working for Watson had been $60,000. He made more than that in his first *half* year with Norman and continued to make more money than he had ever dreamed of in 1990, when Norman won twice, finished first on the money list with more than $1,165,000 in earnings, and continued his globe-trotting, taking Bruce along, and of course paying him for his time when he did.

That was the year when Bruce decided it was time to build a house. He had lived in apartments and small houses shared with others throughout his adult life. Now he was 36 years old, with an income well into six figures, and he was ready to spend some of his money on a place he could truly call home. He decided to build in Ponte Vedra, Florida. It was right near PGA Tour headquarters; he liked the northern Florida climate most of the year, especially in late fall, when he was home the most; and he had a number of friends living in the area. Plus Jacksonville Airport was an easy place to get into and out of, with lots of flights to Atlanta, where he could connect to just about anyplace he needed to go.

As soon as Bruce began telling his caddying buddies what he was doing and showing them the plans, the home-to-be was given a name: The House That Norman Built. Years later, when Watson talked about Bruce's decision to go work for Norman, he used the house as proof that it was the correct thing for Bruce to do. "Greg made Bruce enough money so he could build that house," he said. "The way I was playing back then, there's no way that would have happened."

Watson and Bruce missed each other. Watson continued to struggle with his game after Bruce's departure, and, he admitted, playing golf wasn't the same without Bruce walking down the fairway with him. "Every player has his own quirky habits," he said. "Bruce knew mine so well. I remember one of the first tournaments after he left, I bent down to mark a ball and, without looking, flipped the ball back over my shoulder. That's the way I always did it, and Bruce was always there to catch the ball, because he knew that. This time the ball just went flying, because the guy working for me had no idea. Not his fault. He just wasn't Bruce. He didn't know me like Bruce did.

"Plus I enjoyed his company. We had fun together. We gave each other a hard time, we got each other's humor. None of the guys who worked for me were bad guys or bad caddies. They just weren't Bruce."

And Norman wasn't Watson. When the Eagles played the Chiefs, Norman didn't care who won. Watson wanted the Chiefs to win, if only so he could taunt Bruce. The same was true of the Phillies and Royals. When the two teams had met in the 1980 World Series and the Phillies won, Bruce completely wore Watson out reminding him about the outcome. Bruce had felt as if he were part of the Watson family. With Norman he was well treated and felt that Greg was a friend, but he also understood that the relationship was different — had to be — from the way it had been with Watson.

He liked Laura Norman, Greg's wife. In fact to this day, Jay and Natalie Edwards talk about how much they enjoyed walking golf courses with Laura Norman. Gwyn still remembers walking into a New York restaurant with the Normans one night and seeing heads turn because so many people immediately recognized the white-blonde hair of the Great White Shark.

To Bruce the biggest difference was attitude. "I was spoiled," he said. "I had worked sixteen years for a player who never complained about bad luck, never whined, never blamed anyone. There are very few players like that. Only a handful at most. But I got used to that being the way it was. Then, with Greg, it wasn't. It was, I realized later, far more normal." Norman was a long way from being the worst whiner on tour, but he wasn't Tom Watson. Bruce was used to being outspoken with his player, to telling him when he thought he had screwed up. He learned — the hard way — that Norman wasn't always comfortable with that kind of caddy.

"There's no question that Tom and I are very different on the golf course," Norman said. "I don't think I've ever seen Tom get angry, really angry, at least outwardly, when things go wrong. I've never seen him yell or curse or get on himself or his caddy for bad play. I'm just not that way. I'm too intense. I do get upset when things go wrong. I get mad at myself and sometimes I get mad at my caddy. I say things in the heat of the moment I don't really mean. When I did that to Bruce at times, I would try to tell him later that it wasn't personal, it was a heat of the moment thing. But I think it was hard for him to take it that way, because we *were* friends and because he was so used to Tom, who just never took it out on him at all."

Bruce agrees that he did take things personally. He also believes that his outspokenness, which never bothered Watson, simply wasn't the right thing for Norman. With Watson, he said, "when I called him a chicken-blank mother-blank, he knew I was doing it for a reason," Bruce said. "If I told him not to hang his head or that there was something he needed to be doing, he always understood why. Sometimes when I tried to do that with Greg it worked, other times it didn't.

"It really started to go bad at the British the next year," he said, speaking of 1990. "We were tied for the lead with [Nick] Faldo after thirty-six holes and paired with him on Saturday. Well, it was one of those days. Faldo was great, shot sixty-seven. Greg wasn't, shot seventy-six. Ballgame over."

Bruce remembers standing in the fairway of St. Andrews' famous 17th hole, the Road Hole, the place where Watson's last chance for a sixth British title had disappeared six years earlier. "Well, Bruce," Norman said to him. "I guess some days it's better to be lucky than good."

Bruce was stunned. Faldo hadn't been lucky, he had been brilliant. Later he realized that Norman was doing what many if not most golfers will do in that situation: finding a way to avoid the truth, because the truth can really hurt.

"Maybe I was too tough on him," Bruce said. "But right then and there, it kind of pissed me off that he said it. I guess I should have been the supportive caddy, but I just couldn't do it at that moment. So I said, 'Greg, I just want to work for someone who plays with guts and heart, no matter the outcome.' The look he gave me told me he understood exactly what I was saying."

Things began to slide soon after that. It certainly didn't help that Norman followed 1990 with the worst year of his career, failing to win, finishing in the top ten only six times (down from eleven times the previous year), and dropping to 53rd on the money list with $320,196. The overseas income kept Bruce's pay in six figures, but Norman's struggles became a source of constant strain in the relationship. Whether Norman needed a swing adjustment — as many players do at midcareer — or was just worn out from all the years of globe-trotting and never taking a break is hard to say. But his game suffered. He also hurt his wrist at the U.S. Open at Hazeltine Golf Club that June. His game improved in 1992 after he starting working with swing guru Butch Harmon, but his relationship with his caddy did not. In fact by then Bruce was miserable.

"I had become a 'yes-caddy,' " he said. "All I was really concerned about was not getting blamed when things went wrong. If I did speak up, I was afraid of being wrong, so I wasn't as authoritative as I should have been. Greg had lost confidence in me, and I had lost confidence in myself. Things were really tense between us. I had reached the point where I dreaded going to the golf course. For sixteen years I never caddied for the money. Making money was nice, but I caddied because I loved it, and I enjoyed the competition and the feeling inside the ropes and being with Tom when the pressure was greatest. The last year, maybe eighteen months, with Greg, I was doing it strictly for the money. That wasn't the way I wanted to work or live."

"Neither one of us was happy, that's for sure," Norman said. "I was unhappy with my game, baffled by it. No question Bruce sometimes bore the brunt of that on the golf course. I know he was trying to help me, and it frustrated him feeling as if he couldn't. I don't think either one of us was a bad guy, we were just in what added up to a bad situation."

While Norman's game had taken a turn for the worse, Watson was beginning to see some light after more than four years of groping in the dark, looking for his golf swing. It happened, as Watson's swing revelations often do, very quickly and very simply. "I was on the practice tee one Tuesday at Hilton Head," he said. "I started trying a move where my shoulders were more level than they had been. It occurred to me that I had consistently been too steep with my right shoulder on my downswing for a long, long time. It was as if a light switch had finally turned on.

"I took the thought with me to the golf course the next day and started hitting shots focusing on keeping my shoulders level. There it was. The ball started flying for me again like it hadn't flown in years."

The only move missing was the pleasure of turning around at impact and saying to Bruce, "I've got it."

But he did have it, and he began striking the ball far more

consistently. His scoring didn't improve much at first, because he was still learning the swing and because he was beginning to struggle with a different facet of his game — putting; specifically short putts. But at least he didn't dread every tee box, every iron shot. "I felt," he said, "like I could play again."

By late summer 1992, Bruce could see the end coming with Norman. Playing at the International, outside Denver, they reached the 11th hole, a straight downhill par-three. Norman wanted to hit a nine-iron. Bruce, who at that stage would normally have said nothing, couldn't resist telling him he thought wedge was a better choice. Norman agreed, hit the wedge, and uppercut it just enough that it came up short in a dry creek bed. Norman slammed the club back into the bag and said, "My son [then age six] could have pulled a better club than that one."

Bruce was embarrassed and angry. "What I wanted to say was, 'Your son probably could have hit a better shot too,' but I would either have been fired or had to quit right there, so I kept my mouth shut."

Norman doesn't remember the incident but doesn't doubt that he made the comment. "By then we were both very frustrated with the way things were going," he said. "It was almost as if we both sensed at the same time that each of us needed a change."

Bruce was convinced that Norman was going to fire him, and the more he thought about it, the more he realized that getting fired would be a relief. He had never felt as unhappy on a golf course in his life as he had during the months when Norman's game had gone awry. The next stop was Milwaukee on Labor Day weekend. After two near silent days between player and caddy on the golf course, Bruce decided to tell Norman he was going to quit. He had already made arrangements with another caddy to take over for him on the weekend if Norman didn't want him to finish the tournament.

He waited in the parking lot for Norman after the round was over and said to him, "Greg, I'm not doing you any good right now, and working for you isn't doing me any good. I've decided to quit."

Norman was stunned by the way the news came out, but not by the news. "He had it exactly right," Norman said. "We weren't doing each other any good at that point, and he was right that it was better for both of us this way. I think I had reached that conclusion too, but pulling that trigger was going to be hard for me, because as bad as things were, I still considered Bruce a friend."

In fact when Bruce told Norman that he had lined up another caddy for the weekend if he wanted to make the separation immediate, Norman said no, that he would really like Bruce to finish the tournament. Bruce agreed.

"The funny thing is, the weekend was the best time we'd had together in a long time," Bruce said. "It was as if the pressure was off both of us. At one point he said to me, 'Why do you think I lose it at times during rounds?' I told him I thought he should think about seeing a sports psychologist." Norman listened to that advice — almost. "I should have seen a sports psychologist when I was younger," he said. "I think it could have made a difference then. When I was older I was probably too stubborn and set in my ways to listen to someone else who hadn't been in the situations I'd been in. But I did start studying some Zen soon after that, and I do think that did help me."

Norman eventually hired Tony Navarro, who was then Jeff Sluman's caddy, to replace Bruce. Navarro has been with him ever since. Norman says he learned something about player-caddy relationships from his time with Bruce. "I learned that even if a caddy is your friend, maybe especially if he's your friend, you have to be aware that what you say on the golf course, no matter how you meant it, can hurt," he said. "There are times when I snap at Tony, but now when I do, I make sure he knows before the end of the day that it wasn't personal, that it was just me getting upset with something I did wrong. I've even written him letters to make sure he understands that."

When Norman holed out on that Sunday in Milwaukee, Bruce walked over to him, hand extended, and said, "Thanks for the opportunity."

Norman remembers being very emotional at that moment. "I cried," he said. "You don't meet many people in life much better than Bruce Edwards, and I was sorry we had reached that point. But he was right. It was the best thing for both of us." He paused and thought for a moment. "You know, I really believe things happen for a reason. The way things have turned out for Bruce, he was meant to be back with Tom. I really and truly believe that."

Before he headed for the golf course that morning, Bruce had called the Watsons. It was Tom's forty-third birthday, and Bruce had always made a point of calling Watson on his birthday, even after he stopped working for him. Linda answered. Tom wasn't home, she said, but she was really glad he had called to say happy birthday. "I was glad to hear her sound friendly again," Bruce said. When Linda asked Bruce how things were going, Bruce told her he had quit Norman on Friday and that this would be his last day working for him. He paused and then, figuring he had nothing to lose, said, "Do you think Tom would be interested in having me back?"

Linda's response was immediate. "Bruce," she said, "I can't think of a better birthday present."

After he had said his goodbyes to Norman, Bruce called the Watsons back that night. This time Tom answered the phone. "So," he said, "are you calling to wish me a happy birthday or to ask for your job back?"

"Both," Bruce answered.

They both laughed, and Bruce felt all was right in his world again. They talked for a few more minutes about Tom's schedule and about Bruce's salary and deal. At one point when Tom was talking about money, Bruce heard Linda say in the background, "Give him whatever he wants!"

"That," he said, "made my day complete."

He was back with Watson. Back on the bag that looked right on him. Back, he thought, where he belonged.

10

Home Again

SINCE WATSON DIDN'T PLAY much in the fall, Bruce actually had some downtime after Milwaukee, which worked out well, since The House That Norman Built was just about complete and he had some time to enjoy the fruits of those three years. His first tournament back on Watson's bag came late in the fall of 1992, when he and Watson flew to Japan to play the Dunlop Phoenix Open, the one overseas event Watson always played in the fall because Dunlop was one of his longtime sponsors. Playing in Japan had become something Watson looked forward to each fall. It had been there, in 1976, that Watson had hit the nine-iron shot he felt led to his emergence as the world's best player the following year. Now it also became a place for reuniting.

Being back with Watson was a little bit like returning to his old bedroom at home for Bruce. He felt completely comfortable right away. Which made sense. There hadn't been any hard feelings between player and caddy when they had split. They had remained friends. Any concerns Bruce had about Linda had been wiped away on Watson's birthday. "It was like old times," Bruce said. "Except that we were all twenty years older."

By then the Watsons' children were thirteen and ten, which was a major reason Watson was picking and choosing where he would play. He now felt comfortable again on the golf course, confident with his swing and with the way he was striking the ball. There was a new problem, though: short putts. Once the greatest putter in the world at any distance, Watson was still dangerous from long range; but he had lost his confidence on the short ones. "You miss a couple that you think you're going to make and you start to think more about them the next time around," he said. "The next thing you know, it's inside your head, and people start whispering that you have the yips."

Next to the shanks (hitting the ball dead sideways), the yips may be the worst malady that can afflict a golfer. Quite simply, having the yips means you get jumpy and nervous over putts, almost always short ones. Johnny Miller, winner of two major championships, is the most notable exception to that rule: "I never had the yips on short putts, just ten-to-fifteen-footers," he has said. Most players experience the yips in some form as they get older and their nerves begin to lose their sharpness. The reason so many players on the Senior Tour use long putters nowadays is to combat the yips.

No one knows exactly what causes the yips to kick in. In Watson's case it may just have been the shock to the system he found in being competitive again after several years of wandering among the modern-day rabbits. In the 1970s, rabbits were players who didn't have fully exempt status and had to hop from Monday qualifier to Monday qualifier on tour. Today, on the all-exempt tour, rabbits are players who are up early on Saturday and Sunday morning to lead the field at tour events. The closer he came to a breakthrough, the more pressure he felt over short putts. Fortunately he was distracted throughout most of 1993 by the Ryder Cup captaincy. He had been named captain shortly after the 1991 Ryder Cup, the infamous War by the Shore at Kiawah Island, when the behavior of the American fans and of some members of the American team had gone way over the line of the sportsmanship considered so important to golf.

Watson was absolutely determined to do two things: tone down the rhetoric going back and forth between the U.S. and European teams and, just as important, be the first American captain to win in Europe since 1981, which had been one of the four Ryder Cups Watson had played in. He met with key European players, with key American players, and with Bernard Gallacher, his European counterpart, to discuss what had gone wrong at Kiawah and leading up to Kiawah. There was no questioning the fact that American desperation had played a part in the bad blood in 1991; the Europeans had held the cup since 1985 and had won in the United States in 1987. Watson wanted his team hungry to win, but he wanted them to win the right way.

"We should be able to play as hard as we can to try and beat our opponent," he said often, "and then be able to hoist a toast to one another when it's all over."

Watson took the job very seriously. He spent time with Kansas basketball coach Roy Williams to learn about leading a team — something golfers are almost never asked to do — and about tactics during competition. Williams gave him one piece of advice he had first learned from *his* mentor, legendary North Carolina coach Dean Smith. "Coach Smith always told us that there was no better feeling than to go on the road and quiet the crowd down," he said. "He always told our players to 'listen for the silence,' because there was no better sound you could hear in the other guy's building. And then to watch the crowd leave early."

Watson and the Americans were going into the other guy's building — specifically, the Belfry, a fairly ordinary golf course in the British midlands that was owned by the European PGA. The Americans had lost the cup there in 1985 and had allowed the Europeans to retain it there in 1989 with a 14–14 tie that would have been a U.S. win if four Americans hadn't found the water at the 18th hole on Sunday during the twelve singles matches.

Ten of Watson's twelve players were decided for him by a points system. When the PGA Championship ended at Inverness that year, Watson had to announce his two captain's picks. Actually he made three: Lanny Wadkins and Raymond Floyd, both veterans of many

Ryder Cups, would be the eleventh and twelfth players. Watson's third captain's pick was Wadkins's caddy: Bruce Edwards. He and Wadkins had agreed that Bruce should be part of the Ryder Cup team, and with Watson not playing, this was the logical way to do it. Wadkins knew Bruce well because he and Watson had been playing practice rounds together — with some intense money matches going on throughout — on Tuesdays for most of twenty years.

The 1993 Ryder Cup turned into one of the most dramatic in years. This time the Americans trailed by three points on Saturday morning, rallied to within a point that afternoon, and then came from behind late on Sunday to win. There were all sorts of twists and turns to the plot, including European veteran Sam Torrance's coming up with an infected big toe on Saturday night, which meant that Torrance, who would later be a Ryder Cup captain himself, would not be able to play in the singles matches on Sunday.

Under Ryder Cup rules, if a player on one team can't play singles, one player from the other team sits out the singles matches and each team receives a half-point for the match not played. Before Watson could give any serious thought to who should sit out for his team, Wadkins insisted it should be him. It wasn't fair, he reasoned, to make one of the ten players who had made the team on points sit out. It should be Floyd or it should be him, and Floyd was playing better golf than he was, even though Wadkins's reputation as a Ryder Cup singles player was peerless. Watson decided he was right. Of course that meant that Bruce also sat out — as a caddy. Many of the American players remember him that Sunday bouncing from match to match, handing out encouragement, relaying instructions from Watson, or just cheerleading.

Most vivid among those memories is that of Davis Love III, who, as things turned out, found himself locked in the match that would decide the outcome against Costantino Rocca of Italy. Love had just won the 17th hole to even the match and was walking up the hill to the 18th tee when he saw Bruce standing directly in front of him.

"His eyes were as wide as I've ever seen them and completely full of fire," Love remembered. "He just grabbed me by the arms and screamed at me" — the noise was so loud only screaming could be heard — " 'You are going to win this match! Do you hear me, you are going to win this match. You're a great player. You're going to win.' "

The other end of the emotional spectrum at that moment was Watson, who stood waiting for Love on the 18th tee, hands dug into his windbreaker. "We could use this point," he said quietly.

Love, remembering the day, laughs at the memory. "All hell was breaking loose right there and Tom just says, 'We could use this point.' If I hadn't been so nervous I might have said, 'No shit, Tom.' "

Instead, hearing Bruce's voice in his head from tee to green, Love hit a superb drive and made a memorable, curling six-foot par putt to win the match and clinch the cup. "Usually in golf, under pressure you want calm," he said, years later. "Not at that moment in the Ryder Cup. You really need someone to scream in your face that you can do it. Years later [1999] I was walking on the last day with Justin Leonard" — Love had already won his singles match — "and he was losing to José María [Olazábal] and getting down on himself, and I thought about Bruce at the Belfry and kind of grabbed him and said something like, 'Dammit, you're going to beat this guy. Just be Justin Leonard and you'll win.' " Like Love in '93, Leonard ended up the hero, draining one of the great putts in Ryder Cup history, a 50-footer for birdie, to clinch the cup for the Americans.

To the surprise of no one who knew him, Watson read the "Man in the Arena" speech during the closing ceremonies and declared the U.S.'s 15–13 victory the highlight of his career, placing it even above his eight majors because he had shared it with so many others and so much work and planning had gone into it. Sportsmanship had been returned to the Ryder Cup; the victors and the vanquished toasted one another that night, and Lee Janzen walked in on Watson at 3 a.m. sitting with his feet up, a cigar in one hand, a glass of wine in the other, watching the BBC replay of the final holes with the sound turned all the way up. It was as happy as Janzen or Bruce or anyone could remember seeing Watson in years.

*   *   *

Watson's first real chance to break his seven-year victory drought came early in 1994 at one of his favorite venues, Pebble Beach. In addition to his victory there in the 1982 Open, he had won what had then been the Bing Crosby Pro-Am in 1977 and 1978, and in his college years had often beaten the dew-sweepers onto the golf course at sunup. The corporate takeover of the PGA Tour had reached the Monterey Peninsula in 1986, when the tournament had been renamed the AT&T Pebble Beach National Pro-Am. Those who have been around golf long enough still insist on calling the tournament the Crosby, in part to make the PGA Tour corporate people cringe.

The "Pro-Am" part was a reference to the fact that, unlike at most tour stops, where amateurs play only on Wednesdays, at Pebble Beach the amateurs play in the actual tournament. Each pro has an amateur partner, and many of the amateurs are celebrities from the acting and entertainment worlds, the sports world, even a stray TV newsperson sprinkled here and there, in addition to the corporate moneymen who ante up the big bucks to participate. Watson's amateur partner is usually Sandy Tatum, the former USGA president, who has been a friend and mentor since his days at Stanford.

Watson's swing that week was about as close to perfect as it had been since the glory days. He was confident, his tee shots were finding the fairways consistently, and he went into the final round at Pebble Beach (the first three rounds are played on three golf courses) two shots behind young Dudley Hart and one behind old Johnny Miller, with Tom Kite two shots further back. This was a 1970s leader board: Miller was forty-six and had been retired to the TV booth for five years. He only played in the AT&T because he was a two-time champion and had grown up playing the golf course with his dad. Watson was forty-four and had already been a Ryder Cup captain. Kite was forty-two — and had won *his* U.S. Open at Pebble Beach two years earlier. Hart must have figured he had taken a wrong turn and ended up in a grainy old highlight film.

Naturally the Sunday weather was cold, windy, and rainy — classic Crosby weather. After nine holes, Watson, Miller, and Hart were tied for the lead. Bruce couldn't help but think it was all right there: Watson in bad weather on a golf course he loved, trying to beat a kid and a TV announcer. He was right. Or should have been right. With Hart fading, Watson led Miller by two shots with five holes to play. He still led by one as he lined up a 12-foot birdie putt on the 16th green. But that putt just missed and rolled four feet beyond the cup — right in what players call the throw-up range, the kind of putt that had haunted Watson in his recent past. His par putt didn't even touch the hole.

He went to 17 still tied for the lead, back to the scene of his most glorious moment in golf. This time, in a howling wind, he found the green safely with a four-iron, landing 35 feet right of the flag. Hoping to give Watson some positive thoughts, Bruce whispered to him, "Let's do something special from *this* side," as he lined the putt up. Watson tried, but the putt slid three feet past the hole. Once upon a time, three feet for Watson was like three inches for most people. Not anymore. He missed that putt too and gave Miller the lead. When he missed an eight-footer for birdie at 18, all Miller had to do was par in to win. Which he did.

The depth of Watson's putting woes was never more evident than that day. As he stepped into the bunker at 18 to hit his third shot, CBS commentator Ken Venturi, who almost never said anything demeaning about any player, much less one of Watson's stature, said quietly and sadly, "The only way he can make birdie right now is to hit this ball about an inch from the cup." Watson came out to eight feet — once almost a gimme for him, now virtually unmakeable.

Bruce knew how devastated Watson was. As Watson said later, "If I had been even mediocre with the flat stick out there today, I think I would have won pretty easily."

He was right. And yet he was still Watson, waiting by the scorer's tent for Miller to finish, offering congratulations and then forcing a smile and saying, "Now get your butt back up in the booth."

Miller was as stunned by what had happened as Watson and Bruce were. "Down the stretch I kept thinking, I never beat Tom Watson, he always makes a putt somewhere to beat me," Miller said.

Not this time. "Early in my career I lived by the putter," Watson said. "Right now, I'm dying by it."

There was hope. Watson had hit the ball plenty well enough to win against a good field. He and Bruce both remained convinced that there was an answer to the putting problems. Of course golf fans had answers. Watson was bombarded with letters from fans suggesting everything from putting cross-handed (he tried it once on a putt at number 13 at Doral and then gave up the idea) to the long putter, to putting lefty, to hypnotism. Other players offered tips. One morning on the putting green at the Tournament Players Club in Jacksonville prior to the Players Championship, PGA Tour commissioner Deane Beman, an excellent putter in his day, gave Watson a lesson. Everyone wanted to help. But the yips have nothing to do with mechanics. Watson knew how to putt, he had been a great putter for years. He was simply at a stage where his mind wasn't allowing his body to do what it was perfectly capable of doing.

What made '94 such a tough year was that Watson was playing better golf than he had played in quite a while. Having both his golf swing and Bruce back made the game more fun for him than it had been in years. He played well at Augusta, finishing 13th, and then headed to Oakmont in June for the U.S. Open.

Watson and Bruce both insist to this day that they love Oakmont. It is without question a classic old golf course, located just outside Pittsburgh. It has been the site of many memorable major championships. It was also the site of two of Watson's greatest disappointments: the 1978 PGA, when he lost a five-shot lead on the back nine on Sunday and lost in a playoff to John Mahaffey, and the 1983 U.S. Open, when he had again led on the back nine Sunday before Larry Nelson's 83-foot birdie putt at the 16th hole on Monday morning (after a rain delay) had beaten him by one shot.

"What I remember the most is the tenth hole at the '78 PGA," Bruce said. "He hit a perfect drive and it landed in a sandy divot on the fairway. He had no shot from there, and he had to purposely hit it fat to try to keep it short of the bunkers, because there was no way he was going to get it on the green. But he ended up with an almost impossible third shot and the ball ran clear across the green. He ended up making double bogey, and that changed everything. He actually had to *rally* to get into the playoff."

The '94 Open may have been the hottest in the history of the tournament. The East Coast was in the midst of a record heat wave and the temperatures each day were in the mid-90s with brutal humidity. Watson weather. Any weather that is uncomfortable is Watson weather on tour. For three rounds, he was right there on the leader board, trailing leader Ernie Els by three shots, in a tie for third place with Hale Irwin and Loren Roberts going into Sunday. On Saturday, after his round, someone asked Watson about his two less-than-happy Oakmont memories. Watson shook his head as if to say they didn't matter.

"This is a great golf course," he said. "I love playing here. Oakmont has been a friend."

Oakmont wasn't anyone's friend that Sunday. The USGA hadn't been happy that heavy rains on Thursday night had slowed the greens to the point where there had been a couple of 65s and 66s and a number of other rounds in thc 60s. Els would be starting the final round at seven under par. The Oakmont members were *still* grumbling about the 63 Johnny Miller had shot twenty-one years earlier on Sunday on a rain-saturated course. That just wouldn't do. So the greens weren't watered on Saturday night, as is standard procedure at the end of a round if there is no rain, or if they were, the hoses were turned on for about three seconds per green. The next day, in the searing heat, they were so hot and fast that players who went out early said they were starting to turn white.

Greens that fast made putting tough for everyone; virtually impossible for Watson. He struggled to a 74 and finished tied for sixth. The condition of the golf course produced a rare outburst from Watson, one of the few times in his career when anyone among the public saw him truly upset. When he walked into the scoring trailer to sign his card, Watson asked Jeff Hall, taking scores for the USGA, a direct question: "Whose decision was it to change the condition of the golf course today?" Hall, who is accustomed to players complaining about course setup and conditions, didn't answer the question because he honestly didn't know. "You just don't do that to a golf course on the last day of a U.S. Open," Watson continued, clearly angry. "Let mother nature decide the condition of the golf course. That was a man-made change and it wasn't right."

At that moment, Bruce, standing behind him as always, gave Watson a gentle tap on the back. Looking up, Watson saw the ABC-TV camera installed in the scoring trailer not so much to capture moments like that as just to show the players going through the routine of handing in their cards. Watson was chagrined. He hadn't realized he was on camera.

Years later, though — not surprisingly — his opinion hadn't changed. "That was just wrong," he said. "They changed the golf course overnight and then didn't tell anyone they had done it. At the very least they should have had someone on the first tee to say, 'Fellas, we only watered for two minutes instead of seven last night, you can take that for what it's worth.' Let us know what we're dealing with."

Again, a disappointment, but one laced with hope. Playing a tough golf course, Watson had been right there in contention until the finish. The British Open was coming up. It would be played at Turnberry, a golf course that might be described as Watson's best friend.

It had been seventeen years since that glorious weekend when he had dueled with Nicklaus in the final two rounds. Returning to Turnberry and being back in Scotland was like going home for Watson. Having won the British Open five times and having made it clear how much he had come to love Scottish golf, Watson was an adopted son to the Scots. Everywhere he went they yelled his name — "Toom," or "Toommy" — and it was clear that he loved being there among them. Illness had forced Alfie Fyles to retire from caddying by then, so Bruce was there, thrilled to be in Scotland with Watson, delighted to finally see Turnberry in person.

The week prior to the Open, the Watsons had taken a vacation in Ireland with Lee Trevino and his wife, Claudia — who, in the small world category, had grown up in a house no more than 100 yards from the 16th tee at Wethersfield Country Club and not far at all from the spot where Watson had almost been arrested while sticking up for Bruce during his only appearance at Wethersfield for a GHO.

Watson had come to play in the tournament in part because he knew it would mean a lot to Bruce to come back to Wethersfield on the bag of the world's number one player. During a practice round, Watson and Bruce were crossing a public road that runs between the 15th green and the 16th tee when a car going way too fast came within inches of running Bruce over. Angry and a bit frightened, Watson yelled, "Hey, watch what you're doing, you SOB!"

The car braked to a fast halt. Sure enough, it was an unmarked police car. The policeman got out, marched over to Watson, and said, "What did you just say to me?"

Watson never blinked. "I said, 'Watch what you're doing, you SOB.' You just about ran my caddy over just now."

In the mind of the policeman, that wasn't the right answer. "He wanted to arrest him," Bruce said, able to laugh at the memory years later. "I'm standing there thinking, 'Great, I'm going to have to walk the bag back to the clubhouse and then go bail Tom out of jail.' Fortunately, a bunch of people jumped in and pointed out to the cop that they saw him driving too fast and this was Tom Watson and he should just let it go. The guy finally let it go."

Watson got to finish the round, but he never did make it back to Wethersfield, although he did play Hartford in later years when it moved to the TPC at River Highlands.

Watson loved spending time with Trevino because Trevino could make him laugh as few people could. "Just one of the great wits you'll ever meet," is the way Watson describes him. During the week Trevino, just as aware of Watson's putting woes as everyone else in golf, gave Watson a putting lesson, moving his hands slightly forward on the putter. Watson felt comfortable with his stroke and when he began to make putts on the relatively slow Scottish greens during the practice rounds at Turnberry, his confidence soared.

On Wednesday he played his final practice round with Nicklaus, Nick Price, and Greg Norman. It was the old men vs. the young men; the past stars vs. the current stars — Price and Norman being ranked 1–2 in the world, Norman the defending champion. Watson and Nicklaus hammered them, winning 100 pounds each. The gallery appeared to be every bit as big and enthusiastic as it had been that last day back in 1977.

Watson had to play very early Thursday and struggled while trying to wake up the first nine holes, but he posted a solid 68. The next afternoon it was 1977 again — he shot 65 to take the lead. "Not bad for a has-been," he said, laughing, when the round was over.

Watson would never say it, but he was convinced he was going to win. This was *his* championship, *his* golf course, *his* crowd, and he was hitting the ball as well as he had in years. Even a couple of missed short putts on the back nine on Saturday that dropped him a shot behind the coleaders, Fuzzy Zoeller and Brad Faxon, didn't shake his confidence going into Sunday. Or Bruce's. Mindful of the ugly pattern of Sunday that had developed during the year — 74 at Pebble Beach, 74 at Augusta, 74 at Oakmont — his last comment to Tom as they left the golf course that night was direct: "I have a feeling," he said, "that tomorrow is going to be the best Sunday we've had this year."

He was right. For seven holes. Watson was near perfect for that long. When he birdied the seventh hole, he was leading the golf tournament and his smile was as wide as the nearby Firth of Clyde. The weather was mild — Watson would have loved to have seen the Giant roll in — but that was fine. He was going to win. He was convinced, so was Bruce.

And then, in a space of twenty minutes, it all collapsed. A slightly hooked drive that caught the left rough at eight. A too-hot five-iron through the green. A difficult chip that ran 20 feet past the hole.

And three putts — the second one a four-footer. A double bogey. He had gone from leader to tied for third on one hole. Watson was flashing back. "Dammit, Tom," he said, pulling the ball out of the hole. He was so pumped up and angry that when he tried to toss his putter to Bruce, he put so much into the toss that he almost hit Bruce in the face with it. Bruce tried a brief pep talk walking to the ninth tee, which might be the most scenic spot in all of golf — it sits on a tiny promontory of land, water on three sides, the famous Turnberry lighthouse down the fairway to the left. Watson stared at the water while waiting to tee off, as if searching for something — ghosts from 1977 perhaps.

He hit what looked like a good drive, over the directional flag in the fairway. "Good one, Tom," Bruce said, "Come on, let's get going again."

Something had gone out of Watson on the eighth hole. As he walked up the hill from the tee to the fairway, his head was down. For the first time, he didn't respond to the encouraging shouts from the Scots. His tee shot had actually gone too far right into the deep rough. He missed the green from there, tried to do too much with a chip, then chipped (again) to four feet. There wasn't much question about what would happen next. He missed.

Back-to-back double bogeys. It was over.

Two hours later, after signing for another Sunday 74, Watson stood next to the 18th green and patiently answered all the questions . . . again. Someone asked him what he would take away from the week. For once Watson couldn't think of the birdie that might follow the double bogey. "Nothing," he said. "Nothing."

Did he still think he could win again?

"You bet," he said.

Why.

"Because," he said, his eyes flashing some anger, "I believe it."

A few yards away, Bruce stood waiting, still shouldering the bag. "It's so damn close," he said. "I know you can if and but forever, but if the drive at eight is two feet more to the right, the way he's rolling at that point, it all might have been so different."

He forced a smile. "At least he's still got those five. They can't take them away."

What Bruce didn't say — and wouldn't say — was that he would have loved to have had just one.

Years later, talking about high and low moments in his career, Watson brought up Oakmont in '78 — especially since he never did win the PGA — and Oakmont again in '83. He still remembered Winged Foot in '74 and Olympic in '87. But number one on the list, he said, was Turnberry in '94.

"I thought I was going to win," he said. "In fact I was convinced all week I was going to win. It would have been the perfect way, the absolute best way, to end the [seven-year] drought." He paused. "And I really wanted to win one over there with Bruce. That would have been really special."

Even with all the putting problems, Watson had his best year in a long time in '94. The T–11 at the British was certainly disappointing, but he finished the majors season with a T–9 at the PGA, meaning he had finished in the top 15 in all four majors — even with 74 on three of the Sundays. It was the first time in five years he had made the cut in all four majors and the first time in seven years that he had been in the top 15 in all four. Even spending a lot of money with his Sunday putting problems, he finished 43rd on the money list, the highest he had been since finishing 39th in 1988 and fifth in 1987.

Bruce was just happy to be back where he belonged. The two men were very much partners and, in many ways, peers now. Watson was the boss and always would be, but he almost never had to give Bruce any kind of order, because Bruce knew exactly what needed to be done before Watson asked. And Watson knew that when his caddy spoke sharply to him at times, it wasn't out of disrespect. It was, to put it bluntly, out of love.

Bruce's love life away from the golf course was a different story. With all the traveling he had done through the years he had met many women, dated many women, and enjoyed relationships with many women. But he had never really fallen in love. The lifestyle was certainly a factor, but so was Bruce's personality. As Watson always says, "a gypsy at heart."

Bruce turned forty in November of 1994. It may or may not have been coincidence that he met Suzie Marciano a couple of months later in a bar near Pebble Beach. Watson was to play a Shell's Wonderful World of Golf match against Jack Nicklaus the next day, after the conclusion of the '95 AT&T Pro-Am. "All the other guys had left, since the tournament was over, and I just went into the bar at Mission Ranch to have a drink and she was in there," Bruce said. They started talking. "She told me she had come up from San Francisco to take a tennis lesson." He laughed. "I guess that should have told me something right there — coming over a hundred miles to take a tennis lesson."

Suzie Marciano was short, well-built, and friendly from the start. Bruce had never had trouble meeting women and Suzie was no exception. She had recently divorced ("quite well," Jay Edwards likes to say, since her ex-husband was an executive for the Coach clothing line), and even though she knew very little about golf, she certainly knew who Tom Watson and Jack Nicklaus were. Almost casually, Bruce invited her to the match the next day.

"She showed up for the last four holes," Bruce said. "That started it."

It became something of a whirlwind romance, Bruce flying in to San Francisco when he could, Suzie eventually coming out on tour to spend time with him. Everyone was impressed — initially. "On the face of it, she was everything you would look for," Bill Leahey said. "She was good-looking, very striking, and smart. She had a lot of flair and a good sense of humor. It was only later that we all started to wonder."

Jay and Natalie Edwards were impressed too. Suzie's father had been an operatic singer, her mother a pianist. She played the piano and spoke three languages. She seemed to be the real deal.

They were engaged in the fall. The wedding was set for the Monday after Pebble Beach — a year and a day later on the golf calendar than the day they had first met — and it would be held in the place where they had met, Mission Ranch. Bruce's friends were happy to see him finally settle down. Then they started to learn more about who he was settling down with. She had a daughter from her previous marriage who lived with her father. That was certainly unusual. She traveled in prominent circles — San Francisco mayor Willie Brown, for instance, was to be one of the guests at the wedding. Bruce's sister Gwyn still remembers Suzie's maid of honor getting up at the rehearsal dinner and tearfully talking about how much Suzie meant to her; after all it was Suzie who had given her her first pair of Chanel earrings.

"What in the world," Gwyn whispered to the rest of the family, "is this all about?"

"We had the sense," Jay Edwards said, "that she thought she was marrying a golfer and would be living the life of a golf wife, not the life of a caddy's wife — albeit a well-paid caddy."

Watson was also concerned. He wasn't about to tell Bruce what to do — Bruce admits that at that stage no one could have changed his mind anyway — but at the rehearsal dinner he pulled Suzie aside for a minute and said quietly, "Don't ever hurt him."

"I won't," Suzie said. "I promise."

Watson, like everyone else, was skeptical. "We did everything but set up an over-under for how long it would last during the wedding," Gwyn said. "Bruce was certainly enamored of her. But it didn't feel right to any of us."

It didn't feel right to Bruce for much longer. After the wedding Suzie moved into The House That Norman Built and was miserable. Ponte Vedra, Florida, is a long way from San Francisco in more ways than one. She missed her friends and the social life. The tour, when she was out with Bruce, wasn't nearly as glamorous as she had envisioned — especially since she was a caddy's wife. She began talking about moving back to San Francisco. For Bruce that wouldn't have been practical in any way, financially or logistically. Suzie got very involved in gardening and that distracted her for a time. Then she went back to San Francisco for a while to take a cooking course and train to be a caterer. But when she returned to Ponte Vedra, she found that the law in Florida wouldn't let her run a catering service from her home.

Gwyn, who was working in Atlanta at the time for Turner Sports, remembers going to lunch with a client one day at an expensive restaurant. The golf tour was in town, the tournament being played at a course about an hour north of Atlanta. "There was Suzie, sitting there all by herself eating lunch," Gwyn said. "It just struck me as strange. When she saw me, she sent over a ridiculously expensive dessert. It was nice of her, but all I could think was, 'What is she doing sitting in this place all alone?'"

By the time Watson transitioned from the regular tour to the Senior Tour at the end of 1999, the marriage was clearly floundering. Bruce wasn't happy, neither was Suzie. "There was just no way she was going to be happy in Ponte Vedra, especially with a husband who was away twenty-five weeks a year," he said. "I should have known that right off the bat, but I didn't."

Bruce may be one of the most nonconfrontational people on earth, but it seemed he and Suzie were fighting all the time now. In March of 2000, he was in Arizona with Watson, who was playing his first Senior major at the Tradition, one of those faux majors cooked up by the PGA Tour. Suzie called to say she had decided to move back to San Francisco. The marriage obviously wasn't working for either one of them.

"I was so relieved," Bruce said. "She was right, and now I was off the hook. I didn't have to pull the trigger."

Except that Suzie called back the next day. She wanted to try again. Bruce thought that was a bad idea and told her so. Suzie hung up on him.

The Tradition ended on the Sunday before the Masters, Watson losing in a playoff to Tom Kite. Bruce then flew on a private plane with Tom to Augusta, got to the house he shared during the week with Greg Rita, turned off his cell phone, and went to bed, exhausted.

When he woke up the next morning he turned his phone on and checked for messages. "There were twenty-seven messages," he said. "All from Suzie."

The calls had started out friendly and calm. "I saw you on TV today. You looked great. I was pulling for you guys." But with each passing one they became a little angrier, a little more desperate. Finally one of them said, "If I don't hear from you in five minutes, I'm going to start breaking things."

The next one was Suzie telling him to listen and then the sound of glass being broken in the background. Then another call. And another. "You aren't going to have much memorabilia left," she said at one point.

Panicked, Bruce called his close friend Mike Rich and asked him to go over to the house, find Suzie, and see how much damage she had done. Rich called back a little later to say he had only found one broken item, a framed picture that actually belonged to Suzie. "She'd been bluffing," Bruce said. "So I called her at that point and asked her why she was threatening to break all my stuff. And she said, 'I wanted you to call me.'" Bruce explained that even if he hadn't had his cell phone turned off so he could get some sleep, threatening him was not the best way to get his attention. She told him she was staying in Ponte Vedra till he got home.

Bruce went straight to the house Watson always rented for the week, played the last several messages for Watson, and asked Watson what he thought he should do. "You need to talk to Chuck," Watson said, referring to Chuck Rubin, Linda's brother, who had been his agent since early in his pro career. Rubin, as always, was in Augusta for the Masters. His advice was blunt: "You need to get her out of the house," he said. "She sounds like she's close to some kind of breakdown. The next time might be worse."

Bruce didn't want to believe that, although he knew it was certainly possible. But he was in the middle of a three-week trip: the Tradition, the Masters, and the Senior PGA Championship the next week in Palm Beach, a tournament that was important to Watson, because even though he didn't really think of the Tradition as a major, he did think of the Senior PGA (and the U.S. Senior Open) as a major. "Maybe she'll be okay until I get home," he told Rubin.

Watson missed the cut at Augusta, and he and Bruce flew to Palm Beach to get ready for the PGA. Suzie called to say that movers were coming to the house the next day, bringing back things of hers that she had taken with her to San Francisco during her cooking school sojurn. What, she asked Bruce, should she tell the movers? "I would tell them not to unpack, to turn around and take the stuff back to San Francisco," Bruce said. "I really think that's the best thing for you and for me."

Suzie sounded calmer, more reasonable. Maybe, Bruce thought, she would realize the marriage was over and leave peacefully.

The third round of the PGA Seniors, on Saturday, wasn't completed because of a midafternoon Florida thunderstorm. That meant the players still on the golf course, Watson among them, had to return early Sunday morning to finish the round before the start of the final round. Bruce's 6 a.m. alarm had just gone off when his cell phone rang. He sighed, hoping it was Watson calling about something; hoping it wasn't Suzie.

It wasn't either one of them. "Bruce Edwards?" a voice said.

"Yes?"

"This is Sergeant Smith from the St. John's County Police Department. I think you should come home immediately. Your wife has burned your house down."

Bruce stared at the phone for a second in disbelief. He knew instantly this wasn't a joke or a prank. "How much damage?" he asked, almost afraid to hear the answer.

The police sergeant hesitated for a moment. "It's basically destroyed," he said finally.

He went on to explain that Suzie had been found two doors down at a neighbor's house after police and firefighters had been called to the scene. She had confessed to starting the fire and had told the police officers who questioned her, "I should have burned all his memorabilia by the pool, like I was originally going to." The police thought initially that she had started the fire by burning Bruce's memorabilia, but fire investigators later told him that the fire had been started in the attic with gasoline poured on the floor and a match thrown on the gasoline.

Bruce was staying that week at the home of Kevin Dennis, another old caddying buddy, who had worked years earlier for Tom Weiskopf and had settled in Palm Beach after getting off the tour. Dennis was working with NBC that week as a spotter. Bruce asked him to go straight to the golf course, meet Watson, tell him what had happened, and caddy for him that day. Dennis agreed. Another old caddying friend, Tim Thalmueller, had driven down from his home in Ponte Vedra to spot for NBC that week and was also staying at Dennis's house. He insisted on driving Bruce back to Ponte Vedra. "I'm not letting you get behind the wheel right now," he said. "You'll drive a hundred and that won't do anybody any good."

Bruce, knowing Thalmueller was right, agreed. By the time the two men had made the drive up I-95 and gotten to the house, the fire was out. Suzie was under what the police call Baker Watch, because she had told the police she might commit suicide. That meant she was in protective custody for seventy-two hours. Bruce was allowed to go inside the house. Almost everything inside had been destroyed. Suzie hadn't started the fire in the memorabilia room, but she had made absolutely certain that his most cherished souvenir — the flag from the 18th hole at the '82 Open — had been destroyed. "She had smashed the frame, pulled it out, and set it on fire in the kitchen sink," Bruce said. "All that was left was the three ringholders that held the flag in place. When I saw that, I lost it completely."

His marriage was clearly long gone, he had lost his home, and he had lost many of the artifacts he cherished most from twenty-seven years on the tour.

The police asked him if he wanted to press charges against his wife. No, he told them, he didn't. Clearly she was disturbed and needed help. The state of Florida had no choice but to charge her with felony arson since she had confessed to the crime. Suzie pleaded guilty, and since Bruce was the victim, the prosecutors asked Bruce what kind of sentence he would like them to recommend to the judge.

"I didn't want to see her thrown in jail," Bruce said. "I still don't think she was evil or malicious. I didn't think her daughter or her parents, who I really liked, should go through having to see her in jail. So I asked them to put her on probation for fifteen years *and* place a restraining order on her for that time to keep her away from me. I don't think the judge was thrilled. He wanted to give her jail time. But he went along with it."

Suzie moved back to San Francisco and Bruce started dealing with rebuilding his home and rebuilding his life.

Insurance rebuilt the house. Friends and family helped him begin to rebuild his life. One other person, someone he hadn't heard from in years, provided the finishing touches on the second job.

11

Winning . . . and Moving

THE YEARS DURING WHICH Bruce's marriage deteriorated and moved toward its unhappy finish were also the closing years of Watson's career on the regular tour. Watson turned fifty on September 4, 1999, and started playing the Senior Tour the following week. In fact he won in his second start on that tour, a quick indication that he was going to have a good deal more success playing against the older guys than against the younger ones.

"They shouldn't even let him out there. It isn't fair," Fred Couples, a good friend of Watson's, had said a couple of years earlier. "He hits it better than most of the guys out *here* [on the PGA Tour]. It won't be a contest if he's really into it playing against the Seniors."

Watson had indeed enjoyed a genuine renaissance as he approached fifty. After enduring the near misses of 1994 and a similar year in 1995, he finally won again in '96. Given that Jack Nicklaus had been in the middle of the most dramatic moments of Watson's golf career, it was somehow appropriate that when Watson broke his nine-year nonwinning streak, it was at the Memorial, the tournament created by and for Nicklaus on a golf course he had designed and built. Watson had won the Memorial before, in 1979, shooting a

69 during the second round on a frigid, windy day when the field's stroke average was almost 10 strokes higher. That had been during his heyday. This was different. This was Watson at forty-six, finding the old magic again to beat an elite field.

"It didn't start out to be that kind of week, that's for sure," Bruce remembered. "His dad had just had a stroke and he wasn't even sure he wanted to play. I think he came because he knew his dad would want him to and because by then he and Jack had become very close. But he was really uptight in the practice rounds."

On Wednesday, Watson came to the 18th hole during the last practice round in what would best be described as a lousy mood. He tried to hit his tee shot from left to right to keep it away from the creek that runs down the left side of the fairway. Instead he hooked the ball and it took one hop and landed in the creek. Furious and frustrated, Watson flipped his driver to Bruce and said, "You know, I hate this damn game."

Now it was Bruce's turn to get angry. He knew Watson was worried about his father and unhappy with his game, but he just didn't think he could allow him to continue with that kind of attitude, regardless of the circumstances. "Plus that wasn't him," he said. "Tom almost never talked that way on the golf course, even when he was really playing poorly."

Bruce decided it was time for a lecture. He was about to say something when Watson took out a four-wood, dropped a ball next to the hazard, and proceeded to hit the flag with what was his third shot. That gave Bruce the opening he needed.

"I said, 'Yeah, this game really sucks, doesn't it? Don't you just hate this damn game?' He kind of smirked at me at that point, but I wasn't done with him yet. I said, 'You know, Tom, your father taught you this goddamn game, and considering that he just had a stroke, I would think you might want to dedicate the week to him.' He didn't say much after that, which told me I had gotten through to him. So I didn't say anything else, just handed him his putter and walked to the back of the green.

"He had an eight-foot putt for par and he rolled it in. When he handed me the putter I said very softly, 'Your father would have really liked that four.'"

Getting Watson to straighten out his attitude was one thing — and not usually that difficult. Getting him to make short putts, especially under pressure, was another. Bruce decided to play another mind game with him that week. "I've always been a good putter," he said. "Tom gave me lessons back in the '70s and that really helped, but one thing I've always done when I'm playing is every time I've got a putt under ten feet, I pretend it's for birdie — whether it's for birdie or par or bogey or double bogey. Doesn't matter. I just say to myself, 'Knock this one in for birdie.' Maybe it's pure coincidence, but I've always been good at making those putts.

"So that week, I played the same game with Tom. Every time he had a putt under ten feet I was in his ear, regardless of what the putt was for. 'Knock this in for birdie,' or, 'This will be a good birdie when you make it.' I remember a few years ago when someone asked Tom once what my role was, he said, 'Bruce is always the voice in my ear.' That made me feel good, because it meant he was listening."

Trying to make putts for birdie all week, Watson took a one-shot lead into the final day and was paired with Ernie Els. On the first hole, he missed a three-foot "birdie" putt — and bogeyed. Walking off the green, Bruce said quietly, 'Okay, that's out of your system now. It will be the last one you're going to miss all day.'"

From that point on, Watson was almost perfect. With David Duval, then a rising star, closing in on him in the final holes, he kept making shots when he had to. He missed one very makeable putt — about a six-footer at 16 — but still held a one-shot lead playing the 17th hole, with Duval already in the clubhouse. Watson's second shot ran just through the green. He had about two feet of short rough to putt through and took out his putter, since he was only about 15 feet from the flagstick. At that moment, for the first time in twenty-three years as a caddy, twenty of them with Watson, Bruce broke his code of never telling a player what to do around the green.

"I just thought he was going to have to hit it too hard with the putter to get it through the rough, and then it would be hard to get it to stop near the flag," he said. "I said, 'Let's chip this, you're a great chipper.' Tom agreed, took out a nine-iron and left the chip three feet short. For a moment my heart sank, but then he stepped up and knocked the putt right in — another 'birdie' — and I breathed a sigh of relief. Because he made that putt, I'm a great caddy at that moment. If he misses . . ."

Still leading by one, Watson hit a perfect drive on 18. As he pulled out a six-iron, Bruce said, "Remember the shot you hit last year?" Watson had nearly holed a six-iron shot on 18. "Just do the same thing."

Watson smiled and hit his shot right at the flag, landing it 12 feet past the pin. "That what you had in mind?" he asked as they walked up to the green, hearing the roars from a crowd that was thrilled to see Tom Watson about to win again. Just as he had done at Pebble Beach in 1982, Watson used one putt when he had two to work with, knocking the birdie putt dead center for a two-shot victory.

"It was like winning for the first time all over again," Bruce said. "That hug was almost as special as the one at Pebble . . . and a long time coming."

Needless to say, the win and the hug had just as much meaning for Watson, who did dedicate the victory to his father. It was his thirty-eighth PGA Tour victory and came after he had gone 139 starts in a row without a win. It was the catalyst to what was then the most lucrative year of his career — he made more than $761,000 to finish 25th on the money list — and even though he continued at times to struggle with the putter, he had at least proved that he was right on that disappointing day at Turnberry when he said he would win again.

And he won again, in 1998 at the Colonial, making him one of the oldest players (he was four months shy of forty-nine at the time) to win on the PGA Tour. That victory and another top-30 finish on the money list — 29th — had Couples and others telling him there was no reason for him to move over to the Senior Tour when he turned fifty. He could still hit it long enough and straight enough to compete with the kids, so why not keep competing with them?

Part of Watson wanted to do just that. Most of the best players are dragged kicking and screaming to the Senior (now Champions) Tour when they turn fifty. Nicklaus never fully embraced it, never playing more than seven events there in any single year. Tom Kite, Watson's contemporary, told people he would only go over when he knew he couldn't compete on, as most players call it, "the real tour" anymore. Watson liked being around the younger players, liked competing against the best. But even though he could still hit it long and straight, his body kept reminding him that he *was* fifty, not twenty-two or even thirty-two or forty-two.

"I can't practice the way I used to practice," he said. "Sometimes my hip bothers me, sometimes I just get sore, period, if I'm out there for long stretches. I used to love to practice for hours. I can't practice that way anymore. I like the fact that I can go back and play on the regular tour a few times a year, I enjoy that. But the fact is at this stage of my life, the Senior Tour is the right place for me."

Both Watson and Bruce found the adjustment to their new life difficult at times. Watson and Linda had divorced in 1998 and Watson had remarried just before joining the Senior Tour. His new wife, Hilary (who had previously been married to South African pro Denis Watson), had three children, who were thirteen, ten, and eight when their mother remarried, so Watson had a new family in addition to a new tour. At the same time, Bruce's marriage was in its final throes, climaxing with the loss of his house eight months after Watson began playing the Senior Tour.

Both men knew that the Senior Tour would be different from the regular tour. On the one hand, it was a homecoming of sorts, Watson reunited with players he had known for years: Nicklaus, Arnold Palmer, Jim Thorpe, Andy North, Bob Murphy, Lanny Wadkins, Hale Irwin, and others. The same was true for Bruce. His old buddy Mike Boyce was working for Gil Morgan; Lynn Strickler, a longtime pal, was with Crenshaw. "Sometimes it was as if we were back in the '70s again," he said.

But they weren't back in the '70s. When Watson arrived on the Senior Tour, with Wadkins and Kite arriving a couple months afterward, the hope was that their arrival would pump new life into the tour at a time when interest in it was fading. The Senior Tour had sprung up in the late 1970s, following on the success of an annual event called the Legends of Golf, which had been held as a team event in 1978 and 1979. Noticing that Arnold Palmer, the most popular player in golf history, had turned fifty in September of 1979, the PGA Tour decided to experiment with a couple of Senior events in 1980. At the same time, the USGA decided to hold a U.S. Open for Seniors, although in that first year, players had to be fifty-five to compete. The following year, the age limit was dropped to fifty, and much to the joy of the USGA, the winner was the fifty-one-year-old Palmer.

Palmer's popularity, and the country's fascination with nostalgia in the 1980s, built the Senior Tour. Older golf fans loved to watch Sam Snead still tee it up every now and then, in addition to Palmer and Gary Player and Julius Boros and Chi Chi Rodriguez — and, ten years in, Lee Trevino and Nicklaus, even if Nicklaus didn't play that often. Corporate America loved the Senior Tour because the core audience was, generally speaking, middle-aged and older people who fell into the upper income brackets — the perfect audience for Cadillac, Mercedes, high-end banks, and credit cards.

But as the tour grew, it wasn't dominated by the great players but by players who had been journeymen on the PGA Tour or in some cases hadn't played the PGA Tour at all. Among the legendary players, only Trevino (twenty-nine victories) and Player (nineteen wins) truly embraced it. It was difficult for those who had been the very best in the world to get excited week in and week out about playing in 54-hole no-cut events on golf courses that were set up short and easy in order to encourage low scoring. The money got bigger and bigger, but dominant players weren't motivated by the money. They had plenty. The players who were motivated by the big purses were the midlevel players who had played in an era when one had to be a consistent top-ten player to get rich. This was their chance.

"The Senior Tour," the late, great Dave Marr once said, "is life's ultimate mulligan."

The dominant players on the tour were men like Jim Colbert and Gil Morgan and Bruce Fleisher, all of whom had solid careers but were hardly stars in their prime. Hale Irwin, the all-time leader in victories on the Senior Tour (thirty-eight through 2003), was a superb player who won three U.S. Open titles, but he wasn't the kind of charismatic figure who was going to bring fans to the golf course or to their TV sets. Trevino was, but once injuries and age began to slow him in the late 1990s, there was really no one to fill the void he left. That was where Watson, Wadkins, and Kite were supposed to step in. They had all been born in 1949 and had been rivals throughout their careers on the PGA Tour. Watson had won eight majors, Wadkins and Kite only one apiece. But Wadkins had won a total of twenty-one times on tour and was a popular, charismatic figure. Kite had won nineteen tournaments and for a long period had been the tour's all-time leading money winner.

They would be the Senior Tour's new triumvirate. Their continuing rivalry would bring people back to the over-fifty set. Only it didn't happen that way. Kite played remarkably well in the Senior "majors" his first year out — a first, a second, a third, and a tie for fifth — but had trouble getting excited about the nonmajors. Wadkins never seemed to get excited about playing against his peers. His first three years out, he won once and had only six top-ten finishes in sixty-one starts. Watson played only forty-two times those first three years. After his victory in September 1999, he managed a total of three wins in three years: two of them in the season-ending Tour Championship, one in the 2001 Senior PGA. That victory, by one stroke over his friend Jim Thorpe, had great meaning, since he had never won the PGA Championship. It was hardly a coincidence that all three of those victories took place in 72-hole events played on relatively tough golf courses. Watson likes tough golf courses. The Senior Tour was not the best place in the world for someone looking for challenging venues.

"Look, the Senior Tour is fine," Watson said in 2003. "I do prefer tougher golf courses, but I've enjoyed myself out here. I enjoy being around the guys and I enjoy still having a chance to compete. Is it the same as when I was on the regular tour? Of course not. It's different because it has to be different. Once you understand that, it's just fine."

That's exactly what it was to Bruce, just fine, nothing more. He missed the tension of the PGA Tour, the golf courses, and his friends, who were for the most part still working over there. He also missed the crowds. Most Senior Tour events draw small, quiet crowds. Only the real Senior majors — the PGA and the U.S. Open — are apt to draw crowds that make players and caddies feel as if they are back playing with, as Trevino likes to call them, "the flat-bellies."

Bruce's feelings about the junior tour vs. the Senior Tour may have been best summed up when, as he walked toward the first tee for Watson's first practice round at the Masters in 2000, he stopped under the famous tree outside the clubhouse, looked at the sky, held out his hands, and said, "Real tour *air*. I feel like I can breathe again!"

During Watson's first years on the Senior Tour, Bruce had offers from several top players on the junior tour — notably David Duval and Ernie Els — to go work for them. As he had with Greg Norman, Watson would have understood if Bruce had chosen to make the jump. This time, though, it was never an issue for Bruce. No doubt he could have made far more money working for Duval or Els, who played worldwide schedules as Norman had, probably played twice as much in a year as Watson, and were winning consistently and often. "I learned once that money can't buy happiness," Bruce said. "I knew I belonged with Tom. If he had told me, 'Go do it,' I would have told him no way. But it never came up because I never thought about it seriously."

He did keep his hand in on the regular tour by working several times a year for Lee Janzen and a couple of times a year for John Cook. Watson was only playing about eighteen times a year — thirteen or fourteen Senior events and about four regular tour events — so Bruce had free time to work for Janzen and Cook. Cook didn't have a regular caddy, and Janzen's caddy at the time, Dave Musgrove, lived in Great Britain. Several weeks a year, rather than ask Musgrove to fly over just to work one tournament and then fly back, Janzen would hire Bruce. That worked perfectly for the player and both caddies.

"I already knew he was good from watching him with Tom through the years," Janzen said. "But I found out *how* good one of the first times he worked for me. I asked him for the yardage to a hole, and he said it was something like one fifty-six but I needed to play the shot as if it were one forty-six because there was a little ridge short of the pin that would make the ball hop forward. I pulled out my yardage book and there was no notation about a ridge on that part of the green. I said, 'Are you sure, Bruce? There's nothing here about a ridge.' He said it was there, he had seen it yesterday when he checked the dot." (Caddies nowadays check every green the first three days of a tournament to see where the rules officials have marked a small white dot. That tells them the next day's pin placement and allows them to check around the area for any ridges or plateaus, things that won't always show up in a yardage book or on a pin sheet.)

Janzen was convinced by Bruce's certainty and played the shot as if it were 146 instead of 156. Pros are that exact in their yardage. As Watson says, "When we're on, we can hit any club to within plus or minus two yards of our target." Janzen watched his shot land, take a big hop forward, and settle hole high. "If Bruce doesn't see the ridge, I hit the shot ten yards farther and I'm probably over the green," he said. "Instead I've got a makeable birdie putt. After that I never doubted him again."

Bruce enjoyed working for both Janzen and Cook. He liked both men, he liked the extra income, and he liked getting back to the regular tour whenever he could. He was one of the few caddies who could handle Cook's mercurial temperament. One of the tour's nicest men off the golf course, Cook could become a dervish on the golf course, often beating himself to a pulp when he played badly. "Bruce, as much or more than any caddy who ever worked for me, could handle me," Cook said. "What's more, he was never afraid to tell me to just stop it — which is exactly what I need to hear sometimes."

But his best weeks were still with Watson, especially at the two Senior majors Watson really focused on and those rare weeks when Watson went back to play the regular tour. As a two-time champion, he played Augusta every year; he played the British Open every year; and he played the two tournaments he had won late in his career — the Memorial and the Colonial — every year.

It was at the Colonial in May of 2002 that Marsha Cummins came back into Bruce's life once again.

She was actually Marsha Moore by then, mother of four, two grown, two from a marriage that wasn't working. She and her husband, Jeff, had recently agreed to file for divorce.

It was Marsha's first marriage, but her third serious relationship. Since last dating Bruce in 1984, Marsha had gotten a job as a flight attendant for American Airlines, so for a while she was traveling almost as much as Bruce. Her parents would take her kids, Brittany and Taylor, when she was on the road, and she finally had a job that she truly enjoyed. In 1987, she met Jeff Moore, who was then a senior at SMU.

"I was looking for a car," she said. "I read an ad in the paper and went to see the guy about the car. He was very nice, and I bought the car. Then I get a call from him saying he had left his CDs in the glove compartment. Could he come over and pick them up? He did, we got into a long conversation and, well . . ."

Jeff was twenty-one at the time, Marsha was thirty-one. They dated for six years before Marsha finally got over her phobia about being married and married him. "I had to wait for him to grow up," she jokes.

They had two children: a son, Brice, who was born in 1993, and a daughter, Avery, born eleven months after that. It was not long after Avery's birth that Kay Barton called Marsha with some news about an old friend of theirs: Bruce Edwards had at long last gotten married.

"I probably hadn't seen Bruce a half-dozen times since 1984," Marsha said. "But when Kay called and told me he had gotten married,

I was devastated. I mean, completely devastated. It made no sense. Here I was, married, with young children, and I was carrying the torch for a man I had hardly seen at all for years. But I was crushed. Completely crushed. I remember saying to myself, 'Marsha, it just wasn't meant to be. Now move on.' But it was a lot easier said than done. I guess there was a part of me that just always figured some- how, some way, we'd end up together," she said. "And then there was Kay on the phone, in essence telling me no way it was ever going to happen. I tried to put him out of my mind at that point." She smiled.

"But I guess I never really did. I guess my first clue should have been when my son was born and I wanted to name him for Bruce, so I named him Brice," she said.

She and Jeff had gone from Texas to Florida to Texas, hoping to find happiness in their marriage. He had changed jobs twice. She had gone back to work, as a ticket agent for Southwest Airlines. Then she decided to go back to school, enrolling in the nursing pro- gram at the University of Texas at Arlington. "I was searching," she said. "I didn't know what for, but for something."

And then Bruce showed up again.

Marsha had read in the papers about the house burning down and the divorce. She felt awful for Bruce and had asked Kay Barton, who still kept in close touch with Bruce — he is godfather to her two daughters — how Bruce was doing. "Kay kept me updated on Bruce," she said. "But that was as far as it went."

Until Colonial week. Kay and her sister, Ruthann, both knew that Marsha and Jeff had split. They also knew that Bruce was coming to town. They invited Marsha to a party at Kay's house, not ever men- tioning that Bruce was coming to the party too.

"I walked up to the porch and there he was, sitting in a chair, drinking a White Russian," Marsha said. "My heart just about stopped when I saw him. All of a sudden it was 1974 and I was a seventeen-year-old Nelsonette again."

They started talking, and all the memories flooded back. By the time the night was over, they were sitting on the couch together watching an NBA playoff game while everyone else was off in another room watching some reality show. "So it started up again just the way it had the first two times," Marsha said. "We had a great week together. He took me to a great Mexican restaurant for my birthday, and when it was over we went to a bar and sat and watched a hockey game."

Clearly any woman who actually *wanted* to watch a playoff hockey game on her birthday was a woman after Bruce's own heart.

Which, in fact, was exactly what Marsha had decided she was — after his heart. "When the week was over, he left town and I went to see Kay," she said. "I said to her, 'This time he's not just walking out of my life again. I'm not going to make it that easy for him.'"

Kay was all for the notion of Bruce and Marsha together, but she knew that Marsha's saying she wanted them to be a couple didn't mean it would happen. She explained to Marsha how awful the end of Bruce's marriage had been, how much he had gone through in the aftermath of the fire, the trial, and the divorce. "She said, 'If you'll forgive the expression, he's been burned,'" Marsha remembered. "I said, 'I know, but Kay, I'm a woman on a mission.'"

Bruce and Marsha began talking — occasionally on the phone, but more often by e-mail. Their instant messages went back and forth so often that when Brice and Avery were on their mother's computer and spotted Bruce's e-mail address popping up in the instant messaging corner of the computer, they started screaming, "Mom, Mom, he's back!" For a while they only knew Bruce by his computer sign-on. Bruce was very intrigued by Marsha and greatly enjoyed her company. But as Kay had pointed out, he was in no rush to get serious with anybody.

"I was a long par-four over water," he said. "To a narrow green."

That was okay with Marsha. To carry on with the golf metaphor, she was through laying up where Bruce was concerned.

He invited her to come visit in Ponte Vedra. She scrambled around for a babysitter and went. Then he invited her to a tournament. She went again. She began planning ahead. Bruce's birthday was in November. She wanted to do something truly special, something that would tell him how much he meant to her without her having to say the words. "I've always been a planner," she said. "I wanted to do something unique. I knew he'd lost a lot of stuff that meant a lot to him in the fire, so I came up with an idea to try to get him some of those memories back."

She told Kay her idea: track down every clipping she could possibly find — every photo, every newspaper or magazine story, anything — on Bruce's career with Tom. "That's going to be an awful lot of work, especially to get original clips, not just stuff out of the computer," Kay said.

"I know," Marsha answered, then repeated her mantra: "I'm a woman on a mission."

The mission to find anything and everything about Bruce Edwards took her to libraries and newspapers and magazines around the state of Texas. She spent hours going through microfiche, making copies, then taking them to Kinko's and convincing the people there that she wasn't infringing on any copyright laws, just trying to complete a mission. She found special paper and finally a binding that she knew would get Bruce's attention: It was Eagles green.

As she worked, things were getting better and better with Bruce. He was inviting her to more and more tournaments, e-mailing more and more often. It was all going according to plan — until San Antonio.

"He had invited me to come down for the week, which was great since it was an easy trip from Dallas," she said. "We had a wonderful time. And then I made a horrible mistake. I said those three words."

The three words that often send men, especially recently divorced men, running for cover: I Love You. Marsha knew the instant the words had escaped her mouth that she had made a mistake. She could tell by his response, "something along the lines of, 'Yeah, okay,'" she said, but more by the look on his face. "Terror," she said. "I had terrified him."

The rest of the weekend was as awkward as a first date. Marsha went home to Dallas and reported back to Kay. "I screwed up," she said. "This is a setback, but I can still rally."

Still sticking to the golf metaphors, Bruce's description of San Antonio was simple: "She needed to lay up and she went for the green."

Splash.

Marsha knew she was in some trouble but didn't think she was finished yet. The e-mails went from a torrent to a trickle. "The killer would have been if he called and told me not to come to Las Vegas," she said. "I'm not sure what I would have done if he had done that."

Bruce was scared by the three words, but he wasn't about to stop seeing Marsha because of them. In retrospect, he knows now he was pretty well hooked already. He just hadn't admitted it to himself. "Hilary Watson had walked with her at a couple of tournaments and really liked her," he said. "She said to me, 'So are you pretty serious with this girl?' I said, 'Me, serious with someone? No way. Not again.'"

Hilary knew better. She told Tom that she thought Bruce really liked this woman but didn't want to admit it — to himself or anyone else. Bruce was working Vegas for John Cook. The week went well — not overwhelmingly well, but Marsha thought she detected some thawing around the edges. At the end of the week, she asked Bruce if he still wanted her to come to Ponte Vedra for his birthday. Yes, he said, he did. That was good, she thought, because that was when she was going to give him The Book.

"It was the book that put me over," he said, looking back. "I couldn't believe it when she gave it to me, because so much work had gone into it. I think deep down, I knew then that I wanted to marry her, but I was still scared."

Marsha understood that. After her mistake in September, she wasn't going to push the envelope again. She was thrilled with his reaction to the book but was determined not to get ahead of herself again. When she returned to Dallas, she called Kay and said, "I'm back in the ballgame."

She was very much in the ballgame by then. Bruce took the book to his parents' house in Vero Beach (Jay Edwards had retired in 1997 after forty-three years of dentistry) and showed it to them.

"He said a friend of his had done it for him," Natalie Edwards said. "We looked at each other and thought, 'There is no way some-one who is just a friend does something like this. He's way beyond friendship with this girl — whoever she is.' "

Bruce invited Marsha back to Ponte Vedra for New Year's Eve. He had decided by then to ask her to marry him but told no one — not even Watson. When Gwyn invited him to come spend Christmas in Boston, he turned her down, saying someone was coming to visit him right after Christmas. "I knew it was a girl, that wasn't any big deal," Gwyn said. "But from the tone of his voice I had a feeling it wasn't just any girl."

On New Year's Eve, Bruce and Marsha went to a party at the Ponte Vedra Club, a place where Bruce had gone on New Year's Eve for several years. When the ball dropped and the balloons fell, Bruce kissed Marsha, wished her a Happy New Year, and said, "Will you marry me?"

Marsha was stunned for a second, but quickly recovered. "Absolutely," she said.

Mission accomplished. The long par-four over water had been birdied.

They toasted 2003 and the future, which had never looked brighter to either one of them than it did at that moment.

12

"A Black Thought"

WHEN MARSHA WALKED onto the porch of Kay Barton's house on that warm Texas evening in May 2002 and saw Bruce sitting there, White Russian in hand, he might have been, as far as she was concerned, the same dashing nineteen-year-old she had met in her Nelsonette days.

Except when he started to talk.

"There was a thickness to his speech," she said. "It wasn't a big deal, and I just figured he'd had a couple of drinks already. But it was still there at other times that week when I knew he hadn't been drinking. Nothing serious, the kind of thing where you think maybe he's just really tired. But I did notice it."

She wasn't the first. In fact as far back as February, Bruce had bumped against the issue when he walked into a bar one night in Naples, Florida, during the tournament held there and asked for a glass of wine. "The bartender looked at me and said, 'Sir, I'm really sorry I can't serve you in your condition,' he remembered. "I said to him, 'What condition?' He said, 'You've had too much to drink.'

"I told the guy he was crazy. I'd had one glass of wine all night. But I wondered what in the world was going on."

The slurring in his speech came and went. Some days it was gone completely. Other days it was more noticeable. Both Tom and Hilary Watson noticed it too and initially thought little of it. But when it continued and became more frequent, they also began to wonder what was going on.

"I'd been on Bruce for years to get a complete physical," Watson said. "He's had a smoker's cough for almost as long as I've known him, that deep hacking that sounds so bad sometimes. I wanted him to get his lungs thoroughly checked. I knew it had been a long time since he'd gotten a physical, and periodically I would tell him he needed to go and get a physical. But I knew he never did."

In fact Bruce hadn't had a complete physical since he had first left Wethersfield in 1973 to pursue the caddying life. Like most caddies, he had never bothered to get medical insurance even after he started to make real money. "It was just something I never gave any thought to," he said. "I figured I'd get it when I needed it."

Of course insurance never works quite that way. By the fall, more and more of Bruce's friends were starting to notice the slurring and were concerned about him. But they hesitated to say anything. Greg Rita, his closest friend still in caddying, thought he'd had a minor stroke. "My mother had a stroke about a year earlier, and the symptoms he had were similar, though not as serious," Rita said. "I wasn't sure what to do. I guess I just hoped it would disappear."

So did Bruce, who had a second episode with a bartender in Las Vegas in early October 2002. This time he was with Marsha and hadn't had anything to drink. "The bartender looked at Marsha and said he would give me a drink but only if she was driving," Bruce said. "Rather than argue, Marsha just said she was driving."

By now Watson too was concerned that Bruce might have had a small stroke. "The slurring was getting worse with time," he said. "At first, I thought he was tired when I heard it or that he'd had a late night. But when it persisted, I began to think there had to be more to it. I wanted him to get up to the Mayo Clinic and see Ian Hay [Watson's doctor] and get a complete physical. When I told Ian about what I was seeing and hearing, he told me that Bruce needed a complete physical sooner rather than later."

Watson's concerns were crystallized on the morning of October 24. He was playing in the Senior Tour Championship in Oklahoma City, and the weather was cold and blustery when he and Bruce walked onto the first green. Watson marked his ball and, as he always did, tossed it to Bruce so he could clean it before he putted. Bruce reached out with his left hand to catch the ball and couldn't close his hand around it. The ball dropped to the green and Bruce began looking at his hand to figure out what was wrong.

That was when he noticed the cleft — a deep indentation between his thumb and index finger. He tried again to make a fist, failed, and waved Watson over.

"Hey Tom," he said. "Take a look at this. Something's wrong with my hand."

Watson walked over and looked at the spot where Bruce was pointing. A chill that had nothing to do with the weather went through him. "I had a black thought right then and there," he said months later. "Can't tell you why, I just did."

Firmly, Watson told Bruce the time had come to get to a doctor. Shaken, Bruce nodded, wondering what the heck was going on. First the speech problems, now this. Still, he tried to keep the outlook as bright as possible. "I'm probably getting arthritis," he said, walking off the green. "I'm getting old, you know."

Watson forced a smile in response. He seriously doubted that Bruce had arthritis. As the day warmed, Bruce's hand loosened up. But the cleft was still there. Watson went on to win the tournament, and Bruce had no more trouble with his hand. Still, Watson reminded him again that he wanted him to get a physical as soon as possible. "You let me know when you can go up there, and I'll set you up at the Mayo," he said. Bruce told him he would. When he got home, he began — finally — looking into getting medical insurance. He got all the forms and began filling them out. He didn't want to tell Watson he didn't have insurance, so his hope was to get insurance, then set up the appointment at the Mayo. He wondered what was wrong. He knew his lifelong smoking habit was dangerous and was hoping he didn't have emphysema or lung cancer.

It was the off-season now, and he was resting and feeling better back home in Florida. Marsha visited on his birthday, and he went to see his parents on Thanksgiving. They had noticed some slurring in his speech, but said nothing. "We were sitting around at night drinking wine," his father said. "We figured it was nothing more than that. His spirits were good, and even though he wouldn't admit it, we thought something was clearly going on with this girl who had put together this incredible book for him for his birthday. He seemed as happy as we could remember seeing him in a long time."

By the time the Christmas holidays rolled around, Bruce knew something was wrong with him. The cleft in his hand had grown and he was losing weight, something he never did during the off-season, when he wasn't walking five miles a day with a forty-pound golf bag on his back. His parents went to Boston for Christmas to spend time with Gwyn and Lenny and their kids. On Christmas Day, Bruce called to wish everyone a Merry Christmas.

Gwyn answered the phone. "I said, 'Geez Bruce, I can't put you on with Mom and Dad, you're hammered,'" she remembered.

Bruce hadn't had anything to drink. He didn't argue with his sister, because he knew by then that he probably did sound drunk, even though he wasn't. When Marsha arrived the next day, he kept hiding his left hand from her, because he was convinced she would notice how deep the cleft had gotten. By now he was scheduled to have blood drawn by someone from an insurance company in early January. That would be, he hoped, the last step toward getting insurance. Then he could have his physical, find out what was wrong, and start getting better.

When he proposed on New Year's Eve, he and Marsha agreed they would get married sometime in the summer. Watson was tentatively planning to take a month off after the Senior British Open in July. That would be the perfect time to schedule the wedding and give Marsha time to do all the planning that was needed — not just wedding plans, but moving plans. The day after New Year's, she flew home to Dallas to tell Brice and Avery they were all moving to Florida, that she was marrying the guy who kept sending her all those instant messages on the computer, and that they were going to live in a house with a swimming pool. A few days later, she flew back to Ponte Vedra to look for an apartment — "I wasn't going to just move in with two kids when we weren't married" — and to get Brice and Avery enrolled in new schools. On the night before she was supposed to fly back to Dallas, Bruce woke up in the middle of the night coughing.

And couldn't stop.

"It went on a long time," Marsha said. "It was scary. I thought we were going to have to go to the hospital. He couldn't stop for a long time. When he finally did, he was out of breath, exhausted, and, I think, a little scared. He'd had coughing fits before, but never anything quite like that."

The next day Marsha called Hilary Watson, whom she had become friendly with, and told her about what had happened. When Hilary passed the news on to Tom, he again called Ian Hay and described all of Bruce's various symptoms. "He didn't make any comment to me about what he thought it might be," Watson said. "But I guessed he had suspicions. What he said to me was direct: Get him up here now."

Tom called Bruce to tell him in no uncertain terms he was making an appointment for him for the next week. There would be no more negotiating or stalling. That was when Bruce finally confessed that he had no medical insurance. "Forget about it," Watson said. "You get up there, get checked out, and tell them to send the bills to me."

Bruce argued briefly, saying something about getting blood drawn that week. Watson didn't want to hear it. "I'll call you back and tell you when you're going up there," he said. It was no longer a suggestion or a request. Bruce understood. Watson called back a little while later to say he was expected at the Mayo Clinic on January 14. He would need to be there at least two full days for the battery of tests Dr. Hay was planning. Bruce called Marsha to tell her about the appointment. "I'll go with you," Marsha said. Bruce told her she didn't have to do that, he'd be fine. Like Watson, Marsha wasn't in a mood to argue. "I'm going," she said. "In fact, I'll make all the travel arrangements and meet you up there. You just rest."

Bruce rested. On the Saturday night before he was scheduled to fly to Minnesota, Greg Rita and Mike Rich, a close friend who worked as a bartender in Ponte Vedra, came over to the house to watch the Eagles and Atlanta Falcons' playoff game. The Eagles won, and Bruce decided that was a good omen for the week to come. He told his friends he was going to get a physical, that Tom had set him up at the Mayo Clinic. Both were glad he was finally going to see a doctor.

"I didn't make a big deal out of it," Rita said. "But I was glad he was going."

Bruce had told Rita and Rich about proposing to Marsha shortly after New Year's. At that stage, he hadn't told anyone else — not even his family or the Watsons — because he wanted to do it in person. Both men were delighted, especially Rita, who had first met Marsha back in 1984 and had thought *then* that she was the best woman Bruce had ever dated. He was happy to hear that Marsha was going, because he sensed that his friend was just a little bit scared. "Or maybe," he said, "I was a little bit scared." Without telling Bruce, he called Marsha in Dallas and gave her his cell phone number. "I want you to call me from up there and let me know what's going on," he said. She promised that she would.

Bruce told no one else he was going to the Mayo Clinic except his brother, Brian. "I just thought someone in my family should know I was there and what was going on," he said. "I didn't want to alarm my parents or my sisters, so I told Brian."

Hearing his brother's voice, Brian was concerned — but not panicked. "I was actually happy he was going," he said. "I told him just to do whatever the doctors told him to do and whatever Tom told him to do. When he told me about the insurance and what Tom was doing, to be honest, I wasn't surprised. That sounded like Tom, especially where Bruce was concerned. In his own way, Tom is every bit as much Bruce's brother, every bit as much a part of his family, as I am or any of us are. It's been that way for a long time now."

Marsha had coordinated their flights so they could meet in the Minneapolis airport early on Tuesday afternoon, January 14, and then take a cab from there to the Mayo. "The people at the clinic told me they were a ten-minute cab ride from the airport," Marsha said. "So we got there, jumped in a cab, and asked to go to the Mayo Clinic."

The cab driver's response was surprising: "The Mayo Clinic?" he said. "You want me to take you to the Mayo Clinic from here?"

Bruce and Marsha were baffled. Was that a problem? "Not a problem," he said. "But it's at least an hour and a half away."

Marsha knew that was wrong, because she'd been told the clinic was ten minutes from the airport. When she told the driver that, he nodded understandingly. "That's true," he said. "Unfortunately, it's ten minutes from the airport in *Rochester*."

Whoops. Marsha had figured that Rochester was a suburb of Minneapolis. It wasn't. The driver was sympathetic and told them he thought there was a van that ran from the airport to the clinic that would be a whole lot cheaper than a cab ride. They piled out of the cab, went back into the airport, and found the van. By four o'clock they were sitting in Ian Hay's office.

They liked him immediately. He was calm and friendly and clearly trying to make them as comfortable as possible. He explained that Bruce was scheduled for an MRI at six o'clock that evening, "to get it out of the way." The next day would be the long one, starting early in the morning with a full physical. Then there would be more specialized testing from different doctors — pulmonary test, neurological tests — checking thoroughly to see what could possibly be wrong. He recommended a good Italian restaurant near the hospital and sent Bruce off to the MRI, saying he would see them first thing in the morning. Marsha called both the Watsons and Greg Rita that night to tell them what was going on. She said she would call the next night after Bruce had been through the battery of scheduled tests to give them an update.

The last thing she remembers saying to Tom and Hilary that night is, "We just have to pray that it's nothing serious."

It was Tom who answered. "Don't worry," he said. "We're praying on this end too."

Bruce had always told Marsha that Tom wasn't that religious. Maybe he had said it just to comfort her, but it struck her — again — how deeply Tom cared about Bruce. "I told him that night, almost as a reminder, how fortunate he was to have a friend like Tom. He just nodded his head and said, 'I know. Trust me, I know.'"

They were up early the next day to make the short walk to Bruce's first appointment. They were staying at a hotel inside the clinic grounds that was, like the other buildings in the complex, connected to the hospital by an indoor walkway. The weather was gray and snowy, a typical January day in Minnesota.

They started the day with Hay, and then Bruce moved through examining rooms and doctors and nurses in a blur. His last appointment of the day was with Dr. Eric Sorenson, a neurological specialist. Sorenson ran him through a number of tests, starting with an electromagnetogram to measure muscle activity. Sorenson checked both his left arm and left leg, inserting needles in the arm and the leg to take the readings. "It wasn't painful," Bruce remembered. "But it was uncomfortable." Sorenson then went through a series of what Bruce would come to learn were routine neurological tests: having him walk on his heels; testing his reactions to a rubber hammer on the knees; having him hold his arms out and pushing on them to test his resistance; then the same test on the legs. There was very little talking as he worked, and Bruce remembers how tired he was starting to feel. The various tests took about forty-five minutes. Sorenson took notes throughout. It was after four o'clock and Bruce had now been getting probed and tested and marched around the hospital for close to nine hours. Sorenson finally finished and told Bruce to wait in the examining room. "I'll be back in about ten minutes," he said.

Bruce, dressed in a hospital gown, sat on a gurney in the small room and waited, alone, for Sorenson to return. Finally Sorenson came back into the room and stood a few feet away from him.

"Bruce," he said, "do you know what ALS is?"

Bruce remembers his tone as matter-of-fact, although he concedes that the doctor might just have been making an effort to sound calm.

"ALS," Bruce said. "Yes. I think I know what it is."

He was pretty certain he knew what it was, but was hoping he was wrong.

"It's also known as Lou Gehrig's disease," Sorenson said. "There's no cure. In all likelihood, you have one to three years to live." He paused for a moment. "I would advise that you go home and get your affairs in order."

Bruce was dazed. He looked at the doctor for some sign: warmth, concern, humor — anything. Nothing. His face was blank. "I want to talk to Marsha," he said. "Can I see her now?"

"Of course," Sorenson said. "She's right outside."

Bruce pulled himself off the gurney, took a step toward the door, and felt the room starting to spin. He thought he was either going to pass out or get sick. "I don't feel very good," he said. "I need to lie down. Can you go get her?"

Sorenson nodded and went outside while Bruce stretched out on the gurney and closed his eyes. ALS? Lou Gehrig's disease? One to three years to live? He had just turned forty-eight. He was about to get married and inherit a family. This wasn't possible. Maybe he was dreaming. He opened his eyes and Marsha was there.

"Are you okay?" she said softly.

"No," he said. "I'm not okay."

Marsha looked at Sorenson. "Bruce has ALS," the doctor said. "Lou Gehrig's disease."

Marsha held her hand up. "I know what it is," she said. She had lost a close family friend — "someone I called 'uncle' because we were so close," she said — five years earlier to amyotrophic lateral sclerosis. She not only knew it was fatal, she knew that the way victims died was about as awful as any death can be — the mind still healthy while the body collapses around it.

Sorenson went on for several minutes about tests that needed to be done the next day to confirm his diagnosis. One would be a spinal tap to make sure Bruce didn't have chronic Lyme disease, which sometimes manifests the same symptoms as ALS. It wasn't likely, he said, but they would check. His tone never changed. By the time Bruce had put his clothes on and he and Marsha went back to Ian Hay's office, he was as angry with Sorenson for his attitude as he was shocked and horrified by his diagnosis. Sorenson had briefed Hay on what he had found. The smiling, friendly man they had sat with twenty-four hours earlier was far more somber when they walked back into his office.

Bruce, looking to lighten the gloom in the room just a little, smiled at the doctor as they sat down and said, "How about that shit, huh?"

Hay smiled, shook his head, and told them how sorry he was that this was the news. Bruce was still angry about Sorenson's approach and told Hay. He apologized and tried to explain to Bruce what he had to do the next day, starting with coming back for more testing. Then, if the diagnosis was confirmed, there were things he needed to learn more about — speech therapy, a feeding tube . . . Bruce wasn't listening after the first couple of minutes.

"All I wanted to do was get out of there and go home," he said. "What was the point of staying? I just wanted to get out of there."

He didn't tell Hay this, just listened — or pretended to listen. He was in shock. So was Marsha. He perked up only when Hay asked about the restaurant the night before and recommended another one.

"You know what I'm gonna do when I get out of here, doc?" Bruce said. "I'm gonna go buy a pack of cigarettes" — he hadn't smoked for a week since the coughing fit — "and a nice bottle of wine."

Hay smiled. "Have one on me," he said.

By the time they got back to their room, the gray day had become a bleak evening. Neither of them felt like going out, so Marsha went down to the hotel lobby and brought some sandwiches back to the room. While she was gone, Bruce cried for the first time, still disbelieving what had happened to him in the last two hours. Marsha came back and they ate quietly. "We have to call Tom," Bruce said.

"Do you want me to call?" Marsha asked.

Bruce nodded. He couldn't bear the thought of delivering the news. Marsha took her cell phone and went into the hallway so Bruce could watch *Seinfeld,* which had always been his favorite TV show. "It was the first time in my life," he said, "that it didn't make me laugh."

Marsha dialed the Watsons. Tom and Hilary were sitting in Hilary's office in their home when Marsha called. "I've got some news," Marsha said when Hilary answered. Something told Hilary instantly that it wasn't good news, and she handed the phone to Tom, who was sitting on her desk. Tom took the phone, and Hilary sat and watched his face. "After he said hello, he listened for a few seconds, and a look came over him that told me that whatever the news was, it was as bad as it could possibly be," she remembered. "He didn't say anything for a while, just sat there, tears coming. Then finally he said, 'What can we do?' "

Marsha had come straight to the point when Tom took the phone. There was no way to soften the blow at that moment. "Tom," she said simply. "I'm afraid I have awful news. Bruce has ALS."

That was when Watson started to cry. Marsha waited, and when he asked "What can we do," her response was immediate: "You need to convince him to stay here for the testing tomorrow. He wants to go home."

Watson nodded. "Let me talk to our boy," he said, the words so soft Marsha could barely hear him.

She walked the phone back into the room and handed it to Bruce. "Tom wants to talk to you," she said.

Again Bruce tried to lighten the moment. "You heard," he said. "I made quad."

Watson almost laughed at Bruce reverting to golf terminology, calling ALS a quadruple bogey. He gave his boy a pep talk: There's a lot we can still do, we're going to find out all we can about this thing and fight it. *But,* he added, you have to stay and finish all the testing.

"Tom, I just want to get out of here and go home," Bruce said.

Watson became Watson — adamant. Firm. "No Bruce, you're not

going to do that," he said. "I understand how you feel. But you have to stay. We start fighting this thing tomorrow. Okay?"

"Okay," Bruce said, knowing Tom was right.

Then he had a thought. "You know, Tom," he said, "it could have been worse."

"Worse?" Watson couldn't imagine how it could possibly have been worse.

"Well, I could have had a disease named after Liberace or something," Bruce said. "At least Lou Gehrig was a great athlete. I'd rather tell people I have Gehrig's disease than Liberace's disease."

Watson almost laughed. "You never quit, do you?" he said, smiling through his tears.

Bruce was crying too, even as he did the best he could to maintain his sense of humor. He told Watson he would stay and finish the testing and hear what the doctors had to tell him. They were both crying again by the time they hung up the phone.

Bruce and Marsha were emotionally drained by then, but Bruce asked Marsha if she could make one more phone call — to Brian, who knew they were at the Mayo and would be wondering why he hadn't heard from them. "The worst part of these phone calls," Marsha said later, "was that there was absolutely no way to soften the blow." When Marsha told Brian she had terrible news, Brian, his heart suddenly pounding, said, "Is it terminal?"

Marsha paused for a second, took a deep breath, and said, "Yes." Then she told him it was ALS.

Back at the Watsons', Tom and Hilary had to tell Hilary's children, all of whom knew Bruce well. When they told thirteen-year-old Paige, Hilary's middle child, she went into her room and after a while came back with several pages of computer printouts. "When you told me about Bruce's symptoms, I went on the computer," she said. "This is what I came up with."

She handed them several pages of information on ALS. That was what the computer had told her Bruce had, based on Tom and Hilary's description of his symptoms. Tom read everything Paige handed him that night. The next morning he was up shortly after sunrise at his own computer. He began looking for every piece of information he could find on ALS — history, funding, doctors who were experts, drugs that had been tested, drugs that hadn't been tested. When Hilary asked him what he was doing, his answer was direct:

"I'm trying to figure out a way," he said, "to find a cure for ALS."

At fifty-three, Tom Watson had a new mission in life. He would tackle it with every bit as much zeal as he had mustered in becoming a star on the PGA Tour. And then some.

Following Watson's orders, Bruce returned to the hospital the next morning for more testing. Sorenson had given them a sliver of hope the day before by telling them there were tests that needed to be done to confirm the diagnosis, one of them being the spinal tap for chronic Lyme disease, the disease carried by deer ticks that had first been discovered in the town of Lyme, Connecticut. Bruce and Marsha met with Sorenson again in the afternoon, this time in his office. He walked into the room, sat down, and according to Bruce looked at the test results and said, "Yup, I was right. You have ALS."

"Thanks for coming, take two aspirin and call me in the morning," Bruce said. "That was his tone. Except for sounding victorious because he was right. I wanted to slug the guy."

Instead he asked Sorenson if there was any hope at all beyond his gloomy one-to-three-years prognosis of the previous day. "Well, I should tell you that there have been a few patients who have lived longer than that," Sorenson said. "In fact there's one man who has lived twenty-two years." He smiled, by far the warmest gesture Bruce or Marsha had seen from him in two days. "In fact the first two doctors who treated him have both retired. They're both out fly-fishing every day and he's still alive."

That story made Bruce angrier — "Why the hell didn't he tell me this the day before?" — but also gave him hope. Not everybody died in one to three years. Heck, he thought, in twenty-two years, I'll be seventy. He went from completely defeated and angry to angry and ready to fight — for his life — by the time Sorenson finished the story. When they stood up to leave, the image of Watson on the 17th green at Pebble Beach flashed through his mind, and he pointed his finger at Sorenson just as he remembered Watson pointing at him on that glorious day almost twenty-one years earlier.

"I'm gonna beat this damn thing," he said, pointing. "You have a nice life, and someday I'll see you fly-fishing."

He walked out, still shaking with anger, adrenaline, and resentment. "I wish tragedy on no one," he said to Marsha. "But I would like to see what his tone would be like if someday he had to tell a member of his family that they had ALS."

The last morning at the Mayo — Friday — was devoted to learning about the disease and what to expect. It was not a pretty picture. There is no way to tell someone what the final days of ALS will be like in a gentle manner. "The people who we talked to that day could not have been nicer," he said. "I almost felt sorry for them having to tell us what they were telling us. Even so, it was hard to hear."

They took the van back from Rochester to Minneapolis late in the afternoon and checked into an airport hotel there. They both had early-morning flights out on Saturday — Marsha to Dallas, Bruce back to Jacksonville, with a stopover in Cincinnati. Marsha would connect in Dallas to Jacksonville, and they would meet at the airport there, where Bruce's car was parked. Then they would drive to Vero Beach to have dinner at Jay and Natalie's house. The evening had been planned before the trip to the Mayo so that Jay and Natalie could meet Marsha. Bruce had savored the idea of walking into the house, introducing Marsha, and saying, "Mom, Dad, I want you to meet your future daughter-in-law."

He was still planning to say that. But he was a long way from savoring what would come after that. At some point that night, he was going to have to tell his parents that he was dying.

13

It Can't Be True

WHEN MARSHA AND BRUCE KISSED each other goodbye in the Minneapolis airport on the morning of January 18, it was the first time they had been apart — other than for short periods while Bruce was undergoing tests at the clinic — in four days. The three days since the diagnosis were still a blur to both of them. Marsha had made one more phone call, the one she had promised to Greg Rita, before they left. They had told no one else. Brian had promised not to tell anyone else in the family until Bruce could get back to Florida and tell his parents.

As they boarded their flights that morning, Bruce and Marsha each had a chance to think, for the first time, about what had just happened to them. Marsha had forced herself to remain calm and strong most of the time since Wednesday afternoon. She knew that anytime she started crying, Bruce was going to cry, so she tried not to except when he cried and she had to comfort him. Bruce had said to her on that first night that if she didn't want to go through with the wedding, especially knowing how her "uncle" had died, he would understand completely. She had told him very firmly not to think or talk that way.

But now, as the plane left Minneapolis and banked away from the airport and began climbing, she heard the calm voice of the pilot telling the passengers that if they looked out from the left side they could see the famed Mayo Clinic below them. Against her better judgment, Marsha looked down and there it was. She recognized the sprawling Mayo campus, could even pick out the buildings they had been in the past few days.

"That was when I lost it," she said. "Completely lost it."

Once she started to cry, she couldn't stop. A flight attendant brought her some tissues and sat down in the empty seat next to her to try to comfort her. Marsha was grateful and kept apologizing for not being able to stop crying. "But I just couldn't stop," she said.

It was then, for the first time, that she thought about what lay ahead. She had her children to consider. They hadn't even met Bruce yet, and now they would be meeting him and finding out he had a fatal disease almost at once. As a devout Christian, Marsha believed that she and Brice and Avery would see Bruce again even if he did die young, and she took some comfort in that. On Wednesday she had urged Bruce to revisit his Christianity and his faith, and he had told her that he would do so. But the specter of going through the months and, she hoped, years ahead was frightening. She cried most of the way to Dallas.

Bruce's plane was late leaving Minneapolis for Cincinnati. As he sat by the window and watched the plane being deiced, he looked around at the blank faces of the other passengers. "The thought occurred to me," he said later, "that I was probably the only person on the plane who really didn't care one way or the other if the plane crashed. I was thinking about telling my parents and my sisters, and about Marsha and her kids. Everything was so bleak. I wanted to care, but at that moment it was tough."

Marsha got to Jacksonville before Bruce and was waiting for him when he got off the plane. "I had dealt with all these thoughts and fears all day long," she said. "But when I saw him come off the plane with his carry-on bag slung over his shoulder, giving me that smile of his when he saw me, I just said to myself, 'No way am I leaving him now. I love him and I'm going to be with him every minute I can.' Once I made that decision, right then and there I started to feel better."

Bruce wasn't feeling good about anything — except being out of snowy Minnesota and back in the warmth of Florida — as they drove down I-95 to Vero Beach. "All I could think," he said, "was that I was about to break my parents' hearts."

There was one consolation awaiting Bruce when they arrived at his parents' condo. Waiting for them, in addition to Jay and Natalie, was Bruce's aunt Joan, someone he had been very close to since boyhood. Joan Walsh is Jay's older sister. Knowing how heartbreaking the news would be for his parents, Brian had made a unilateral decision to call her and tell her what had happened so she could be there to help soften the blow in any way possible.

There was probably no one in the family Brian could have called who would have been more of a comforting presence than his aunt Joan. Even when Bruce was a boy, Joan had been his number one defender in the family. She was about as different from Jay, her younger brother, as a sibling could be. Jay was careful — belt-and-suspenders — Joan was bold, a traveler, an experimenter, always looking for a new adventure. Jay was a conservative Republican; Joan a liberal Democrat. Jay saw his oldest son as troubled; Joan saw him as charming — the same sort of rebel that she had always been. "I always thought he was special," she said. "I'm glad that Jay and Natalie came to see what I always saw in him — even if it wasn't until he was an adult."

When Joan hugged Bruce coming in the door, she whispered, "Brian called," and Bruce knew that she knew. Brian was right. Knowing Aunt Joan would be there to lend another shoulder allowed Bruce a small sense of relief. Bruce introduced Marsha to his parents as their future daughter-in-law, just as he had planned before the trip to Minnesota. They were thrilled and not all that surprised. "When Bruce brought the book home at Thanksgiving and showed it to us, it was pretty clear something serious was going on," Jay Edwards said. "When he had called to say he was going to bring her down to meet us, we figured something was up."

Dinner was a happy time, Marsha and the three elder Edwardses getting acquainted. The only problem was the salmon Natalie made. She had called Bruce's house several times to ask what Marsha would like for dinner, but Bruce hadn't been checking messages. She made salmon, not knowing that Marsha was allergic to fish. Marsha didn't have the heart not to eat, so she ate little bites and hoped it wouldn't affect her too badly. Seeing his parents enjoying Marsha during dinner was almost more than Bruce could bear. "I knew what I was about to do to them," he said. "I had to keep myself from starting to cry before I told them."

Finally, as everyone was finishing dessert, Bruce took a deep breath and decided it was time to get it over with. "There's something I need to tell you," he said with all eyes at the table on him. "You may have noticed that I've had some problems with my speech lately. Well, this week I went up to the Mayo Clinic to have some tests done to find out what was wrong." He paused for a moment, took a deep breath, and then let it out. "They said I have ALS — Lou Gehrig's disease."

The gasp from both his parents was audible. Bruce could not remember ever seeing his father cry. Now, like Natalie, he was crying inconsolably. Joan and Marsha both went into action, Joan with an arm around her younger brother, letting him cry on her shoulder. Bruce heard himself saying, "I'm so sorry to have to tell you this."

When his parents began to regain their composure, he filled them in on the details, none of which really mattered. "We both knew exactly what ALS was and what it means to have the disease," Jay Edwards said. "I kept trying to get hold of myself, but every time I thought about my son . . ."

His voice trailed off, remembering that night.

Natalie couldn't help but wonder if her own Parkinson's disease was somehow connected to the ALS, since both are neurological disorders. There was no evidence of that, but it bothered her nonetheless to think that it was even possible.

Later in the evening, Jay pulled Marsha aside. "I just want you to know that none of us here will think any less of you at all if you feel you can't go through with this marriage," he said. "You shouldn't feel guilty if you have second thoughts."

Marsha explained to him that any second thoughts were already behind her. "I've let him walk out of my life in the past," she said. "I'm not letting it happen again."

Jay Edwards decided right then and there that he loved this woman he had known for only a few hours. He also told Bruce that even though he and Natalie had said earlier the couple would be expected to stay in separate bedrooms when they came to visit — they were not, after all, married — that as far as they were concerned Marsha and Bruce could stay together that night. "It was the only good news of the entire week," Bruce said.

Brian had been instructed to break the news to his sisters after Bruce had told his parents. Chris was in New Orleans with John, celebrating her fiftieth birthday, Gwyn was home in Boston. Brian had decided to hold off until Monday, in part because he was dreading his assignment but also because he saw no need to ruin their weekends, especially Chris's birthday weekend.

Bruce and Marsha were en route home the next morning when Bruce's cell phone rang. It was Bill Leahey, calling to give Bruce a hard time about that afternoon's Eagles–Tampa Bay Buccaneers game. The winner would go to the Super Bowl, a place the Eagles had not been since 1981. Bruce had been trying hard to focus on the game, which would be played in Philadelphia, looking forward to it as an escape from the reality he was dealing with now. Leahey was surprised when a woman answered Bruce's phone.

"I'm sorry," Leahey said. "Maybe I dialed wrong. I was trying to get Bruce Edwards."

Marsha quickly showed Bruce the phone number that had popped up on the cell's screen and he told her who it was. "Is this Billy Leahey?" she said, having heard enough stories from Bruce about his pal to feel as if she knew him.

"Yes," Leahey said, now completely mystified.

"Hi Billy," Marsha said. "My name is Marsha Moore and I'm a very close friend of Bruce's."

Leahey knew right away who she was, because he had called to invite Bruce to spend Christmas in New Jersey with his family and Bruce had said he was staying in Florida and was expecting a friend — clearly a female friend — to visit right after Christmas. He had heard reports from the caddying grapevine about an old girlfriend coming back into Bruce's life. Clearly that was who he was talking to now.

"I was standing by the window, talking on my cell phone, looking out at the lake behind our yard," he said. "It was a pretty day for January, and I was really looking forward to busting Bruce's chops about his Eagles, because I knew how much the game meant to him."

Bill and Marsha small-talked briefly, then Bill heard Bruce talking in the background. "Bill," Marsha said. "There's something Bruce wants me to tell you. We're engaged and we're going to get married."

Leahey suppressed both a laugh and the comment that ran through his mind at that moment. "What I almost said was, 'Marsha, I know Bruce pretty well, and I don't think he's dumb enough to make the same mistake twice.' I didn't, though. I just said, 'Congratulations, that's great.'"

Marsha thanked him, then paused and went on. "There's something else I have to tell you. Bruce and I were at the Mayo Clinic this week. He had some tests done and . . . he's been diagnosed with ALS."

Leahey found himself staring at his phone in disbelief. It had to be that he somehow hadn't heard right. "It was impossible," he said. "Not Bruce. Not my buddy. It couldn't be true."

He was fighting tears by the time Bruce came on the phone. "I need you to do something for me," he said.

"Anything."

"Call Gary [Crandall] and Drew [Micelli]. Marsha and I have already had to tell Tom and Hilary and my parents and Brian and Greg [Rita]."

Leahey understood. He promised to make the calls. "Anything I can do, anything at all?"

"Yeah," Bruce said. "Pray. Pray that the Eagles win today."

Leahey hung up the phone, sat down on his couch, and cried. Then he prayed. But not for the Eagles.

There were others who had to be told. Greg Rita and Mike Rich were coming to the house that afternoon to watch the football game. Greg already knew and had promised not to tell Mike. Before the game began, Marsha took him into a bedroom and told him. Each new set of tears, whether from his family or his friends, reminded Bruce that the pain involved in this disease wouldn't be his alone. They watched the game quietly, in large part because the Eagles, heavily favored, were beaten soundly. Bruce had desperately hoped that the game would give him a release, give him something to feel joyful about. Instead it was just another reminder of how awful he felt.

In Boston, Len Dieterle was also watching the game. Gwyn, who didn't care that much if the Eagles won, went into the kitchen to make her weekly phone call to her parents. "It's not anything written in stone," she said. "But most Sunday nights I give them a call."

The moment she heard her father's voice on the phone — "I mean on the word 'hello,'" she said — she knew something was very wrong. Her first thought was about her mother.

"Dad," she said. "What's the matter?"

Jay Edwards was stunned. He had thought Brian would have called already to give Gwyn the news. "Brian didn't call?" he asked.

No, Brian hadn't called. What was it? As with Marsha and Bruce, Jay Edwards had no way to deliver the news that wasn't going to be stunning.

"Bruce has ALS," he said.

Gwyn isn't exactly certain what happened next. She knows she dropped the phone, cutting her father off. The room began to spin and she thought she might faint. She heard the phone ringing and picked it up. It was Jay. "Are you okay?" he asked.

"I think so," she said, not really sure.

After he had given her the details, Gwyn half walked, half stumbled into the room where Lenny was watching the end of the game. "My first thought was that something had happened to Jay," he said. "We've worried all these years about Natalie [who was diagnosed more than fifteen years ago with a very mild form of Parkinson's disease], and I thought Jay had had a heart attack. When she told me it was Bruce and ALS, I had no idea what to say."

John Cutcher, Chris's husband, was put in an even worse position. Concerned that Chris would somehow hear in the kind of unplanned, sudden way that Gwyn had, Jay called John's cell phone in New Orleans. John and Chris were having dinner in a small restaurant, celebrating her birthday, when John saw Jay's phone number pop up on his cell. Thinking Jay and Natalie were calling to say happy birthday to their daughter, he answered the phone.

"John, I have to tell you something and you have to promise me not to gasp and that you won't tell Chris tonight," Jay said. John was baffled, but agreed. Chris, expecting to be handed the phone for birthday greetings, sat looking at him, confused. Jay gave John the news. In spite of the warning, John couldn't help himself. "Oh my God," he said. "That's awful." Jay talked for a few more seconds while John recovered, looking at Chris and nodding. Then he hung up.

"What was that about?" Chris demanded. "What's awful? Why didn't you let me talk to him?"

"Oh, the Eagles are losing," John said. "Jay was upset about it. He said he wanted to go back and watch the end and to wish you a happy birthday and they'd try to call you later."

"I never should have bought the story," Chris said later. "For one thing, John could care less about sports, and the 'Oh my God' was clearly genuine. But we were drinking wine and having a good time and I had no reason to be suspicious, so I bought it. Looking back, I shouldn't have, but I'm glad I did."

The next day, when they got back to their home in Annapolis, John quietly sat down with Chris and told her the news. "When he said Bruce was very sick, my first thought, to be honest, was AIDS," she said. "All those years on the road, being single most of that time. Gwyn and I had worried about it at times. When he said ALS, I found myself wishing it was AIDS, because these days at least there's some hope there."

Telling his family and closest friends was a step Bruce knew had to be taken. He had prepared himself for it almost from the night of the diagnosis. He knew that the inevitable next step was the word getting out on the tour and then to the media and the public. He dreaded dealing with all of that, but he knew it was unavoidable. The regular tour had been in Hawaii the week he was diagnosed and would be in Phoenix the next week. The Senior Tour — newly renamed the Champions Tour in a marketing ploy by the PGA Tour — would begin the week after that in Hawaii with the MasterCard Championship, the seniors version of the Tournament of Champions. Watson had qualified for the event with his victory in Oklahoma City. Bruce was planning to caddy in Hawaii and take Marsha with him. He knew that by then the word would be out.

Actually it was out sooner than that. Once it was on the caddy grapevine, the news spread through Phoenix like wildfire. Bruce's phone began ringing off the hook. Most of the time he screened the calls and simply listened to the messages. They were all heartfelt. Caddying buddies, players, equipment reps. Someone in the media was bound to hear the news quickly. Someone did, Melanie Hauser, a longtime golf writer who had written for years for the *Houston Post* and as a freelancer after that paper folded. When she initially heard about the diagnosis, she called Watson to ask him if it was true.

Watson knew Hauser well and knew she would handle the story sensitively. So he confirmed it for her, not realizing that she would write the story almost immediately and post it on PGATour.com, the tour's website. As luck would have it, Bruce wanted to check something on his upcoming schedule on the website later that day. "I think I was double-checking the dates of the tournament in Naples," he said. "I clicked onto PGATour.com and there was this huge headline, WATSON'S CADDY EDWARDS DIAGNOSED WITH ALS. It rocked me, just seeing it that way in a headline. I saw Tom quoted in the story, so I knew what had happened. He was trying to help me by being my spokesman, I understood that, and he knew it wasn't going to stay secret anyway. He felt badly that he hadn't been able to reach me before I saw it, but again, there's no easy way to do something like that. He made it easier for me, because he did all the talking and explaining."

Hauser's story made it official that he would have to deal with the issue when he got to Hawaii. It also engendered another week of phone calls — many now coming from the media.

Sometimes, when he heard the voice of a close friend, Bruce picked up the phone. Even those conversations were difficult, because whoever the caller was could find little to say. "They all wanted to help," Bruce said. "They all wanted me to know they were thinking about me. They all said, 'Anything I can do.' I knew they were all sincere, but it was hard — for them and for me."

One of the early calls came from Greg Norman. He was in Australia, playing in a tournament. Tony Navarro, who had replaced Bruce on his bag in 1993, had gotten a call from Phoenix from one of the caddies there telling him the news. As soon as he heard, Norman put in a call to his brother-in-law, a surgeon, because he wanted to understand the disease thoroughly. "I knew what it was and I knew about Lou Gehrig," he said. "And I knew about Jeff Julian" — a tour player who was stricken with the disease late in 2001 — "but I wanted to hear from a doctor exactly what was involved. The more he talked, the more despondent I got. I finally just told him, 'Enough. I can't listen anymore.'"

Bruce was touched that Norman took the time to call from Melbourne. The conversation was similar to the others: Anything he needed or wanted, call. He was thinking of him, praying for him. By now Bruce was almost becoming immune to these talks. He understood, though, that each person who was calling needed to talk to him, to tell him that he was in their thoughts. He did remember one thing Norman said: "I can't think of anyone who will have more people pulling for him than you."

Norman wasn't the only one who wanted to learn more about ALS. Most people knew as soon as they heard "Lou Gehrig's disease" that the disease is incurable and fatal. Few knew how quickly most people die once diagnosed, or how they die. Many, searching the Internet for details, had the same reaction as Norman. "I got to a point where I simply couldn't read any more," Greg Rita said. "I kept looking for something that would give me some hope, anything, but the further I went, the bleaker the picture got."

Ten days after the diagnosis, Bruce and Marsha flew to the Hawaiian island of Kona for the MasterCard Championship. In a sense, this was the perfect event for Bruce to return to the tour. There were only thirty-six players in the field and the media coverage would be tiny, even by Champions Tour standards, because of the location of the event. He would have to deal with being the subject of TV coverage, but even that wouldn't be full blown, since the tournament was on the Golf Channel as opposed to being on one of the networks. Still, being out on tour meant Bruce could no longer screen whom he talked to. Everyone was going to want to say something to him, and he spent most of the long flight to Hawaii preparing himself.

It was on Monday that Hilary Watson proposed marriage to Marsha — as in Bruce marrying Marsha there, in Hawaii, that week. "I was thinking it's such a beautiful spot to do it," she said. "And I knew Bruce was concerned that if they waited until the summer he might have trouble saying his vows. So I asked Marsha if she wanted to do it."

Marsha and Bruce talked it over and decided to go ahead with the Hilary Plan. "Being realistic, there was no way to know how much time we were going to have," Bruce said. "I knew my family would want to be there, but I also knew they would understand."

Hilary did most of the work, finding a minister, arranging for a spot on the beach right near the hotel where all the players were staying, putting together invitations that could be slipped into lockers on Friday. The wedding was at sunset on Saturday after everyone had completed the second round of the tournament. It was, to say the least, an illustrious guest list: Jack Nicklaus, Arnold Palmer, Gary Player — the famed Big Three of the 1960s, winners of thirty-four majors among them — were all there. So were Hale Irwin and Fuzzy Zoeller and Bruce Fleisher and Gil Morgan, recent stars of the Champions Tour. Wives came, and so did all the caddies. The best man, as at Bruce's first wedding, was Tom Watson. This time, though, Watson was beaming, full of enthusiasm for this union.

"It was so beautiful," Marsha said. "It was like something straight out of a movie. I can't imagine having a more beautiful wedding than that one."

After joking about the Eagles and Cowboys, Watson talked about his friend of almost thirty years. "The one thing I can tell you about Bruce," he said quietly, "is that there's not a mean bone in his entire body."

That was a theme Watson would return to often throughout the year when he was asked — over and over again — to talk about his friendship with Bruce. Like Bruce, he understood that he was going to be asked the same questions over and over on a subject that was painful to discuss at all. But both of them — along with Marsha — came to understand that it was critical that they deal with those questions; with the media attention; with the public outpouring. Watson's "mission," as Hilary described it, could only have a chance for fulfillment if millions of dollars could be raised for research.

"The toughest part of this disease is that so few people live for very long with it," Watson said. "I don't blame the drug companies for focusing research on diseases that afflict more people, but the statistics are, in a way, deceiving. Nowadays there are people who live very long, productive lives after being diagnosed with cancer. It isn't that way with ALS. That's why we've got to raise the money *now,* while the awareness level is up, because it is so difficult to get people to understand just how powerful and destructive the disease is."

Watson's goal wasn't just to find a cure for ALS; it was to find a cure for ALS in time to save Bruce. Right from the beginning, he was very conscious of a ticking clock, more conscious every time he saw Bruce looking thinner, tiring more easily, having more difficulty speaking.

But that night on the beach, even though everyone was aware of the clock, there was a strong sense that a wonderful thing was happening. Watson, who isn't a believer in destiny or getting over-philosophical about things, looks back on that night and says, "I don't know why Bruce had to get this disease. But when he did get it, the fact that Marsha had come back into his life and has been willing to take on everything that she's taken on is something approaching a miracle."

No one who knows Bruce or Marsha would argue with that.

14

Media Darling

DEALING WITH THE MEDIA had never been a problem for
Bruce during his thirty years on the PGA Tour. Because he was
friendly and outgoing by nature, he was always approachable when
reporters wanted to talk to him and never felt uncomfortable talking
to anyone.

"Most of the time, though, the attention I got was because of who
I was working for, whether it was Tom or Greg," he said. "More
often than not, I would get questions about what club we had hit or
what I might have said or he might have said at a given moment. I
never had any trouble with that. It was easy."

Occasionally it would go beyond that. Because he had been on
tour for so long and knew so many people, there were occasions
when someone would do a feature on the guy who had been Tom
Watson's partner for all those years. "Even then it would always be
someone I knew," he said. "It wasn't as if some newspaper or magazine was going to send some guy who had never written about golf to
do a story about a caddy."

The only time he had ever been the least bit uncomfortable with
the spotlight had been when he left Watson for Norman and then
when he left Norman for Watson. In both cases there were ques-

tions about whether any sort of rift existed, but even then it was eased by the player. First Watson made it clear that he had supported Bruce's decision to leave. And then, even though most people in golf knew that Edwards and Norman were clearly at odds by the time they split, neither man ever said a bad word about the other publicly.

Now, though, Bruce was in a completely different arena. He had become the story. That would not have made him happy under any circumstances. Under these circumstances, they made him miserable. Even when dealing with media members he knew and liked and trusted, the act of talking was becoming more and more difficult. It frustrated him that he was hard to understand, although he joked about it. "Sorry I sound like the town drunk," became his standard line. The toughest part was suddenly finding himself the focus of attention from media people he didn't know, some of whom asked sensitive questions like, "So about how long do you think you have to live?"

Bruce first began to understand how different his life was going to be when he arrived for Watson's first full-field Champions Tour event of the year in Naples, Florida. After an entire lifetime of answering questions about his player, Bruce realized that his player was now answering questions about him. No one asked him anymore about how Watson was playing or what his club selection had been at a particular hole. After years of finishing a round or a postround practice session, taking the bag back to the bag room, and heading for the parking lot, Bruce found he couldn't do that anymore. Always there were reporters or camera crews who just wanted a minute. People wanted autographs. He had gone from being recognized by some in golf as Watson's caddy to being recognized by almost everyone as "Bruce Edwards — the guy with ALS."

Bill Leahey saw that difference almost instantly. Several years earlier, he and Bruce had been playing golf one afternoon at Leahey's club in New Jersey. Leahey was standing in the rough on one hole midway through the round when a wayward drive from an adjoining hole smacked him on the forehead, just above his right eye. Stunned and hurt — though not seriously, as it turned out — he grabbed a towel, yelled over at Bruce that he had been hit by a ball, and proceeded to lie down with the towel underneath his head to try to recover from the wooziness he was feeling. "Bruce came running over," Leahey said. "So did the guys from the group that had hit me. I was lying there with my eyes closed when I hear one of these guys say to Bruce as he's getting there, 'Hey, you're Tom Watson's caddy.'"

Now when Leahey mentioned Bruce's name to people, they knew exactly who he was long before Bill added those three words that had identified him to the public for so many years: Tom Watson's caddy.

Intellectually Bruce understood that virtually everyone who stopped him, whatever the reason, meant well. Strangers would want to talk to him about their relative who had ALS; about a friend who had lived five years with it; about a doctor who had a new drug or a new theory. He and Watson were both bombarded with e-mails and phone calls with advice, remedies, doctors, new drug protocol suggestions, and, in many cases, simply good wishes from people who wanted them both to know they were thinking of Bruce and praying for him.

Emotionally it was tough to take. As Watson would say later in the year, "I love the outpouring of affection people have directed at Bruce. I *hate* the reason for it."

That summed up well the way Bruce felt. He knew why people wanted to tell him their stories, give him a hug, or pat him on the back. He knew why one reporter after another wanted to talk to him. He and Marsha both went through a period early on where they were resentful of the press, feeling that what they were going through was private, that they were entitled to not talk about what was going on everywhere they went. But after a while they realized that life doesn't work that way when you are a public figure, and Bruce had gone from being a semipublic figure — Tom Watson's caddy — to being a very public one.

Bruce's private life had also undergone a radical change. Soon after they returned from Hawaii, Marsha went back to Dallas to get the children and move them to Ponte Vedra. There was now no need for an apartment, so Marsha, Brice, and Avery all moved in together. Bruce had vowed to Watson on the night of his diagnosis that he was going to marry Marsha, enjoy every minute he had with her, *and* buy a dog — something he had never done in the past even though he loved dogs, because there had never been anyone at home to care for the dog when he was on the road. Now he had an instant family, so he decided not to waste any more time before getting a dog. The dog, a Labrador, was quickly named Nabby, after Eagles quarterback Donovan McNabb, in spite of their miserable failure in the conference championship game.

After living most of his adult life alone — and certainly never with kids or a dog — Bruce found the suddenly full house an adjustment. But he was, overall, very happy to have Marsha, the kids, and Nabby with him, even when the latter three ran amok on occasion. "At this time in my life, having people around, especially people who love me, can only be a good thing," he said.

After a while, both Bruce and Marsha began to understand that the fight they were now in, the one Watson was leading every chance he got, was a very public one. The only way to raise awareness about ALS, about the funds that were needed and about the horrors of the disease, was to talk about it every chance they got. By coincidence, Lou Gehrig had been born in 1903, and ALS fund-raisers were already using the 100th anniversary of his birth as a jumping-off point to try to raise more money for research. Watson and Bruce became new voices and symbols for that campaign.

"I think it was hard for all of us to see how public the whole thing had become," Bruce's sister Gwyn said. "To us, at least in the beginning, this was a very private family thing. Reading about it, hearing about it all the time in the media, was hard for all of us. It wasn't as if we weren't used to hearing or reading Bruce's name or seeing him on TV, that had been going on for years. But this was an entirely different context. Because I worked in public relations, I understood why it was happening. But that didn't make it any easier."

Each time he arrived at a tournament, Bruce felt as if he had to deal with a new wave of questioners and well-wishers. In Hawaii there had been just a trickle of attention, and he had been distracted for much of that week with plans for the wedding when he wasn't on the golf course. Naples meant more attention, more media, and a whole new round of players and caddies and officials coming up to tell him how they felt. No doubt if he could have, Bruce would have worn a sign that said, "I know how sorry you are that I'm sick. I'm doing okay right now and I appreciate your support and your concern. Now, can we talk about something else?"

Since he couldn't do that, Bruce often made the effort to change the subject as quickly as possible. He would ask about a player's or caddy's family, or comment on how they were playing. This came naturally to him because it was what he had been doing all his career. He readily admitted that he was in denial about what his future held. Both Marsha and Watson had been studying the Internet constantly, talking to doctors and ALS experts to learn everything they could about the disease. Both remained convinced there was time to find a cure; both were encouraged when they heard about doctors working with new drugs and progress that was being made in research. Several ALS fund-raising organizations explained to them how Bruce's illness could benefit fund-raising for research, a role Bruce was more than willing to take on, even if it meant talking about his condition far more often than he wanted to talk about it.

"It almost became part of my job," he said. "In one sense, the speech impediment helped me there, because I could beg off things, say it was just too hard. Most of the time I was telling the truth, but every once in a while with a reporter, I'd say I was too tired to talk just because I really didn't feel like doing any more talking on that particular day."

Once he had made the rounds on the Champions Tour and heard all the words of concern and sorrow, Bruce had to go through it again on the regular tour. As he had done in the years since Watson moved to the Senior Tour, he caddied for John Cook at the Players Championship at the end of March. This was an event Bruce always enjoyed because he got to sleep in his own bed during the week, the

Tournament Players Club at Sawgrass being only a few miles from his front door. This time, though, it was different. One player after another whom he had not yet seen came up to him. In some cases words escaped them and they would literally collapse in his arms, speechless, leaving Bruce in the awkward position of having to say something like, "It's okay. Thanks. I know what you're thinking."

"All I could think when I heard it was that it was so unfair," said Billy Andrade, who never forgot how Bruce went out of his way to help him when he first arrived on tour in 1988. "Here's a guy who the main sound in his life has always been laughter — his and everyone around him. I was on the range in Phoenix when one of the caddies came up and said, 'Did you hear about Bruce?' You know it's something bad when they start the sentence that way, but when he said ALS, my knees buckled. I called him that night."

Andrade was one of the few people Bruce picked up the phone to talk to. "When I heard his voice, all I could think to say was, 'I know you'll fight this and I love you,'" Andrade said, his voice choking with emotion as he remembered the conversation. "We all deal with tragedy in our lives. Some just hit you harder, especially when they're so unexpected, than others."

Many players hadn't seen Bruce before the Players. Some were shocked by how thin he looked, even though he said his legs felt fine and joked about his speech problems.

Andrade's closest friend on the tour, fellow Rhode Islander Brad Faxon, had the same weak-in-the-knees reaction when he heard the news while sitting at home watching the Golf Channel one night. "The first thing I thought about was coming on tour in 1984 and there was one caddy everyone in golf knew: Bruce. I mean, who didn't remember him and Watson at Pebble in '82. So as luck would have it, the first time I'm paired with Watson is the last round at Pebble that year. I was almost as excited about being paired with Bruce as Watson. The first nine holes, Watson shot even par and it looked more like ten over. I mean, he was all over the place. As we're walking off the ninth green, I hear Bruce say, 'Okay, we've got all that out of our system, let's make our move *now.*'

"And Watson looks at him and says, 'I'm going to shoot thirty on the back nine and win.'

"I'm thinking they're *both* nuts. Watson was lucky not to shoot forty on the front and he's talking about thirty, and there's Bruce saying, 'That's what I want to hear, let's get going.'

"So Watson birdies ten, the first time he's even had a chance to make birdie all day. Next thing I know, we're standing on the eighteenth green and he's got a putt for thirty-one. And there's Bruce with the flag in his hand whispering to him, 'This could be for the win.' As it turned out, he finished third, but the two of them were thinking win the whole time. I remember thinking to myself, 'These guys are the essence of a team. I want something like that someday.'"

A year later, Faxon, still struggling to establish himself on tour, went over to play in qualifying for the British Open — something unheard of for American nonstars at the time, since money made in the British didn't count toward making the top 125 on the money list. Watson told him he would play a practice round with him on Tuesday if he qualified. When Faxon ran into Bruce on Monday morning before playing his second 18 holes in the qualifier, Bruce said to him, categorically, "Hey, we're playing a practice round tomorrow."

"I said, 'Yeah, if I get in,'" Faxon said. "And he looked at me and said, 'Like I said, we're playing a practice round tomorrow.' When I made it, I walked onto the putting green the next day and the first person to come over and high-five me was Bruce. You don't forget things like that."

Almost everyone on tour has a Bruce story along those lines. Even Watson, who knew Bruce better than anyone, was amazed by the number of people who felt the need to tell him how Bruce had touched their lives and how much they were thinking of him and pulling for him. One who didn't surprise him was Ben Crenshaw. As Ryder Cup captain in 1999, Crenshaw had asked Lynn Strickler, his longtime caddy, to join the team for the week as an assistant captain to work with the caddies. That's not unusual. Watson had wanted Bruce at the Belfry in 1993 when he was captain. But Crenshaw asked Bruce to be an assistant captain too.

"I knew he would add something to the effort," Crenshaw said simply. "All the players like and respect him. All the caddies like and respect him. He would work hard and do anything I asked him to do to help. And when he said something, whether it was about pairings or the matches or anything, people were going to listen. It's easy to find people who are going to jump up and down and say, 'Let's go get them.' It isn't as easy to find people whose words are going to mean something to the people involved."

Davis Love, who had won his '99 Ryder Cup match early on Sunday during the singles, remembers standing by a green watching another match when Bruce drove up in a cart. "He just waved me over and said, 'Get in.' I didn't even ask why, because I knew he wouldn't be doing it just for fun. When I got in, he took off and while we were driving said, 'Ben wants you to go over and watch Justin [Leonard]'s match. He's behind and down on himself. Maybe you can talk to him.'"

It was Love's ensuing pep talk that Leonard later cited as a key to his coming back to halve his match with José María Olazábal and clinch the cup. "I take full credit," Bruce said later. "Someone had to give Davis a ride to get over to Justin."

During the Players NBC's Jimmy Roberts asked Bruce about doing a piece on him for the weekend telecast. Part of Bruce didn't want to do it, didn't want the entire world hearing his speech problems while he talked about what he was going through. But he remembered what Watson and others had said about the platform he had to talk about the need for funding ALS research. So he agreed. Roberts is a good interviewer and an eloquent essayist. Although everyone in the cult that is the PGA Tour knew about Bruce's illness, there were still millions of Americans watching the telecast that day who did not. The piece brought another outpouring of sympathy, phone calls, e-mails, and good wishes.

It was Roberts's piece that Gwyn, at home in Massachusetts, walked in on during the Sunday telecast. She was stunned by how her brother looked: still smiling and brave, but so thin. She had heard the thick speech on the phone, but seeing him struggle to talk on camera hit her hard. "We had all been talking since the wedding about getting the family together to celebrate, probably in Florida, maybe in the spring or the summer. After I saw Bruce that day, I said to Lenny, 'We have to make sure this gets done soon.' It wasn't as if I said to myself, 'He's going to die soon.' I wouldn't let myself think that way under any circumstances. I just decided someone in the family had to step in and make sure this got organized and it might as well be us."

As much attention as he had received at the Players Championship, Bruce knew it was going to be even worse at the Masters. The golf media covers the Players; everyone in the media covers the Masters. Plus he was back with Watson, working at the scene of two of Watson's most glorious victories. "Normally that's the week I look forward to more than any other," Bruce said. "I always stay in the same house with Greg [Rita]. It's always a good time, seeing the same people you see there year after year. But I knew this time it was going to be different, with all the attention and all the questions. I was excited about Marsha seeing Augusta for the first time, but I also knew she was nervous about the media. She hadn't really dealt with it very much up until then. I told her to expect it and she said she understood. But I don't think she really could understand until she was there."

On the first day, when she walked outside the ropes with several writers following in her wake, Marsha found out what Bruce was talking about. After consulting with a number of doctors, Marsha and Tom had decided to have Bruce work at least initially with a California biochemist named Tim Cochran. Cochran would test Bruce's blood, pinpoint specific deficiencies, and prescribe various vitamins to counter the low readings he saw. In all, his protocol called for Bruce to swallow 162 pills a day. That meant Marsha had to carry some of the pills with her on the golf course to give to Bruce as a round progressed. The last thing in the world either Bruce or Marsha wanted was to call attention to the regimen. But this was Augusta, and there was no place to hide.

"That week was the most difficult one for me," Marsha said. "I had spoken to reporters here and there a couple of times prior to that, but nothing like this. Nothing could really prepare me for what it was going to be like. I felt like I was walking around under a microscope."

Bruce was more accustomed to it but still found it a struggle. The thought had crossed his mind before he even arrived in Augusta that this was Marsha's first Masters and might be his last. He wanted to savor every moment he could but found that hard to do, because every time he turned around, someone else wanted to talk to him. On Wednesday afternoon he was talking to several reporters under Augusta's famous tree on the veranda outside the clubhouse when Ernie Els walked up to him and said, "I'm going to win this for you." Needless to say, that made headlines. Every columnist in America, or so it seemed, felt compelled to do a Bruce column that week. All were kind and flattering, full of quotes from golf people about why Bruce was so popular and why this was such a shock to the golf community.

The disease had attacked his throat first, but by this time Bruce was beginning to feel it in his legs as well. Not seriously — yet — but he was aware of the fact that he was tiring more easily than he had in the past. Watson was aware of it too. Without saying anything to anyone, he began doing small things to make Bruce's life easier. He left his umbrella and rainsuit in his locker to lighten the bag except on days when it was actually raining. Instead of playing two full practice rounds at Augusta, he played nine holes on Tuesday and nine holes on Wednesday, trying to save Bruce's legs for the tournament itself. "How many years have I played Augusta?" he said. "It isn't as if playing eighteen more holes is going to make a big difference to me."

On Wednesday night, Bruce and Marsha and Tom and Hilary attended the annual Golf Writers Association awards dinner. They had been invited by Jeff and Kim Julian. Jeff Julian was being given the golf writers' Ben Hogan award for courage in the face of adversity and a physical handicap and had invited the Watsons and the Edwardses to be there. Julian, who had played on both the PGA Tour and what is now the Nationwide (triple-A level) Tour for a number of years prior to his ALS diagnosis late in 2001, had reached the point where he couldn't actually talk anymore but carried a tiny hand-held computer called a voice synthesizer that allowed him to "talk." He would press a few buttons, hold the synthesizer up, and his words would come out through the computer.

In accepting his Player of the Year award, Tiger Woods mentioned the guts both Julian and Bruce had shown since they had been diagnosed. "I'm inspired by what they've done," he said. Julian opened his acceptance speech by typing into the synthesizer, "I've made it. Tiger mentioned my name." He was both humorous and inspiring in his remarks, which he claimed would not be brief — "You would think a guy who can't talk wouldn't talk long," he said. He spoke eloquently about the support he had received from fellow players and from others on the tour and, most notably, from Kim. Near the end, running out of energy, his eyes filling with tears, he had to ask Kim to come up and help him finish. He concluded by signing to her, and she spoke on his behalf. It was one of those speeches that leaves everyone in the room taking a deep breath and wondering how Julian could still continue to go on and keep his sense of humor in the face of all he had gone through.

Bruce was very quiet during Julian's speech and afterward too. "He couldn't help but look at Jeff and think, 'This is my future,'" Marsha said. "It was a very difficult night for all of us."

"I was amazed at his guts," Bruce said. "But I knew everyone in the room had to be looking at me and thinking, 'Bruce is going to be like that in the not too distant future.'"

Nonetheless, Bruce thought it was important to be there that night, in part because Julian had invited him but also because there was no sense running from what he was going to be facing. "That's the tough part," Watson said. "As wonderful as all the support has been, as much as everyone has been trying to do for him, he's the one who is going to have this thing in the end. There's no escaping that fact."

With the memory of Julian fresh in his mind, Bruce couldn't wait to get to the golf course on Thursday. There was one problem: rain. It started in the morning, and after pushing the tee times back on several occasions, Masters officials finally gave up and called play off for the day. That not only left everyone with an unwanted free day — there's not a whole lot to do on a rainy day in Augusta — it also meant that the players would be asked to play as many holes as possible before dark on Friday. Eighteen holes a day up and down Augusta's hills wasn't going to be easy for Bruce. More than that would be brutal. Even so, Bruce didn't mind the chance to catch his breath a little after the interviews he had been doing and the emotions of Wednesday night.

It didn't help that the golf course was still wet and muddy Friday morning, making walking that much more difficult. Marsha again had a coterie of reporters following her, and CBS had now joined the fray, with essayist Dick Enberg preparing a piece on Bruce that would air Saturday. Many of the fans following the group of Watson, Mike Weir (who would go on to win the tournament), and Padraig Harrington were aware of Bruce's condition. Throughout the day, Bruce heard shouts of encouragement and had people coming up to him to offer their prayers and words of hope as he walked from green to tee at places on the course where fans could get near the ropes. It was a long, emotional day for both Bruce and Watson.

They ended up getting in 30 holes before dark, meaning they would have to come back Saturday morning to complete the last six holes of the second round. Watson was four over par for the tournament when the horn blew Friday evening, right around the cut line, which most people were figuring would come at four or five over par. At this point in his career, when Watson starts a major, his goal, realistically, is to make the cut. Anything beyond that is a bonus. Since finishing fourth in 1997, he had only made one Masters cut, a year earlier, when he finished tied for 40th. This was a cut both he and Bruce wanted to make badly.

Because of the rain, Augusta officials had sent the players off of two tees on Friday — almost unheard of at the Masters. Only poor weather would occasion such a drastic step, and this was only the third time in tournament history it had been done. Watson's group had gone off the 10th tee for the second round, meaning they finished play Friday on the third green. Watson was tired; Bruce was exhausted but upbeat. "The last few holes I was going on pure adrenaline," he said. "The crowd actually helped me, because they kept yelling encouragement and telling me I could do it. I'm sure they could see I was tired too. But there was no way I wasn't going to make it. I had to. And we were in the hunt for the cut. I felt pretty good when we finished."

The hardest part was the walk back to the caddy barn. A half-dozen reporters had been following the group strictly for the purpose of monitoring Bruce so they could write about his day. Bruce understood why they were doing it and also why they wanted to talk to him after play was called. But he was tired and emotional and wanting to get home for a hot shower and dinner. Still, he answered the questions patiently, knowing that the reporters were doing their job just as he had been doing his. "The longest walk of the day was the one back to the caddy barn answering all the questions," he said.

The next morning, with the sun shining brightly, they were back at the golf course to play the last six holes. Forced to start the day on the fourth hole, the toughest par-three on the course, Watson hit a solid four-iron onto the green and made par. Then he parred the fifth hole. Four more pars and he would make the cut for sure; one over the last four holes might get it done too. The sixth hole is a straight downhill par-three with one of those Augusta National greens that can bring disaster at any moment. Watson hit the green with a six-iron but had almost a straight downhill putt. With no chance to stop the ball, he was 15 feet past the cup. From there he three-putted for a double-bogey five.

Disaster. "Now we've gone from pars being okay to feeling like we needed at least one birdie, maybe two," Bruce said. Pressing on the seventh hole, Watson's second shot from the middle of the fairway found the front bunker. From there he made another double bogey, trying desperately to make his par putt and rolling it 10 feet past the hole. Right there his chances to make the cut evaporated. Two pars on eight and nine left him eight over par, three shots out.

There were cameras everywhere when Watson holed out on number nine. Reporters too. Seeing the crowds and the cameras and the beauty of the day, it occurred to Bruce that he might have just caddied for the last time at the Masters. He had worked at Augusta every year since 1984. He and Watson had almost won the tournament in 1991, when Watson came to the 18th tee on Sunday tied for the lead only to double-bogey the hole and lose by two to Ian Woosnam. His legs hurt, something he wasn't accustomed to feeling. Walking off the green, everything crashed. He cried, first on Hilary's shoulder and then on Marsha's.

He had learned since his diagnosis that once he started to get emotional about something, it was very difficult to bring his emotions back under control. That was why he had tried during the two days not to focus on the shouts and cheers he was hearing but on doing his job, because he didn't want to get caught up in the emotions. Now it was all too much. When he walked outside the ropes a woman came up to him, tears in her eyes, and said, "Bruce, I have a relative who has ALS. Seeing you doing what you're doing right now is inspiring for my whole family."

"That got me started again," he said, shaking his head at the memory. He thanked the woman, took Marsha by the hand, and walked briskly up to the clubhouse area, not wanting to talk, not wanting to break down again. A CBS camera followed him all the way. Finally he and Marsha walked around the clubhouse to the porch area where caddies normally wait for their players to pull up in the morning or to walk from the locker room to the range.

Bruce lit a cigarette, hands shaking, and, arm still around Marsha, tried to calm down.

"I wanted to make that cut so badly," he said softly. "Just wasn't meant to be."

He brightened, his trademark smile returning. "Next year," he said, "we'll win this thing."

He was being brave and he knew it. The tears came again. He

turned realist again. "I just want to walk up eighteen with Tom on a Sunday at this place one more time," he said. "If I can do that, I'll be happy."

That afternoon CBS aired the piece Enberg had done, ending it with Watson hugging Bruce on the ninth green and Bruce, after hugging Hilary, walking away with Marsha. In the piece, Enberg, who writes his own material, talked about how the tables had turned for Watson and Bruce. After years of Bruce carrying the load for Watson, now Watson was trying to carry the load for Bruce.

The Masters is the highest-rated golf tournament of the year. Its TV audience is probably triple that of the Players Championship. Around the country, more and more people were hearing Bruce's story for the first time. Most golf fans knew him because of all his years with Watson. Anyone even vaguely familiar with golf remembered The Chip, The Point, and The Hug at Pebble Beach. Between the Enberg piece and all the columns written that week about what Bruce was going through, the attention level increased dramatically.

Back in New Jersey, Bill Leahey watched the piece on CBS and tried in vain not to cry. In the weeks since the diagnosis, Leahey had been working almost nonstop on putting together a fund-raiser for Bruce at Caves Valley Golf Club outside Baltimore. "All I could think after I heard the news was that I had to do something to try to help my pal," he said. "I'm retired, so I've got free time. My first thought was a golf outing with friends and family and people who wanted to put up some money to help Bruce."

Leahey floated the idea to his old boss at Smith Barney, Tom Matthews, who although he is now a higher-up at the firm, is best known to his friends as someone who once played in Bruce Springsteen's band. "If you can put it together, I can get you a golf course," Matthews said. "I'll get you on Caves."

Caves Valley is a relatively new golf course but it is already considered one of the better courses in the country. Watson and Bruce were certainly familiar with it. It had been the site of the 2002 U.S. Senior Open, in which Watson had lost a dramatic five-hole playoff to Don Pooley. Leahey began contacting friends from Smith Barney and old clients and people he knew were golf fans. He called Watson to see if he might be willing to come in for the day and participate in the outing. "Bill, if you can guarantee $100,000 net to Bruce, I'll definitely come," Watson said.

"Tom, if I have to put the money up myself, we'll raise that much," Leahey answered.

Watson promised to be there. He also called the president of Caves Valley, Leslie Disharoon, a friend of his, to seek his help convincing people to Play-and-Pay. A date — May 20 — was set. The goal was to get a dozen foursomes at $10,000 a foursome and net the $100,000. With Disharoon's help the total ended up being eighteen foursomes. When Leahey called Gary Crandall to tell him about the day, Crandall mentioned that Andy North was doing an outing not far away the day before and might be willing to come over. When North heard what was going on, he was more than willing to take part.

There was one other thing Leahey wanted to do the day of the fund-raiser. He wanted to play one more Hebert Cup.

The Hebert Cup was a four-man competition that had first been played in 1987, not long after Crandall had suffered a mild heart attack. "It reminded all of us that you never know what's going to happen in life," Leahey said. "There had been four of us who really hung out together in the early years on tour: Bruce, Gary, Drew Micelli (who had caddied for Mark Hayes), and myself. Three of us had left the tour, but we had all stayed in pretty close touch. There was no regular get-together, though, nothing we put on our calendars. So we decided we needed to change that." The Hebert Cup was born.

They named the event after Lionel Hebert, who had won the 1957 PGA Championship in what was by far the highlight of an otherwise ordinary professional career. "We decided that the PGA was so humiliated having Hebert win that they changed the format from match play to stroke play the next year. So four mediocre golfers getting together, why not call it the Hebert Cup?"

The PGA's switch to stroke play undoubtedly had nothing to do with Hebert, but that was the foursome's story and they were sticking to it. The initial Hebert was played in Dallas — Crandall getting to host first — and was played with a Ryder Cup format: three days, match play, with best-ball matches, alternate-shot matches, and singles matches. Crandall and Micelli played Leahey and Bruce and won a tense match that went down to the final holes on the final day. Bruce and Leahey had an "Hebert Cup" made and presented it to their two buddies.

Like the Ryder Cup, the Hebert was played every two years at different venues. Leahey hosted one year in New Jersey; Bruce one year in Florida; Micelli one year in California. But after the fourth match, the Hebert had faded away. "It probably didn't help that we just couldn't win," Leahey said. "We'd always be close, but they were just a little bit better than us. After the fourth time, the cup kind of got retired. Or lost."

Or both. Now Leahey wanted to revive the Hebert, at least for one day: 18 holes of best ball on the day of the fund-raiser at Caves Valley. All four Hebertians were game and the match was set up.

Needless to say, Bruce had played almost no golf since his diagnosis. Between work and travel and seeing different doctors and saving his energy, there hadn't been any chance to play. He had never played very much, although he'd become a reasonably good player as an adult, someone capable of breaking 80 when he was playing regularly. "I was always a good putter," he said. "The irony is, I was never a good bunker player, and I took lessons from arguably the best bunker player ever to play the game."

They all arrived in Baltimore on a beautiful spring day. Most of Bruce's family came — only Brian and Laurie couldn't make the trip — even though they all had doubts about what the day would be like. "I think we were afraid it would just be too sad for all of us," Chris said. "But it didn't turn out that way. It was a celebration, and

I know it was a great day for Bruce, which made it a great day for all of us."

Many of Bruce's caddying buddies — some retired, some still working — flew in for the day. Leahey had been able to sell enough foursomes to put the net for the day at over $150,000.

But the highlight of the day was the Hebert.

The underdog team of Bruce and Leahey grabbed an early lead and was two up after nine holes. As they relaxed on the 10th tee before starting the back nine, Bruce said to his friends, "You know, this might be the last nine holes of golf I ever play."

He tried to say it half-joking, but the comment stuck with everyone. It became even more poignant when Bruce, normally the least serious golfer in the group, began to play as well as anyone had ever seen him play. After Micelli and Crandall had rallied to tie the match on 15, Bruce rolled in a birdie putt at 16 to put his team one up again. Sixteen had been the one hole Watson had bogeyed coming down the stretch eleven months earlier at the Senior Open, a bogey that probably cost him the championship.

Micelli and Crandall tied the match again on 17, and after Bruce had just missed a long birdie putt on 18 that would have been the winner, they had finished even. By then Andy North, having finished his round, had driven up in a cart. He asked how the match stood and was told even. "Sudden death!" he screamed and they marched back to the 18th tee. No one won 18. Newly appointed commissioner North decreed that they play 16. Another halve. They went to 17. This time it was Leahey who came through, trickling in a short par putt. Micelli and Crandall could do no better than bogeys.

Bruce and Leahey had won.

"I'm not sure who was happier, us or them," Leahey said. "I mean, they weren't going to give an inch, but when we won fair and square, I think they were thrilled."

In fact Crandall and Micelli went out and had new plaques made up and sent them to the winners, immortalizing their victory at the 2003 Hebert Cup. Leahey has an office in his house that is filled with plaques and photos and memorabilia. The Hebert plaque is right over his desk, in a place where he can see it anytime he looks up from his computer.

The rest of the evening was almost as much fun as the Hebert. By the time it was over, the $150,000 was only part of the story. When it was Bruce's turn to get up and thank everyone, he simply couldn't do it. Finally he whispered something in Marsha's ear. "If you judge a man's life by the friends he has," he said, "then I've certainly had a great life."

That was the moment when everyone was too filled with emotion to do anything but cry.

15

A Great Five Hours

THE OUTING AT CAVES VALLEY came during the last break that Bruce and Watson would have for a good long while. Beginning the first week in June, Watson was going to play three weeks out of four, take one week off, and then play three more weeks consecutively. Each of those six tournaments was, technically at least, a major championship. He would start at the Senior PGA Championship at Aronimink Golf Club outside Philadelphia and then go from there to the U.S. Open, which would be played at Olympia Fields in Chicago's south suburbs. After a week off, he would play the U.S. Senior Open at Inverness in Toledo. All three of those events were majors in Watson's mind, the Senior PGA being by far the longest running of the senior major championships (dating to 1937), and the Senior Open being a national championship always held on difficult golf courses.

After that would come another week off, followed by the Ford Senior Players Championship, an event the Champions Tour insisted was a major; the British Open; and then the Senior British Open, which had just been declared a major by the tour, meaning that there were now five Champions Tour "majors." Bruce had a simple method for deciding if a tournament was a major: "If there's a pro-am, it's not a major." He might have added, if there was a corporate name in the official tournament title it also wasn't a major. That would eliminate the Ford Senior Players and the JELD-WEN Tradition, the final Champions major, which would be held at the end of August. JELD-WEN, for those of you keeping score at home, makes doors and windows.

It could be argued that the three June events were the most important on Watson's schedule for the year: the two Champions events he cared about the most and the event he had grown up dreaming about winning. What's more, he hadn't played in the U.S. Open since the 2000 event at Pebble Beach and was delighted when he got a call from his old friend Sandy Tatum in January asking him if he would accept an exemption at Olympia Fields if it was offered to him.

"You're darn right I would," was Watson's succinct answer.

In its winter meetings, the USGA executive board had decided to offer three exemptions to past Open champions: one would go to Tom Kite, who had won the Open in 1992 and had exhausted his ten-year champion's exemption the previous year at Bethpage Black. It had become an unofficial USGA tradition to invite Open champions of note to play in the first year they were no longer exempt. Hale Irwin, who was offered the third exemption, had benefited more than anyone from this, winning his third Open at Medinah in 1990 on an eleventh-year exemption. He was invited as a three-time champion whose last win had come in the Chicago area. Watson had also been given an eleventh-year exemption, at Baltusrol in 1993, and had used it to finish in a tie for fifth.

Watson would have said yes to an exemption to any U.S. Open on any course but was especially happy to be invited to Olympia Fields, since he had played his first professional tournament there in 1968. He was an eighteen-year-old Stanford freshman then, playing as an amateur, when Olympia Fields had been the site of the Western Open. Watson didn't receive his official invitation to the 2003 Open until May, but he had told Bruce to put it on his schedule before then. It occurred to Bruce, as it occurred to Watson, then fifty-three, that this might be Watson's last Open. There were ways he could qualify again — win the Senior Open or finish in the top 15 at the Open or at a Masters — but at this stage of his career those were accomplishments that, while not impossible, certainly could not be counted on.

Watson arrived at Aronimink with a fairly cranky golf swing. He had hoped to spend a good deal of time on the practice tee during the week, but the weather was awful, limiting practice time and forcing play to be called off completely on Saturday. That made for a very long day on Sunday, slogging 36 holes on another muddy golf course. The only good news was that since this was a senior event, there wasn't much media around, which was a relief to Bruce. Watson finished in a tie for 17th and never really felt comfortable with his swing all week.

"It wasn't all that hard to hit fairways there," he said. "And I was having trouble hitting fairways. You aren't likely to win when that's the case."

The best news of the week came when Watson got a phone call from Andy North, who was in Chicago doing advance work on the Open for ESPN, which has employed him as a commentator for many years. North is one of Watson's closer friends on tour, a fellow midwesterner who loved to tell Watson that his beloved University of Wisconsin was every bit the center of learning that Stanford was and had a better football team to boot.

North had walked the golf course at Olympia Fields while doing his TV prep work. "Tom," he said on the phone, "you can play this golf course. The rough's not that high and the greens aren't all that fast either."

Watson was happy to hear that but was convinced that by the time play began the following Thursday the rough would be higher and the greens considerably faster. "I remembered the greens from '68 as being rock hard," he said. "I figured the USGA would get them there eventually. I was hoping that Andy was right about the rough. Those young guys can slash it out of the high stuff, but I'm not strong enough to do it anymore, especially when I'm hitting a long iron."

What Watson didn't know was that the USGA wasn't going to get the greens as fast and hard as it may have wanted, because Chicago had been saturated by rain all spring and the greens were far softer than the USGA had planned. Obviously the rain would make it easier to grow the rough high, but the USGA has been more forgiving in recent years when it comes to Open rough. "We want to penalize players when they hit it in the rough," said Tom Meeks, who is in charge of course setup at the Open. "But we don't want them pitching out. We want them to have the opportunity to play for the green if they're willing to gamble."

So the rough would be difficult but not impossible.

It wasn't going to matter, though, if Watson couldn't find a swing key to get him hitting the ball more consistently. He and Bruce flew back to Kansas City for a rest day after Aronimink and then arrived in Chicago on Tuesday afternoon. Since he hadn't seen the golf course in thirty-five years, Watson wanted to get in two full practice rounds before the Open began on Thursday. The advantage of arriving relatively late was that most of the media was already busy writing stories for Wednesday about Tiger Woods — who had done his pre-Open press conference that morning — and many of the fans had already left for the day. Watson hit a few balls on the range and then he and Bruce headed onto the golf course alone.

"It was actually kind of nice," Bruce remembered. "There weren't that many people, and without any other players or caddies with us, it was just Tom and me preparing for an important tournament. It was kind of like old times. I really enjoyed it."

Of course both men were working too. Bruce had never seen the golf course, and although he had Gorgeous George's yardage book, he made his usual checks around the greens and the hazards and stepped off some of the more likely yardages that Watson might be facing when the championship began. Watson was, in his words, "trying to remember the golf course." That day he was having trouble remembering the layout of the holes. There had been a number of changes since he'd played it, and as good as Watson's memory for golf courses is, a lot of it wasn't coming back.

"That's why I wanted the two practice rounds there," he said. "The first one you're almost finding your way around. On Wednesday it started to come back, I started remembering shots I had played to different holes and the way each hole was set up. I was a lot more comfortable after practice round number two than I was after practice round number one." One thing he had discovered was that North was right: He could play the golf course. The greens were surprisingly soft, almost attackable, generally unheard of at an Open.

Still, it wasn't going to matter if Watson didn't start hitting the ball better. After they had finished their Wednesday practice round, Watson and Bruce went to the range. As always, Watson was tinkering with different swing moves and thoughts. Bruce watched closely as he hit one shot after another. Watson was trying to get his right arm a little bit farther from his body as he came through the ball. He felt as if he was too tight, a little bit locked up, and wondered if moving his arm outward would free up the swing.

The shots began flying truer and truer. One after another. As had always been the case, Watson said nothing for several shots. "I don't say anything until I've hit a number of shots to confirm that what I'm thinking is working," he said.

Finally he turned to Bruce, the old smile on his face. "I've got it," he said.

"I almost jumped up and hugged him right then," Bruce said. "He doesn't make a habit of saying that unless he's pretty sure he's found something. To find something on the range the day before what might be our last U.S. Open was something. Of course we wouldn't really know until we got onto the golf course the next day, but I went to bed that night feeling confident that he could make something happen."

So did Watson. He was paired with Scott Verplank, a solid American veteran player, and Eduardo Romero, a longtime star on the European Tour who is from Argentina. Verplank was extremely pleased to be paired with Watson. As a youngster, growing up in Dallas, he had been a big Watson fan and remembered watching Watson and Bruce during the six-year period (1975 through 1980) when Watson had won the Byron Nelson Classic four times. "I loved to watch Watson play," Verplank said. "I loved his boldness and his pace of play, the way he attacked every shot. I still remember the year he was going for four in a row [1981] when he lost in a playoff [to Bruce Lietzke], how disappointed I was."

Verplank and Bruce had become friendly after Verplank turned pro when Bruce was still living in Dallas. Verplank had dealt with health issues of his own — he is an insulin-dependent diabetic who wears an insulin pump that hooks onto his belt while playing — but had never complained about bad luck or the unfairness of it all, even though the diabetes and two major surgeries on his elbow had prevented him from reaching the level of stardom that had been predicted for him after he won the Western Open (the first amateur in twenty-nine years to win a PGA Tour event) in 1985 while still in college.

The first time he had seen Bruce after the diagnosis had been at the Players Championship, when he had gone looking for him on the first practice day to talk to him and see how he was doing. "It was exactly what I would have expected from Bruce," he said. "No 'why me,' no whining. He just said, 'Hey, I'll deal with it,' and wanted to talk about me and my game. That's just always been his way. He's been a caddy a long time, but I think — no, I know — that almost every player looks at him as one of us, as a peer in every way."

Verplank came into the Open with high hopes. He was playing well, and he knew that the Open, with its emphasis on keeping the ball in the fairway, was always going to be his best shot at winning a major. He arrived on the first tee thinking he had a chance to be in contention on Sunday afternoon. The Watson-Verplank-Romero threesome would tee off at one-thirty in the second wave of tee times. In 2002 the USGA had given up its longtime tradition of starting everyone from the first tee during the first two rounds, because pace of play had become so slow it was almost impossible to complete the rounds — even with mid-June's extra daylight — before dark. By starting players from the first and 10th tees in a morning wave and an afternoon wave, it spread the field out more and moved the last tee time up from three forty-five local time to two-fifteen.

Bruce woke up on the morning of the first round feeling as good, mentally and physically, as he had felt in a while. He had been able to walk 36 holes on Sunday without feeling that exhausted at the end of the day. He was encouraged by the way his legs seemed to be holding up. There was no doubt in his mind now that he would be able to walk 72 holes this week and again in Toledo at the Senior Open. He was even regretting just a little bit his decision to skip the trip to Great Britain. But he knew the doctors were right about the risks involved if the weather was cold and rainy, which could cause his joints to stiffen. "I couldn't afford to take a chance that I'd get over there and lock up in bad weather midway through the round and have to give the bag to someone in the crowd or something," he said. "It wouldn't have been fair to Tom, not to mention the fact that it would have been embarrassing. Plus I knew a rest after working four weeks out of six was going to be a good idea."

Still, he felt good enough to talk confidently about being able to caddy — maybe even walk — in 2004. This would not be, he told people, his or Tom's last Open.

The weather conditions on that Thursday, June 12, were close to perfect. It was comfortable and breezy, just enough wind to keep everyone cool without really affecting shotmaking. As usual Bruce arrived at the golf course long before Watson, hanging out on the putting green right outside the clubhouse while waiting for him. Since Watson plays so rarely on the regular tour these days, there were still a lot of players and caddies who hadn't seen Bruce or had only seen him briefly since his diagnosis. As had been the case at both the Masters in April and at the Colonial in May, people kept stopping to talk to him, to try to think of something to say. Rich Beem, the PGA champion in 2002, walked up, started to say something, began to bite his lip, and simply threw his arms around Bruce in a hug. "Hey," Bruce said quietly. "I'm fine. Okay?"

Bruce had developed a strategy by this point to deal with the awkwardness he knew people felt. As soon as the first pause in conversation came, he would tell a joke or make a comment about how well a
player was playing. Anything to steer the subject away from ALS or
how he was looking or feeling or talking. At one point, while several
players were standing around trying to figure out what to say, Bruce
began yelling at veteran caddy Mark Jiminez, who was standing a
few yards away from him on the green.

"Hey Mark," he yelled. "Can you caddy for Watson at Inverness?"

Jiminez looked both concerned and confused, as did everyone
else. The Inverness Club was the site of the U.S. Senior Open in two
weeks. Was Bruce saying he wouldn't be able to caddy then?

"You see," Bruce said, without waiting for a response, "I really
want Watson to win the Senior Open, since we lost that playoff last
year at Caves. I was thinking, since you never lose at Inverness, you
might bring him some extra luck."

Jiminez started laughing. So did everyone else. In 1986 Jiminez
had caddied for Bob Tway when he had won the PGA at Inverness.
Seven years later he had been on Paul Azinger's bag when *he* won
the PGA at Inverness. Undefeated and untied at the Inverness
Club. "Best Inverness caddy that ever lived," Bruce concluded.

Watson arrived about ninety minutes before his tee time. All
Bruce wanted to see was how the ball was flying when they got to the
range. Would he still have it?

Yes. The move that had worked Wednesday was still working on
Thursday. By the time they walked to the 10th tee, Bruce was feeling confident that it was going to be a good day. "I take a lot from the
way he warms up," he said. "If he's solid on the range, he's almost always solid on the golf course. Some guys aren't that way. Tom almost
always is."

Most of the morning players were already in the clubhouse by the
time Watson's group was introduced on the 10th tee. The early leader
was thirty-three-year-old Brett Quigley, a seven-year tour journeyman who had bounced back and forth between the PGA Tour and
the triple-A Nationwide Tour since 1997. Quigley had shot a five-

under-par 65 to take the lead. That score, and the fact that quite a few players were under par, was an indication that North's initial call to Watson had been accurate. The only surprise among the early scores was that Tiger Woods, the defending champion, had struggled in with a one-over-par 71, leaving him well back in the pack.

The 10th hole at Olympia Fields is a 444-yard par-four. Watson decided on a three-wood off the tee and proceeded to hit a nervous opening shot into the right rough. Even someone playing in his thirtieth Open can get Open jitters. From there he had a long shot to the green from an iffy lie and pushed it right of the green. He chipped to 12 feet and two-putted for a bogey. Hardly an encouraging start. Walking off the green Bruce said quietly, "We've still got seventy-one holes to go."

Both men later admitted that the opening bogey surprised them, given the way Watson had been hitting the ball on the range. The 11th is another par-four, a tad longer than the 10th, at 467 yards. This time Watson found the fairway, and his six-iron came up just short of the green. From there he putted and ran the putt a good eight feet past the hole. Now, less than twenty minutes after teeing off, things were beginning to look sour. "One bogey, okay, you get it out of your system," Bruce said. "But if you start bogey-bogey, you might begin to think it's a trend and it might be a long day."

Confidence in golf is a remarkably delicate thing, even for the great players. Lining up his ninth shot of the day, Watson was already facing a minicrisis, and both he and Bruce knew it. When the par putt went in the hole, both men breathed a small sigh of relief. "Stopped the bleeding right there," Bruce said. Now they were into the round and, he hoped, ready to start making a move.

At the 12th, yet another par-four — the back nine starts with five in a row — Watson hit a superb drive down the left side of the fairway. He had 170 yards to the hole from there and, with a slight following wind, was between a six-iron and five-iron. Bruce was inclined to hit five, not wanting to end up too far short of the hole. Watson, feeling good about his swing, preferred a smooth six. "I think," Bruce said later, "he called that one right."

As soon as the ball came off the club they could both tell it was a good shot. The question was, how good. "It was at the flag all the way," Bruce said. With the ball in the air, Bruce said, "Be right," meaning, "Be the right club." The ball bounced directly in front of the flagstick, took a big hop, and disappeared. Up at the green, the crowd was going crazy.

Watson has always had good eyes, but at fifty-three, they weren't quite what they used to be. What's more, the shot was uphill, which meant he couldn't see the hole. Bruce, who has always had remarkable vision, still has it. When he saw the ball bounce and disappear, he screamed, "You holed it!" Watson could hear the crowd, but knew they might be screaming because the ball was very close. Then he saw fans behind the green holding their arms up in the touchdown signal and knew that Bruce was right: The shot had gone in for an eagle two. He turned to give Bruce a high-five and could see that Bruce was getting very emotional, far more emotional than he would have in the past, even about a great shot.

"Part of it was the fact that I do get more emotional quickly with the disease," he said. "But part of it was also me thinking, 'Okay, here we go. He's going to do something special today.'"

Watson was thinking the same thing. "That turned the whole round around," he said. "I started kind of shaky with the bogey, then managed to get the par at eleven. But when that shot goes in and I go from one over to one under just like that, I started thinking maybe this was going to be one of those days." Watson remembered playing in another national championship — the 1970 U.S. Amateur — when he stood on the eighth tee on the first day four over par and promptly holed his tee shot for an ace, then birdied the ninth hole. "I went from four over to one over in two holes," he said. "Turned the whole week around for me." He went on to finish fifth, which in those days was good enough to get into the Masters.

Lee Janzen was a few fairways over from Watson, playing the 16th hole when he heard the roar come from number 12. He could see Watson and Bruce celebrating in the fairway and he realized what had happened. "It sent a chill straight through me," he said. "I think we all had the same thought that day: This might be the last time for Tom and Bruce. You couldn't help but root for them every step of the way."

Verplank was in a sour mood at that point, having started out bogey–double bogey. But when Watson holed his shot and he saw the look on Bruce's face, he caught himself grinning in spite of the fact that he was angry with himself for getting off to such a poor start.

Now, with the crowd urging him on, Watson was very much into the round. He kept making pars on the back nine, the more difficult of the two nines at Olympia Fields, until 16, when he hit a huge drive and a wedge to about 18 feet and made his first birdie of the day. That put him at two under, with 17 and 18, two very difficult holes coming up. "By then he was really rolling," Bruce said. "I was worried about seventeen" — a monster of a par-three, at 247 yards — "because he had to hit four-wood. But he hit the ball so well it hit the flagstick. He didn't make the putt, but I was thrilled to make par there." He hit two more good shots and just missed birdie at 18, so he walked to the first tee at two under par with a growing crowd now following the group.

The first hole is probably the easiest one on the golf course, a relatively wide-open par-five. Watson's drive caught the rough and he was forced to lay up. His wedge stopped 12 feet past the hole, leaving him a slick downhiller for birdie. He knocked it in. Now he was on the leader board, and word was starting to make its way around the golf course that something extraordinary was happening.

In the comfortable clubhouse dining room that was the headquarters for USGA officials for the week, many veteran rules officials and volunteers had been watching the goings-on on TV. When Watson birdied number one, many of them decided this was something that needed to be seen in person. "People just wanted to be part of it in some way," said Clyde Luther, who has worked at Opens since the beginning of time. "It couldn't possibly be the same on TV."

It wasn't bad on TV. Since Mark O'Meara had played in the morning, Greg Rita was back in his hotel room watching on TV. "I was shouting and cheering and getting teary-eyed all at once," he said. "I just felt like it was the most amazing round of golf I'd ever seen."

By now Bruce was really in a battle with his emotions. He knew what was going on, knew Watson was being Watson again, but he also knew he had to keep himself steady and do his job. Watson was afraid to look him in the eye, because he knew if he saw Bruce losing it, he might lose it too. "Which I couldn't afford," he said. "There was still a lot of work to do."

They worked steadily through the next few holes, wobbling only a little at number six, the second and last par-five on the golf course. Watson missed the fairway there, and his third-shot wedge was a little long. But he managed to chip to four feet and save par, keeping him at three under for the round, two shots behind Quigley in a tie for second place at that moment.

The seventh is another long par-three, 212 yards, but doesn't play that long since the tee is elevated. Watson decided five-iron and ended up about 35 feet beyond the flagstick. Not a bad shot, but Bruce walked down the hill wishing he had campaigned harder for a six-iron. "Just like I had wished we had hit three instead of two back at Pebble in '82," he said.

It can be argued that Watson has made as many long, dramatic putts in his career as anyone who has ever played the game. He is justifiably proud of his ability to make long putts. He might never have enjoyed making one more than the one he made at the seventh on Olympia Fields that afternoon. The putt had a major left-to-right break to it, maybe 20 feet according to Bruce, but it was tracking the hole all the way. As it rolled closer and closer, the crowd noise grew louder and louder. Watson was tempted to put his arms in the air because he could see it was dead center. But at the last possible moment, the ball stopped right on the lip of the cup. When he saw the replay later, Watson was convinced that the ball hit some kind of ridge on the edge of the hole. "You could actually see it rock backward just a tiny bit," he said.

Standing up by the hole, getting ready to putt after Watson, Verplank saw the ball stop, rock, and then, as Watson started walking, begin to move forward just a tiny bit. "Hey," he shouted over the din. "It's moving, it's going to go."

Watson walked toward the ball, fully intending to wait the ten seconds the rules allow when a ball is hanging on the lip before tapping in for his par. Just as he arrived at the hole, the ball, as if intimidated by his presence, rolled that last inch forward and disappeared. As the crowd screamed — really screamed — Watson kicked his left leg gleefully as if kicking the ball into the hole, then turned to where Bruce was standing and bowed. That was it for Bruce. He was laughing and crying all at once.

"The kick was pure joy," Watson said. "The bow was to everything and everyone: to Bruce, to the crowd, to the moment — everything."

Golf crowds can get very loud — usually more so on Sundays — but they rarely get raucous. When the putt dropped and Watson kicked and bowed, the noise could be heard all over the golf course. "I've heard loud in my day," Watson said. "But that was *really* loud."

Waiting back up the hill on the tee, knowing where Watson stood on the leader board before the putt went in, Billy Andrade saw the kick and the bow and felt himself losing his composure. "I wanted to run down the hill and hug both of them," he said. "At that point it was really hard for me to concentrate on my own golf game. I wanted to go and cheer them on."

It was, by now, very much *them*. What Watson was doing would have been remarkable under any circumstances: fifty-three-year-old past Open champion one shot out of the lead twenty-one years after his Open victory. But everyone in the place knew Bruce's story. The media, which had been sitting around the press tent dutifully telling Brett Quigley's life story while explaining what had gone wrong for Tiger Woods, basically dropped everything for Tom and Bruce. The other 155 players, at least for one day, had become a footnote.

"When the putt went in on twelve, I was thinking, 'Wow, this is really something,'" Verplank said. "I mean, here I was having an awful day" — he would finish with a six-over-par 76 — "and I was like a little kid getting excited for Tom and Bruce. The look on

Bruce's face when that putt went in on seven was something I'll never forget."

Both Watson and Bruce were fighting their emotions as they walked to the eighth tee. "I just felt like we had turned the clock back," Bruce said. "It was as if we were back at Pebble Beach again. We were both young and confident and knew anything was possible. It was just an amazing feeling."

There were, however, still two holes to play. Watson was alone in second place now, one shot behind Quigley. Pumped up, he crushed his drive at the 433-yard eighth and had only a seven-iron to the green. He hit it perfectly, stopping it 12 feet from the hole. "I walked onto the green and said to myself, 'Oh my God, he's going to make this one too,' " Bruce said. "You could just feel it at that point."

Watson was feeling it too. The birdie putt was never going anyplace but the bottom of the hole from the moment it left the putter. "I really swished it," Watson said. "I looked back at Bruce for a second and I could see he was losing it completely by then. At that point, I was really fighting it myself."

So was almost everyone else. Watson was now five under par and tied for the lead with one hole to play. He was one par away from shooting 65, the lowest round he had ever shot in a U.S. Open. It seemed as if every single person on the grounds at Olympia Fields was on the ninth hole. In the locker room, players who normally might glance at a TV as they walked by, had stopped and stood or sat transfixed in front of the sets.

The ninth is the longest par-four on the golf course, at 496 yards, but it plays shorter because the hole plays downhill. Watson took three-wood and found the right side of the fairway. He wanted to play his second shot, a six-iron, right to left to the flag tucked on the left side of the green. Whether it was nerves or adrenaline or just all that was going on around him, Watson hit the worst shot he had hit since his opening tee shot five hours earlier. "Just fanned on it," he said. "It was a bad golf shot."

The ball went right, stayed right, and flew into the right-hand bunker. The groan was audible. Now Watson had to get up and down for par to maintain his share of the lead. One of Watson's great strengths throughout his career has been an ability to stay in the present. Many athletes who have blown leads or not been able to finish strong will admit afterward that their mind wandered, that they started to picture themselves holding the trophy or started thinking about what they would say in their victory speech. Watson has never been that way. "Nerves have come into play at times when I haven't played my best under pressure," he said. "But I've never lost a golf tournament because I couldn't focus on what I needed to do next."

Now, though, as he and Bruce walked toward the bunker, his mind *did* wander. "It hit me right then, as soon as I'd put that bad swing on the ball and saw it go into the bunker, that I *had* to get up and down," he said. "I had to make par for Bruce. If I didn't make par, the round was going to end on a down note and I wasn't going to be tied for the lead. The media would talk to me, sure, but it wasn't going to be the same. I had to make par and be tied for the lead so I could walk into the pressroom and have the bully pulpit and talk about Bruce and ALS and about raising money for research. I was completely aware as I walked toward that bunker that this was a huge moment for me and for Bruce. I'm not sure I've ever faced an up-and-down that, in its own way, was as important as that one."

Handing the club back to Bruce, Watson said, "Lousy shot."

"No problem," Bruce said. "Let's just get it up and down."

Watson walked into the bunker and examined the shot and the lie. He would later say it was "a fairly easy bunker shot." Most players would not have agreed. The lie was good and there was plenty of green to work with, but it was slightly uphill, it was a long shot to the flag, and the ball was going to break hard from right to left as it got near the hole. All of that made it delicate.

Refusing to think about what was at stake, Watson got over the ball and, quick as ever, softly nudged the sand, popping the ball up onto the green. The ball took a couple of hops, swerved to the left, and came to a halt seven feet from the flag. A superb shot. "Typical Watson under pressure," Bruce said.

They took some time over the putt, Watson making sure that Bruce's read was the same as his. "It was just outside right," Bruce remembered. "I was shaking by then, but I knew he was going to make it."

Once he had the read, Watson quickly got over the putt. The silence around the green was deafening. A few seconds later, the roar was ear-splitting when the ball went straight into the cup. Watson had done it. He had shot 65 to tie for the lead in the U.S. Open at age fifty-three, the oldest man to ever do so. "My first thought was, 'I can win this thing,'" he said, remembering the moment. "Then I saw Bruce."

Bruce was crying by now, joined by many around the green and by many others around the country, watching on TV. Instinctively, remembering it was Thursday, Watson put his hand out. Bruce was having none of it. He threw his arms around Watson and whispered in his ear, "Thanks for a great five hours."

That was it for Watson; he was crying now too. "Normally, hugs are for Sunday," he said. "This was just one round, it was Thursday. But the hug was absolutely the right thing to do at that moment. I think Bruce and I have had two very emotional hugs in our life on the golf course. One was at Pebble Beach and the other was that day at Olympia Fields. They both meant a lot to both of us. This one was more emotional because of the circumstances."

Bruce agreed. "Pebble Beach was pure joy. This was different, because there were so many emotions involved."

Verplank and Romero were almost as emotional. Romero offered both men a warm handshake. Verplank hugged them both. "The whole thing was surreal by then," he said. "I mean I've *never* hugged a guy I played with and his caddy on a Thursday. About the only time I've ever done that is when a close friend of mine has won on Sunday. But it was unique, clearly, the kind of moment you just can't make up. I had shot seventy-six and I walked off the green feeling great, excited, so happy for them. I was amazed that Tom still had that kind of magic left and just thrilled that I had been there close up to see it."

The easy part of the day was now over. For once, Watson wasn't talking to the media just because it was part of the job. He practically bolted into the interview room and said, very bluntly, "I have the bully pulpit today and I intend to use it." He then talked about Bruce and about the desperate need for funding to do more research and find a cure for ALS. Patiently he did every TV interview he was asked to, even sticking around to sit on ESPN's *Sportscenter* set. "I had no problem doing any of that stuff," Watson said. "To begin with, it's my duty as a player, I understand that. But on this day, I wanted to do it. This was an opportunity, and I know just how fleeting fame is. I had to grab it and run with it while I could."

Bruce wasn't nearly as eager to meet the media. For one thing, he was exhausted and emotionally drained by the events of the day. For another, his thinking was that Watson had shot 65, not him. He had heard the fans calling his name, *"Bruuuuuce,"* as if he were Springsteen. He was moved by the sentiment. But he didn't want people focusing on him after what Watson had just accomplished. "He shot one of the great rounds in U.S. Open history," he said. "I really didn't think the story should be about me."

But the story was about him. Actually it was about both of them. Clearly Watson had been inspired by the moment and the setting, and by Bruce's emotions and by his understanding that this might be their last time together in this sort of mega-spotlight. Watson knew that and Bruce knew that. But Bruce wasn't eager to talk. Tired as he was, he knew his speech would be slurred and difficult to understand. After Bruce came out of the scoring tent, pressroom volunteer Steve Malchow approached him to tell him that quite a few reporters had asked to speak to him. "I'd really rather not," Bruce said. "They should talk to Tom."

Malchow understood Bruce's reluctance. He is an associate athletic director at the University of Wisconsin, charged with running the sports publicity arm of the athletic department. He was working at the Open as a volunteer in the pressroom, something he had done for three years as his vacation. "Being a golfer, I love having the chance to do it," he said. Malchow is one of a number of sports publicity pros who volunteer to help Craig Smith and his staff Open week. Now he had been handed a slightly more difficult challenge than normal. He followed Bruce into the locker room and found him sitting by Watson's locker, collecting his emotions and taking a deep breath after an exhilarating but draining afternoon.

"Bruce, look, you can tell me to go away and leave you alone if you want to," Malchow said. "But there's something I'd like to say to you, and then if you tell me no I'll go away. It happens that I'm an insulin-dependent diabetic — just like Scott Verplank. And I can tell you for a fact that when I see him out there competing successfully wearing that insulin pump, it inspires me, makes me think I can do things I might not otherwise think I could do. I know how much worse ALS is. I suspect that a lot of people with ALS give up on themselves when they're diagnosed, stop living because they've been given such awful news.

"You haven't given up at all. You're still out there doing what you've always done. What you did today was inspiring, believe me, for all of us, but I'll bet especially for people with ALS. I think it would be great if you came out and talked just for a few minutes about how you've been able to do this. It's an amazing story."

Bruce thought about it for a minute, then lit a cigarette. "I'll be there the whole time," Malchow promised. "If you get tired, or it's too tough, you tell me and I'll stop it."

Bruce agreed. He walked back outside the locker room and found a phalanx of reporters waiting for him — notebooks, tape recorders, and cameras were everywhere. Bruce had talked to reporters for thirty years; he had done a good deal of media at the Masters. But nothing like this.

He spoke slowly, trying to make his words clear, about what the day meant to him. He talked emotionally about all Watson had done for him. "To have a friend like Tom Watson," he said at one point, "is an incredible thing. I can't tell you how lucky I feel."

The tears were coming again, and he paused and looked down to gather himself. When he looked up, he glanced at some of the faces around him and noticed something: Many of those listening — cynical, jaded reporters — were crying too.

"All my years in the business," Malchow said, "I've never seen reporters crying. They did it that day, and I don't think any of them was ashamed to do it."

It was that kind of day.

The last thing Bruce did before he left the golf course was an interview with ESPN. Once he understood that this was an opportunity, that people wanted to hear his story, tired as he was, he agreed to do as many interviews as he could.

Before he left for the evening, Watson had made the comment to people that "if I were to go out and shoot ninety tomorrow, it really wouldn't matter." He didn't want to shoot 90, he wanted to win the golf tournament. The competitor in him was saying it was Thursday and he had played 18 good holes with 54 still to go. But the friend in him, the brother in him, or as Neil Oxman would put it, the closer-than-brother in him, knew that nothing could take away from what had happened that day. It had been magical, and as he said, shooting 90 wouldn't change that.

He went back to his hotel room and was getting ready to go to bed when he flipped on the television set. There was Bruce, doing the ESPN interview, struggling to talk because he was so tired and so full of emotion. The interview wasn't long, but Watson clearly heard the last thing Bruce said: "I know," he said, the tears coming one more time, "that he did this for me."

This time, alone in his room, Tom Watson made no attempt to hold back his tears. As Bruce's image faded from the screen, he sat for several minutes crying quietly out of both joy and sorrow. "I only wish," he said later, "it could have been more about the joy and less about the sorrow."

16

Needle in a Haystack

ANY GOLFER WILL TELL YOU that there is nothing more difficult than coming back and playing well the day after a great round.
It is not the least bit uncommon for a player who has gone low one
day to shoot 8 to 10 strokes higher the next day. The feel is different,
the pressures are different, and when the magic that was evident the
day before isn't there, a player can get frustrated easily and quickly.

In Tom Watson's case all that was in play on Friday at the Open —
and more. He had slept well — "I had trouble sleeping at times
early in my career," he said, "but not anymore" — and came back to
the golf course the next day to find the place still abuzz about what
had happened on Thursday afternoon. One after another, players
came up to congratulate him on his round and on the day. Watson
took the compliments as nothing more than the respect players
show one another after a good round, but many of those who paid
him the compliments felt as if it had been far more than that.

"If all it had been was a great player turning back the clock for a
day, it would have been a wonderful story," said Jeff Sluman, the
1988 PGA champion. "But this was so much more than that. I think
we all believed that he did play that round for Bruce, and I think we
all felt proud of both of them that day."

Watson played early on Friday, which according to Bruce was normally an advantage for him. "I prefer to go late-early when he's playing well, because you get up and get right back at it," he said. "You don't want to sit around and wait to play if you don't have to."

Watson didn't play poorly on Friday, but it wasn't the same as Thursday. Realistically, how could it be? He wasn't likely to hole out another six-iron or have too many thirty-five-footers hang on the lip of the cup and drop in. He shot 72, two over par for the day. That left him at three under par for the championship, four strokes behind the leaders, Jim Furyk and Vijay Singh. Like most people, Furyk, after playing early on Thursday, had watched much of Watson's round. "The good thing was, after a while, it was all Tom Watson," he said. "Normally, as a player, if you're watching on TV you get upset if they just focus on one guy. But this time it was the right thing to do. Some stories are feel-good stories for the viewers. This was different. It was a feel-good story, at least for that day, for everyone."

Even when Watson dropped back on Friday, most of the buzz around Olympia Fields was still about what had happened on Thursday. In fact a truly remarkable thing had happened: Tiger Woods, still struggling, had become almost an afterthought. Story one was Watson and Bruce; story two the leaders. *Then* people got around to Tiger. It was almost unnoticed, since Watson finished the second round in a tie for 10th place, but he had already accomplished his unspoken goal: making the cut. Of course that goal had become a given after Thursday. Watson was still focused at the end of the day Friday on trying to win. Four shots behind the leader with 36 holes to play was far from an impossible task.

By Saturday evening, though, the dream had faded. Each day at the Open, the USGA makes the golf course a little bit more difficult. Furyk and Singh's score — 133 — had broken the Open record for 36 holes, and there were all sorts of red (under par) numbers on the board. In fact twenty-six players were under par through two rounds. A year earlier, at Bethpage Black, the number had been four. That did not make the USGA happy. So the hole locations on Saturday were considerably more difficult. "The weather and wind conditions never really changed all week," Watson said. "The course did get drier and faster. But what really changed were the pin placements. By Sunday they had them tucked pretty well."

Saturday was no picnic either. Furyk was steadily playing himself into control of the tournament. He shot 67, three under par, which gave him a commanding three-shot lead over unknown Australian Stephen Leaney with 18 holes to play. Watson had a tough day right from the start, shooting 75. By the time he finished, he knew he had no chance to win. He was now tied for 32nd place and trailed Furyk by 12 shots. So he and Bruce changed their goal. Since he wasn't going to win, the next best thing Watson could do was guarantee himself a spot in the 2004 Open at Shinnecock. The way to do that was to finish in the top 15. Watson figured if he could shoot 68 on Sunday and finish at even par for the week, he would be a lock for the top 15.

His calculations were right. In fact they were conservative. The combination of Sunday Open pressure, a golf course that was now playing fast and hard, and those always tricky Sunday hole locations sent scores soaring. From twenty-six players under par on Friday, the number had trickled down to nineteen on Saturday. By the time everyone holed out on Sunday, there were only four players under par, led by Furyk, who shot a cozy, conservative 72 to ease his way to a three-shot victory over Leaney, his first major championship after being a very solid player on tour for almost ten years. Mike Weir and Kenny Perry finished tied for third place, seven shots back. It was the least suspenseful Sunday at an Open since Woods's 15-shot victory in 2000, but that had been different since it was Woods in the lead, smashing records left and right en route to his first win in the Open.

A 68 would have tied Watson for fifth place. Unfortunately, he shot 72, which left him tied for 28th. That was a very solid finish for a Champions Tour player, but it wasn't what Watson had hoped for, especially after Thursday. "I never backed up the great round on Thursday with another good one," he said. "I needed one more round in the sixties to confirm the first round and didn't get it. That part was disappointing."

As it turned out, an even-par 70 on Sunday would have put Watson in the top 15, with virtually everyone in the field going in reverse on the last 18 holes. Even though he never made a move on Sunday, the afternoon was still full of emotion for both Watson and Bruce. When they arrived at the first tee, Ron Read, the USGA's longtime Open starter, told Bruce he had something for him. It was, he said, the original flag that had been in the hole at Pebble Beach on the 17th green that day in 1982 when Watson had chipped in to win the Open. Bruce knew that Watson had a framed flag from the 17th hole in his house, so he was a tad skeptical. "We always have two," Read explained. "We keep an extra one for every hole in case something happens to the flag we're using during the round — wind gust, whatever it might be. We sent Tom the copy because it was less beat-up."

Bruce looked at the flag. Sure enough, there were small tears and stains, indicating it had spent time on the green on that windy day. "Of all the things I lost in the fire, losing the flag [from the 18th] at Pebble was the worst," he said. "To get the one from seventeen that way was just unbelievable."

The round itself wasn't terribly gratifying in a golf sense, but it had to be in a personal sense. At every single hole the two men heard cheers that were as loud as Thursday's, only different. These were valedictory cheers. Most fans knew it might be Watson's last Open and that it might also be Bruce's last. "There was a sense," Billy Andrade said, "that Thursday had been a farewell of some kind. It was great that it happened, but it made you very sad to think of why it had been as dramatic a day as it was."

Watson felt that sense keenly. He was trying very hard to focus on playing well, but he couldn't help but hear the cheers, hear the fans chanting, "Bruuuuce," on almost every green. "As wonderful as the cheers were," he said, "the closer we got to eighteen, the more heartbreaking they became."

NBC was now clinging to Tom and Bruce as if they were a ratings life raft. With Furyk in command and no one other than Leaney even remotely having a chance to make a run at him (Woods had faded to 75 on Saturday and was a complete nonfactor, finishing tied for 20th), Tom and Bruce were NBC's story. Every time they walked on a green, the camera showed close-ups of both of them. Whenever Watson made a putt or hit a good shot, there was a close-up of Bruce reacting. It went on that way all day.

Bruce felt as if he had spent all his emotions on Thursday. He heard the cheers and, like Watson, was grateful. Marsha had flown out Saturday to be there for the final round, and he was glad she was getting the chance to feel all the emotions in person. But he was cried out and worn out. As he and Watson walked up the 18th fairway together, the noise was as loud as it had been on Thursday, growing as they got closer to the green. Watson put his arm around Bruce as they approached the green and Bruce whispered to him, "We've still got another shot to get into Shinnecock, you know — if we win at Inverness."

"Absolutely," Watson said. "Let's just do that."

They both had to go through one more go-round with the media when it was over. Watson did an interview with Jimmy Roberts in which he talked about the four days and what Thursday had meant and the importance of raising money for ALS research. At the end Roberts asked him what he would remember most about the week. Watson paused a moment. "Bruce's tears," he said finally. "That's what I'll remember." He was choking up again. "I just want to find something for him." Roberts, pretty close to tears himself by then, managed a "thank you, Tom" and threw it back to Dan Hicks in the 18th tower.

The *Today* show wanted Tom and Bruce to appear the next morning. Since the two of them were flying back to Kansas City that night, that would mean waking up at about 4 a.m. to do the segment. But it was too good an opportunity to turn down. Marsha and Kim Julian had been working on setting up a website called Driving4Life, and this was a chance to talk about it on one of the most-watched programs in the country, and about the work being done on ALS research at Massachusetts General Hospital in Boston, where Bruce was now being treated.

"What this comes down to is simple," Marsha said the next day. "We're looking for a needle in a haystack. It won't be easy. But we've got to find it."

The publicity generated by the Open was overwhelming, dwarfing the post-Masters response. Money came in, good wishes came in, requests for more interviews came in.

And people claiming to know where the needle was came in.

Watson and Marsha were both bombarded with calls and e-mails from people who claimed they knew how to help Bruce. They knew about a drug or a doctor or had a friend who had found a way to slow the progress of the disease. There were also a handful of people who insisted that Bruce didn't need to find a cure for ALS. That's because they didn't think he had ALS. They thought he had chronic Lyme disease. One of the reasons the Mayo Clinic had tested Bruce for Lyme disease in January was because there are times when the symptoms of ALS mimic the symptoms of chronic Lyme. Both are neurological diseases, the difference being that one is treatable if caught in time and one is not. The key, in the case of Lyme, is diagnosing it as early as possible.

Both Watson and Marsha were extremely skeptical when people first began to bring up the issue of Lyme. Bruce had been tested for it. The test had been negative. Doesn't matter, some people insisted; the spinal tap done at the Mayo Clinic wasn't foolproof. Sometimes people have Lyme and it doesn't show up in that test. Further testing should be done. The more Bruce and Marsha heard about this, the more curious they became. Watson remained the skeptic. There were several doctors — notably one in Philadelphia — who kept insisting that Bruce needed to come see them and undergo *their* tests for Lyme. Finally Bruce told Watson he wanted to go see the doctor in Philadelphia.

"What have I got to lose?" he said. "What if he's right? If he's not right, I still have ALS and nothing changes. If he is right, everything changes. It certainly can't be worse than just waiting to die."

Watson understood that Bruce wanted to at least find out if there might be a needle out there. He agreed with Bruce's plan to go to Philadelphia after the Open. Bruce flew in, spent a day in Philadelphia, and underwent various tests. The doctor told him he was convinced he had chronic Lyme disease but couldn't be certain until the test results came back. Bruce rested at home for a few days before the Senior Open and arrived in Toledo believing there was a reasonable chance that he had Lyme disease. "It's also possible," he said, "that the tests might show I have both. I'm trying not to get my hopes up too high, but I can't help but hope at least a little."

That was certainly understandable under the circumstances. What Bruce really wanted to focus on was trying to help Watson win the Senior Open. Watson had finished second the year before and had not won that title in his first three attempts. What's more, a victory, as Bruce had pointed out on Sunday in Chicago, would ensure a return to the Open the following year.

The weather in Toledo was predictably hot and humid. On Wednesday Watson and Bruce taped a public service announcement that would air during the NBC telecasts that week. The USGA is allowed two PSAs during each telecast. They are used, most often, to promote the USGA's role in the game — putting on thirteen championships each year, growing the game, and helping to write and rewrite the rules of the game along with the Royal and Ancient Golf Club of St. Andrews. They are, in essence, thirty-second fundraisers. USGA executive director David Fay had offered to cede one of his PSAs to Watson and Bruce for the week to allow Watson to talk about the two ALS organizations that they were now trying to raise money for in the wake of what had happened in Chicago.

They taped the PSA on the range after Craig Smith, the USGA's communications manager, had written a brief script. "You know Bruce and I have been together for more than twenty-three years," Watson began.

"Twenty-seven years," Bruce interrupted.

"Is it that long?" Watson said.

"Nice memory," Bruce answered.

Watson was ready to try it again. A production assistant held a copy of the script a few feet away from where Watson was standing.

"Can you read that?" he asked.

"Sure I can," Watson said.

"Liar," Bruce interjected.

The stuff that never made it on the air was clearly more entertaining than what did.

Watson got it right in four takes, talking about all he and Bruce had been through together on the golf course, then adding, "But now we're in the fight of our lives, specifically a fight for Bruce's life." He talked about ALS and the fund-raising organizations. When he was finished, Bruce said simply — unscripted — "Thanks Tom, you're the best." Then, turning to the camera like an old pro, he added, "And thank *you* everyone, for all your support."

One take.

He was really getting good at this stuff.

The weather was far more comfortable when the tournament began on Thursday, June 26, than it had been during the practice rounds. That was a relief to both Watson and Bruce. The hot, humid weather had worn Bruce out on both Tuesday and Wednesday. The USGA had told him, first in Chicago and now in Toledo, that he could use a cart whenever he felt the need. Bruce was absolutely determined to make it through the two Opens without resorting to a cart.

"If I do it at a Senior tournament I don't stick out like a sore thumb, because there are carts all over the place," he said. "But at a regular tour event or any USGA event" — where carts aren't allowed — "it would just put more focus on my situation, and I don't want that. Plus I like to walk, I like to be there on the fairway next to Tom. It's what feels normal to me after all these years."

He had gotten lucky in Chicago, where the weather had been comfortable all week. The two practice days in Toledo had been miserably hot, and he had been as tired as he could remember after the Wednesday round. He had given up the 162-pill-a-day protocol in

May and was now receiving a daily B-12 shot, recommended by the doctor in Philadelphia, to help his system. He had lost twenty-five pounds, most of it muscle, since his diagnosis, and now carried a very lean 145 pounds on a 6-foot frame. At the golf course, Watson was almost like an overattentive mother, checking Bruce frequently to monitor how he was feeling. He had arranged for a doctor to give Bruce the B-12 shot each day in Toledo. On Wednesday afternoon, tracking down the doctor after the practice round was a bit of a concern. He finally showed up while Watson was in the player's dining area of the clubhouse sipping a postround soda.

"You have your shot yet?" he yelled in the direction of the locker room at Bruce, knowing the doctor had arrived.

"Did you hear me scream in pain yet?" Bruce answered.

Watson smiled. "The amazing thing to me is that there's been no change in the sense of humor, dating back to that first night when he was diagnosed," he said. "He just won't give in no matter what he's going through, how he's feeling, or through all the poking and prodding from the doctors and different pills and protocols they keep coming at him with."

Watson could see clearly, though, what was happening to Bruce. The loss of weight was obvious, and having walked golf courses with him for so many years, he knew how much more easily he was tiring. "This is three weeks out of four," he said. "The weather doesn't help. We've talked about the fact that when we get to Dearborn [Senior Players Championship] in two weeks, he's going to have to start using a cart. At least there, it won't be as noticeable, because other guys will be using them. That makes it easier for him mentally."

The two men had also decided earlier in the spring that Bruce would not make the two-week trip in July to Great Britain for the British Open and Senior British Open. This was tough for Bruce because, having missed all those years caddying in the British, he loved going over there. The Senior British was being held at Turnberry, a place that held so many memories for Watson — the great one in '77; the disappointing one in '94 — and Bruce had looked forward to going. But doctors had told him that if the weather turned cold and rainy — a definite possibility — his joints might lock up and it would become very difficult for him to walk, much less walk and carry a forty-pound golf bag. On that basis, it had been decided he would stay home and rest after working four weeks in six. Neil Oxman had told Bruce in the spring that he wanted to do some caddying in the summer since he had relatively few elections to work on in an odd-numbered year. He asked Bruce if he could line him up with someone.

Oxman was excited, happy, and disappointed when Bruce told him he had a bag for him for two weeks overseas: Watson. "My attitude was, of course I'd do it and it would be a thrill to work for Tom," Oxman said. "I had always worked with middle-of-the-road type players; good guys and all, but certainly not in Watson's class. But there was another part of me that was hoping he would change his mind at the last minute and go. I booked flights, but I held off on booking a room."

Watson was paired for the first two rounds of the Senior Open with José-María Canizares, a solid player from Spain, and his old friend and rival Fuzzy Zoeller. Playing with Zoeller was always different, because he kept a steady stream of one-liners going all day, directed at himself, the crowd, and anyone within hearing range. The morning was breezy and pleasant, and Bruce, after watching Watson warm up, was very optimistic. His swing looked much the way it had early in the week at Olympia Fields.

Concerned about how tired Bruce had looked Wednesday, Watson asked him how he felt as they walked down the 10th fairway (their first hole of the day). "I feel pretty good," Bruce said. Then he smiled. "I went to bed at nine." That was virtually unheard of for Bruce, but he had understood he needed the extra sleep. "Kept waking up, though. My body's not used to keeping those kind of hours."

The morning turned out to be a mini-reprise of Chicago. After parring the first three holes, Watson played the par-five 13th in Watson-of-old style: He missed the fairway to the right, laid up in the rough, then hit a wedge that ran through the green and stopped against the collar on the fringe 25 feet behind the flag. "When the hell did they move a highway in here?" Zoeller asked as Watson's ball scooted through the hard, fast green. That got a grin from Watson, who then bladed a perfect wedge straight down the hill and into the hole for birdie. Classic Watson: His ball had never come to rest on the fairway or the green and he walked off the hole with a birdie. When the crowd went nuts, Watson smiled and said, "Heck, you're *supposed* to birdie a par-five." Walking to the next tee, when Bruce commented on that being a flashback to the old days, he nodded and said, "Yeah, that really was an old-time Watson birdie."

The rest of the day was pretty much just that way. Watson rolled in a 35-footer for birdie at the next hole and said pointedly, "That was a good read, Bruce."

"Wasn't a bad putt either," Bruce answered drily.

They had a lengthy discussion about a hard-breaking 20-footer at the 15th before Watson made that one too to go to three under par. Zoeller shook his head after that one and said loudly, "What the hell do you do about that except say, 'Damn nice putt.'" Watson saved par at the 17th, making a tricky six-footer, and then made his fourth birdie at number one, drilling a 30-footer. Two holes later, after Bruce had convinced him there was more break in the putt than Watson thought, Watson made a 20-footer from the fringe. "You had it exactly right," he said to Bruce, who was grinning from ear to ear.

Watson was in the lead by that point, but this had a completely different feel than Chicago. For one thing, Watson leading the Senior Open was no surprise. For another, if he were to shoot 90 the second day it *would* matter. He had only one real goal for the week: to win. This was a more typical Thursday. Get off to a good start in order to be in serious contention on Sunday. There were "Bruuuce" chants around the golf course, but both he and Watson had become almost accustomed to them by now.

Watson's first bogey came at the par-four fourth hole, which would be statistically the most difficult hole of the entire year on the Champions Tour. He came back to birdie the fifth, then bogeyed the par-three sixth when his tee shot took another of Zoeller's highway hops and went through the green. "What is this, the British Open?" was Zoeller's comment on that one.

He finished on the par-four ninth, with the gallery seemingly almost as large as it had been in Chicago. It was midday by now, and the weather had warmed considerably. Watson, who had been excellent off the tee most of the day, hit a perfect drive. Standing in the fairway, he and Bruce were between wedge and nine-iron. Knowing the humid air would make the ball fly and that his player was pumped up, Bruce preferred wedge. Watson liked nine. "Okay then," Bruce said, "but just a little one."

Watson smiled and said, "Yes sir." He hit his little nine to within four feet of the flag and nailed the birdie putt for a five-under-par 66. That gave him a little piece of history: He became the only man to lead both the Open and the Senior Open in the same year. More important, it put him right where he wanted to be, setting up the rest of the week. There was no hug this time, because this really was just a Thursday. Watson had his arm around Bruce as they walked off the green to the cheers of the very enthusiastic crowd.

"There's one goal at this event, that's to win," Bruce said later. "The Open was completely different for all the obvious reasons. We finish second here or anything that isn't first, it's going to be a disappointment."

Predictably, the second day was tougher. Watson actually hit the ball just as well as he had on Thursday, but he didn't make the bevy of long putts he had made in the first round. "That was as good a putting round [Thursday] as I've had in a long time," he said. "That's the way I used to play. But these days, that's not the norm. Friday was more the norm."

The result was a one-over-par 72 that dropped him into second place behind Vicente Fernandez, who came in late in the day with a stunning 64 to take a one-shot lead. Watson was still in very good position despite what he and Bruce hoped would be their worst day of the week.

There was one difficult moment that afternoon. As the players and caddies walked toward the third green, the "Bruuuce" chant started again. The third is a par three, the green sitting in what amounts to an amphitheater, with bleachers behind and on the sides. The bleachers were packed and the crowd was loud, going on at length. Bruce had actually learned how to tip his cap in Chicago — there hadn't been much need earlier in his career — so he tipped his cap quickly, hoping that would quiet the crowd.

"Where in the world did all these people come from?" Zoeller joked as the chant picked up again after Watson had two-putted for par. Walking to the fourth tee, the players and caddies walked in between ropes, with fans crowding in on both sides. There were more shouts for Bruce and words of encouragement. The fourth is a forecaddy hole, the players walking back to the tee while the caddies walk forward to meet them in the fairway. The quickest route is down the right side, where the ropes are. Bruce walked straight across the fairway to the far side, away from the ropes and the fans.

"I felt like it was starting to become a circus," he said. "The last thing in the world I want is to be a distraction in any way for Tom or the other players. I needed to get away, just get to a place where it would be quiet for a couple of minutes."

While Bruce fled across the fairway, Cayce Kerr, Zoeller's caddy, another longtime friend, stared at him. There were tears in his eyes. "I know they mean well," he said of the fans. "But all they're doing now, when we're just out here playing and nothing special's happening, is reminding Bruce that he's sick. He doesn't need to be reminded. He can feel it every step he's taking."

Kerr and the other caddies had noticed that Bruce, who had always been one of the fastest walkers on tour, just couldn't keep a fast pace for 18 holes anymore. "He needs it slower," Kerr said. "He won't ever say a word about it, but we notice. The guy has so much guts, but you can see the exhaustion in his face. We got lucky today because it's cooled off, but he's still hurting. I can feel it."

Caddies will often help one another during a round — raking for one another, for example, if a caddy needs to get right to his player after he comes out of a bunker. On 18 that afternoon, Watson found the back bunker. After he played out, Kerr grabbed the rake just to save Bruce a little work. "All the guys are doing that when they can," Watson said. "I notice it when they do it, and I'm grateful. But I know they aren't doing it for me. They're doing it for Bruce."

Watson didn't play badly on Saturday, shooting a one-under-par 70, but Bruce Lietzke, who had started the day two shots behind Watson, in third place, played what he later called the round of his life, shooting 64. That put him at nine under for the week, giving him a four-shot lead on Watson and Fernandez. Sometimes the most frustrating thing about golf is not being able to play defense. Lietzke was a talented player who had won thirteen times and made a lot of money on the regular tour but had never won a major. He had made a conscious decision early in his career to play enough golf to make a good living but took off long stretches during the year to spend time with his two children. If that meant missing majors, he simply missed them. He had never played in the British Open and had last played in the U.S. Open in 1985. Now his kids were almost grown, and like a lot of players, he was finding playing with the over-fifty set quite enjoyable.

"We need a good start," Bruce said Sunday morning. "He's never been in this position before, and he'll definitely be looking at this as a chance to win a major — senior or not. We put some pressure on him early and he might come back to us."

The chance to do that was there early. Just as Bruce had predicted, Lietzke looked tight at the start. He found the bunker off the first tee, missed the green, and made bogey. Watson had a 20-foot putt for birdie that could have sliced the lead in half on one hole, but it just slid by. Both Watson and Bruce looked chagrined, because they knew how important a two-shot swing on the first hole might have been. Lietzke then had to get up and down from a greenside bunker at the second while Watson had another birdie chance. Lietzke saved his par; Watson missed his birdie.

That set a pattern for the day. Lietzke was no different than anyone else coming off a great round: The day was a struggle for him. The fact that he was trying to hold off Tom Watson in a Senior major made it that much tougher. But Watson couldn't make enough putts to really turn the pressure up. Lietzke made a great par save at the sixth, then drilled a 10-foot eagle putt on the par-five eighth hole after his best shot of the day got him that close.

At that moment Watson trailed by six strokes, having missed his own birdie putt. Bruce could see a little sag in his shoulders as they walked off the ninth tee.

"Hey," he said, "how far behind were we last year at Caves? Six wasn't it?"

"Five," Watson said.

Bruce knew that, and he knew Watson would know it too. "Yeah," he answered, "but you made a bogey on sixteen and we still caught up."

The message got through. Watson birdied the ninth while Lietzke bogeyed to slice the margin quickly back to four. Watson got within three and had a 12-foot birdie putt at 13 that would have cut the margin to two. But as had been the pattern since Friday, he couldn't make the putt. A Lietzke birdie from the rough at 16 — when his ball bounced over a bunker and stopped two feet from the flag — sealed the deal. The final margin was two. As Lietzke lined up his final putt, Bruce, knowing the tournament was over, said to him, "Knock it in, Bruce."

Lietzke gave him a big smile and did just that. The handshakes were warm and so was the applause for everyone. But Watson and Bruce both felt let down. Each had believed that Watson would win and, in doing so, clinch that spot in the 2004 Open. It just wasn't meant to be.

"We still have a lot of golf left," Bruce told Watson as they walked off the green.

"Damn right we do," Watson answered.

One week later Bruce made his debut in a cart at the Ford Senior Players Championship. Technically this was a major, just as the Senior Open and the Senior PGA Championship were. But most of the players, especially those who had won real majors during their career, looked at it as a good tournament but a clear notch below the first two majors on the Champions schedule.

The event in Dearborn wasn't all that different from the Senior Open, except that Watson's brilliant round came on the second day — a 64 — and the player who made a big move on the weekend to catch him wasn't Lietzke but newly minted senior Craig Stadler, the 1982 Masters champion who had turned fifty a month earlier. Once again Watson's inability to play defense on the golf course was his downfall, as Stadler shot 65–66 on the weekend to beat him by three shots. Watson had played remarkably well in three straight tournaments but had come up short of his goal in each one of them, especially the last two, where he very much wanted to share a victory with Bruce.

Midway through the week in Dearborn, Watson got a phone call from Neil Oxman. "Bruce should go with you to Europe," he told Watson. "I've been following the weather over there. It's been hot and dry all summer, and they're expecting it to stay hot and dry. He should go."

Watson understood and appreciated Oxman's feelings. He knew why Oxman wanted Bruce to go, but he also knew Bruce was exhausted, and he would have to walk at both British Opens if he went overseas. Hot weather, even Scottish hot weather, would be just as tough on him at this stage as cold, wet weather, just in a different way. Oxman understood. Reluctantly he finally made a room reservation and told Watson he would meet him at Royal St. George's the following Monday.

Watson's two weeks overseas were an almost unqualified success. He finished tied for 18th place in the British Open, his highest finish since a tie for 10th in 1997 at Royal Troon. He did so, according to Oxman, in spite of a series of gaffes by his caddy on the first day, which he comically described to Bruce in a lengthy letter he wrote him after returning home. "By the fifth hole on the first day," he wrote, "I had dropped a towel, had a bag fall over, the umbrella had fallen out of its bottom brace, and Tom threw me a ball that I dropped and it ended up rolling halfway across the green. At that point, Tom tried to calm me down. I actually thought I wasn't that nervous!"

The following week, returning to Turnberry for the British Senior Open (he and Hilary shared a cottage for the week with Jack and Barbara Nicklaus), Watson appeared on his way to yet another second-place finish until Englishman Carl Mason, leading by two shots with one hole to play, double-bogeyed the 18th hole, forcing a playoff. Both men parred the first playoff hole — the 18th — then they played the 18th again. Watson had hit two-iron the first time he played the hole that day, leaving himself 195 yards to the front of the green. On the first playoff hole, he hit driver and had 124 to the front. The third time, he hit driver and "turned it over" (hit a draw that cut the corner), and had 95 yards to the front. "A hundred yards closer to the green than he was in regulation," Oxman wrote. "I just don't think you can give Watson two 'take-overs' (as we would say in Philly) and not have him come out on top."

He did, winning on the second playoff hole. Even though he had needed Mason's help at the finish to win, the victory was gratifying after the near misses earlier in the summer. "I know for a fact that he was tired of finishing second," Bruce said. "Of course I told both him and Ox before they went over that Tom was a lock to win since I wasn't going."

Bruce wasn't there in body, but his spirit was very much present. After Watson had been presented with the trophy and had done his postround media interviews, he returned to the cottage to pack. Oxman was already there, getting things organized, since the Watsons and the Nicklauses were leaving that night to fly home. They sat down for a moment to talk about the week and joked about how Bruce had correctly predicted Watson's victory. "We both started to get emotional, just talking about him, even making jokes about what he was going to say when we got back," Oxman said. "We didn't start out to have a good cry, but that's what we ended up doing."

In his letter to Bruce, after telling him all the funny stories and expressing amazement that Watson had been able to win with him on the bag (it was Oxman's first win as a caddy *ever*), Oxman wrote:

Without exaggerating, fifty or sixty times over the two weeks someone came up to me and began a conversation with the same two words, "How's Bruce." A guy at Turnberry who you gave a signed glove to; someone who first met you at Wethersfield when you were fifteen; spectators in front of the clubhouse at St. George's and Turnberry seeing me standing next to the golf bag; reporters; marshals — all of whom asked in the most genuine and sincere way.

When we were on the practice tee one day, a European Tour caddy gingerly stepped up to Tom and said, "How's Bruce? Please tell him all the caddies over here are thinking of him and wish him well."

It happened every day — lots of times every day.

One more. We were standing in front of the locker room at St. George's and one of the members asked Tom how you were. Coincidentally, the guy was a doctor. Tom got into a very animated discussion about you with him. (I saw this happen a lot as well.) And when this conversation was over there was one overriding conclusion that you could draw from listening to it. Tom Watson loves you Bruce. That is for sure.

And so do a lot of other people — many of whom have never met you. But you know that.

Thanks for letting me see a little bit of the world as you've been able to see it for the past thirty years.

Feel better.

Best.
Ox

P.S. — I packed the flag from the 18th at Turnberry and the bib in Tom's bag for you.

Bruce couldn't help but smile at the P.S. Finally, twenty-eight years after Watson's first win in Scotland, he had gotten a British Open flag.

17

"We're Not Done Yet"

WHILE WATSON AND OXMAN were in Great Britain, Bruce and Marsha made a trip of their own: to Hartford.

The Jaycees who run the Greater Hartford Open had asked Bruce to come home to the GHO to be honored. They had decided to name a scholarship after him. "Imagine that," Bruce said. "Someone naming a scholarship after me, the antistudent."

Even so, he was delighted with the honor and the gesture. The Jaycees were planning to give $12,000 in Bruce's name to a deserving high school senior which would be put toward his or her college education at the rate of $3,000 a year. The Jaycees had asked Bruce and Marsha to fly in to be part of the GHO's opening ceremony on Monday morning, July 21, at which all of their scholarships and grants were presented.

Bruce and Marsha flew in on Sunday, which gave Bruce a chance to give Marsha a tour of his old neighborhood: the house where he had grown up, the schools he had gone to, the places where he had played, and, of course, Wethersfield Country Club. "I guess I was like a lot of people going home to the place where they grew up," he said. "As a kid I couldn't wait to get out. Now, as a grownup, it was great to be back."

It had been a hectic month for Bruce and Marsha. After arriving home from the Senior Open, Bruce had received a call from the doctor who had examined him in Philadelphia. His tests for chronic Lyme disease had come back positive. He was convinced, the doctor said, that the Mayo Clinic had misdiagnosed him in January and that he did not have ALS. This was stunning news, though not necessarily surprising. Marsha had by then done enough research to know that many Lyme experts believed that what appeared to be ALS was chronic Lyme. At times, they believed, ALS was an outgrowth of chronic Lyme. When Bruce told Watson the news, he was skeptical but encouraged Bruce and Marsha to follow up. He had done the same research as Marsha and had come across some cases where people diagnosed with ALS had been treated for Lyme and gotten better.

"There weren't many of them, but they were out there," Watson said. "My attitude was pretty much the same as Bruce's. As long as the testing and the medicines they were proposing weren't going to hurt him, why not pursue it? At the very least, it gave us all some hope."

Watson and Bruce and Marsha agreed then that the best thing to do was go to the Mayo Clinic in Jacksonville and have them test for Lyme again.

"We showed the test results from Minnesota to the doctor there and the Lyme test results from Philadelphia," Marsha said. "I could tell by the look on his face that he didn't believe the Lyme test. I knew when they retested it was going to come back negative."

She was right. The test for Lyme was negative again. The test results said, "Unconventional testing was done with a positive result and through our testing the Lyme diagnosis remains negative."

Who was right? Naturally Bruce and Marsha wanted to believe the Lyme doctor was right. Lyme was treatable. Marsha found a second Lyme doctor, one who was thought of as one of the best in the country. After he finished caddying in Dearborn, Bruce went to Springfield, Missouri, for still more testing. Again he was told he had chronic Lyme disease, not ALS. The doctor prescribed Flagyl, a potent drug which he said would make Bruce feel worse at first, even taken in small doses. But, he said, as Bruce built up the dosage, he would start to see results and would begin to feel better. Bruce and Marsha were certainly willing to try.

"There are two options," Bruce said, sitting in a Hartford restaurant the night before the scholarship ceremony. "One is to try this and hope for a miracle. The other is to go home and wait to die."

Bruce had decided by this point not to caddy in the PGA at Oak Hill in August. Watson had been invited to play by the PGA of America. Bruce wanted to go, but he knew that walking the golf course, especially in August heat, would be difficult. He didn't want to ride. What's more, Marsha and Kim Julian had found someone in the Bahamas who had come up with a "cobra venom" that he insisted halted the progression of ALS. "I guess we were at the point of trying just about anything then," Marsha said. "If it was Lyme, this stuff wouldn't hurt Bruce. If it was ALS, maybe, long shot, it might help."

Jeff Julian's ALS was far more advanced, and he had already been involved in just about every experimental treatment there was, so this was close to being a last-ditch effort. The trip was planned for the week of the PGA.

"One of the things that happens when you are diagnosed with ALS is that you don't want to just accept it," Marsha said. "Looking back, the first two doctors we spoke to — Dr. Sorenson in Rochester and a local neurologist we saw soon after that — were probably the most honest with us. They said, 'This is what it is. Right now, there is no medicine and no cure. Don't waste your time, your money, or your hope on treatment. Live your life to the fullest as long as you can.' They probably gave us the best advice of anyone. But at the time, it wasn't the advice we wanted to hear." In July there was still hope. Or so it seemed. Bruce had heard about the cobra venom soon after his diagnosis and had told Watson about it.

When Bruce Lietzke told Watson that his brother Brian had a friend in Texas who had been diagnosed in 1975 and had taken cobra venom and was still living with the disease, Watson, Bruce, and Marsha were, if nothing else, intrigued. "Again, we knew the odds were long," Watson said. "But we're already dealing with long odds to begin with. Your life is on the line, you try things. I told Bruce if it was me, I'd try it. I didn't expect much, neither did he or Marsha, but there was nothing lost by trying."

Time would tell on the Flagyl, and who knew what would happen with the cobra venom. In the meantime, Bruce was excited to be home, and pleased — if a little bit embarrassed — to be honored with the scholarship. He had decided to kick in $1,000 of his own money to Bonnie Fewel, the high school senior who had won the scholarship. "The money they're giving her is for books and fees and things like that," he said. "I want her to have some money she can use just to have a good time."

Bruce's part of the ceremony was brief. Most of the time was taken up by politicians (including Governor John Rowland, who in spite of a police escort showed up ten minutes late) and local officials congratulating one another on keeping the tournament alive even though there was no title sponsor for 2003. When Bruce was introduced, he received a warm ovation and let Marsha — who was getting used to speaking on his behalf — tell everyone how he felt. "Bruce is thrilled to be back and to be a part of this, because this is where it all began for him," she said. "He's very proud to have this scholarship carry his name." She then surprised Bonnie by handing her the check for $1,000 and telling her that Bruce wanted her to use it to have a good time. Shocked, Bonnie let out a shriek and hugged Bruce, who was both delighted and slightly embarrassed by the commotion being made on his behalf. During forty-five minutes of speeches, presentations, and announcements, there was nothing that touched the warmth clearly felt by everyone involved when Bruce and Marsha made their presentation to Bonnie.

The trip home was fun and nostalgic and a little bit sad. Bruce saw people he hadn't seen for years and couldn't help but wonder if he would see them again. By the time the ceremony was over and Bruce had shaken every hand in the place and struggled through several interviews with local media members, he was ready to go home. "This has been fun," he said. "But I'm a little worn out."

*   *   *

The trip to the Bahamas proved to be about as fruitless as they had expected, although it was still discouraging. "The day after Bruce took the cobra venom the guy said to him that his speech sounded better," Marsha said. "Well, I knew it didn't sound better and he knew it didn't sound better. We were pretty convinced at that point that we were actually dealing with a snake oil salesman. What was discouraging about the trip was that, for the first time, we felt like we were dealing with people who took advantage of desperate people. We didn't want to feel like we were in that category, and yet that's where we were headed."

Even though he doubted that the venom was going to do any good, Bruce came home with an inhaler that he was supposed to continue using, presumably forever once it began to work. Unfortunately it didn't ever begin to work. During this same period it became evident that the Flagyl wasn't having any effect either. The high hopes of July were rapidly becoming the fading hopes of August.

Watson had his first poor tournament of the summer at the PGA. With Bill Leahey caddying for the first time since the 1981 Kemper Open, he shot 75–75 and missed the cut. As with the two British Opens, Watson enjoyed the company of his fill-in caddy but felt Bruce's absence, not so much from a golf standpoint as from a companionship standpoint. "Bill and Neil are wonderful guys, and they worked hard and did everything I asked them," Watson said. "But I missed Bruce. How could I not miss him? I think they both knew I missed Bruce, and there was an emotional tug for all of us."

Bruce was back on the bag two weeks later in Portland, Oregon, for the JELD-WEN Tradition — the fifth of the so-called Senior majors. By this time neither he nor Watson was concerned about whether an event was a major or a nonmajor; they both just wanted to win. They had been close twice and then Bruce had missed the victory in Scotland. "I wanted very much to win again *with* Bruce," Watson said. "I don't think I was pressing because of it, but I was aware of it and so was he. I told him when I got back from Scotland that the only reason I'd won was because he'd put a hex on poor Carl Mason on that eighteenth hole."

For his part, Bruce had told all his friends that Watson had won *because* he hadn't gone to Scotland and that if Watson won at the PGA he was going to demand 10 percent of the purse and then retire.

The week in Portland began on a high note when John Solheim, the chairman of the Ping corporation, presented Tom and Bruce with gold-plated putters. Each bore an identical inscription: "Tom Watson and Bruce Edwards: Friends, Companions, and Brothers Forever."

"Brought tears to my eyes," Watson said. The same was true of Bruce. For both men, the gesture and the words meant far more than the putter itself.

For a long time on the weekend, it looked as if the Tradition was going to be a repeat of the Senior Open and the Senior Players. Watson played well the first two days, shooting a stunning 62 in the second round to take a four-shot lead over Jim Ahern going into the third round. But as had been the case throughout the summer, he struggled on Saturday, shooting 73 to let the rest of the field get back into contention. He entered the final round tied with Tom Kite and Morris Hatalsky for second place, one shot behind Ahern.

There was one good moment on Saturday. At the par-five 16th hole, Watson missed the green to the left with his second shot and caught a hanging lie with the pin no more than 25 feet from where he was standing. It was a shot very similar to the one at the 17th hole at Pebble Beach in 1982. As he pulled his wedge out of the bag, Watson shot a look at Bruce and said, "Aren't you going to tell me to knock it close?"

"I only do that," Bruce answered, "during majors."

They both cracked up, then Watson chipped to three feet and made birdie.

"I'm not sure what's more amazing, that he was thinking the exact same thing I was thinking about the shot and the lie, or that he came up with an answer like that so quickly," Watson said. "Actually, when you think about it, neither is really that amazing at all. They're both just Bruce."

Sunday was an up-and-down day from start to finish. Watson played well on the front nine, then found water on the 10th hole. Peter Jacobsen, the longtime PGA Tour player whose company was managing the event (he is Portland-based), had come out to watch after Watson made the turn, hoping to help push him to the win. "As soon as he knocked the ball in the water," Jacobsen said later, "I said, 'I'm out of here.' I felt like I was a jinx."

Watson made a good up-and-down there to save bogey, righted himself, and got to the 16th — the easiest hole on the golf course — tied for the lead with Kite and Gil Morgan and one shot ahead of Ahern. Kite and Ahern were playing one group behind him. "I was thinking I had to birdie sixteen and then see what I could do on the last two holes," he said.

He didn't birdie 16. Instead he hit his second shot in the water and had to work to save bogey. He walked off the 16th green convinced he had blown the tournament. "I figured Jim and Tom both had sixteen and eighteen" — another par-five — "to play and it was going to be really hard for both of them to not make at least one birdie, if not two, on those holes. I thought I had lost, that I'd given it away right there."

As always, Bruce was in his ear, reminding him a lot could still happen — remember Turnberry? — and that he needed to focus on playing the last two holes well. As always, Watson put the mistake behind him. He parred 17 and was in the bunker at 18 in two, looking at what he thought was a fairly easy bunker shot. "I knew I had, at worst, a good chance to get up and down," he said. "It was the kind of shot you should be able to get to no more than six feet from the flag."

As he walked up to the bunker, Watson checked the scoreboard. Ahern had birdied the 16th. But Kite had not. That left Watson, Kite, Ahern, and Morgan — who was already in the clubhouse — tied for the lead. If he got up and down for birdie, he would have a one-shot lead. "I had been thinking I had to make birdie to have a chance to play off," he said. "When I saw the board, I realized if I made birdie, chances were that I would do no worse than play off."

He knocked the bunker shot to about four feet and, with the wind whipping, managed to nudge the birdie putt into the hole. Now he had the lead. Kite and Ahern had both parred 17. If either or both birdied 18, there would be a playoff. Watson and Bruce went into the scorer's tent and went over the card, and Watson signed for a two-under-par 70. Then they sat together and watched Kite and Ahern play 18.

Kite had to lay his second shot up but, always a superb wedge player, knocked his third shot to about five feet. Ahern was much closer to the green in two, but his chip pulled up eight feet short. Both had makeable birdie putts. But Ahern missed. "At that moment it occurred to me that Tom's just not a good putter inside six feet anymore," Watson said. "I didn't say anything to Bruce, but I was thinking there was a pretty good chance he'd miss. I didn't want to think about it too much, because I had to be mentally prepared to go out there and play off if he made it. But the thought crossed my mind that he could miss."

He did. Watson had won. As soon as the putt slid by the hole, Watson and Bruce hugged — their first victory hug since that cold October weekend in Oklahoma City ten months earlier when Bruce had first noticed the problem with his hand. That seemed like a long time ago at that moment.

"I thought he might miss and he did," Watson said to Bruce.

Bruce's answer was direct: "Hey," he said. "We aren't done yet."

"You're right," Watson said. "We're not close to being done."

Later, talking about that moment, Watson's voice was very soft. "I think we both wanted to take the approach that this was just another win and that there were more to come," he said. "We've always been that way. Celebrate, yes, but then move on to whatever is next. In a sense, we did take it that way, but in another sense, we both knew this was very special."

They weren't the only ones. When they came out of the trailer, the first person to greet them was Jacobsen. "You know I love Tom

Kite," he said. "But I have to admit, I was thrilled when he missed that putt."

The following week, the cover of *Golf World*, the magazine that chronicles all the tours on a weekly basis, did not feature Adam Scott, who had won the new $5 million Deutsche Bank Championship on the PGA Tour. It didn't feature Tom Watson either. The cover boy was Bruce Edwards, and the subhead said, "Caddie Bruce Edwards carries Tom Watson to another major championship."

Bruce, of course, disagreed. "It wasn't a major," he said.

Watson always takes September off, so Bruce had time to rest, enjoy the victory at the Tradition, and travel to Boston for the family reunion. By then he and Marsha both understood that none of the medications he was taking were having any effect. His speech was getting worse, he was continuing to lose weight, and his legs were getting sore and tired far more quickly than they had at the beginning of the summer. Sleep had become difficult because he often had trouble breathing when he was lying down.

Predictably his emotions swung more frequently than they had in the initial stages after his diagnosis. In the spring, when his legs still felt strong, he had talked confidently about caddying throughout 2004, saying he knew he would work the Masters again and that he was still holding out hope that Watson would get into the Open again so they could go to Shinnecock together. By the fall, the constant aching in his legs, the continued deterioration of his speech, and the fatigue he often felt all made it apparent to him that caddying in 2004 would be difficult, if not impossible.

"If I go to Augusta, it would have to be in a cart," he said quietly one night during the family reunion weekend at Gwyn's house. "I know that my legs couldn't take those hills for four days anymore."

There was sadness in his voice as he spoke, as if saying the words were some form of surrender. From the very first day, he had vowed not to give in to the disease, almost convinced that his mind could command his body not to weaken to the point where he couldn't caddy anymore. As strong as his mind and his heart were, each day brought him closer to realizing that they could not stop ALS from wreaking havoc on his body. The idea of giving up the Masters brought home the realization that the day was coming when he wouldn't be able to caddy anymore.

"If he wants me to, I'll call Hootie" — Augusta National chairman Hootie Johnson — "myself and ask him to let Bruce work out of a cart," Watson said. "I would be very surprised if Hootie were to say no under the circumstances. That's all up to Bruce. I'll do whatever he wants." He paused and took a deep breath, knowing, like Bruce, that what he would say next was another step closer to the end of their working relationship. "Knowing Bruce, my guess is he wouldn't want me to do that," he said. "I know he wants to work at Augusta again. But I also know if he works in a cart, it will be a media circus, and he knows that too. It wouldn't bother me a bit. I'll make the call tomorrow if he asks me to. But my guess is, in the end, he won't want me to do it."

Bruce was all over the map on what he expected and wanted from 2004 as the 2003 season wound down. There were good days and bad days, up days and down days. Marsha, a devout Christian, talked to him often about not fearing death, and in many ways he was at peace with what he was facing, except, as had been the case that day in Boston, when he thought about what those who loved him would go through in his final days and in the aftermath of his death.

"There are times," he wrote in an e-mail, which had become his main form of communication by late fall, "when I think it would be better if I went sooner rather than later. I know it will be very tough on Marsha, and I worry about the children [Brice and Avery] when that time comes. I don't want anyone else to suffer through this any more than is necessary. What I worry about is those last days."

On the days when he thought about what was to come, Bruce would get down and depressed. Only on rare occasions did the unfairness of it all make him angry. Even then, he kept almost all of that to himself. When reality would hit him hard on a given day, he shared some of those thoughts with Marsha. But he always managed to snap back and find things that would make him happy. He was still working; he had a great family around him, not to mention all his friends, who he knew would do anything for him. In October he was inducted into the Caddie Hall of Fame — a long-overdue honor that had been held back only because most inductees are already retired — and managed to find humor in the notion. "The best caddies aren't famous," he said. "We're the guys behind the players who are famous. They're the ones who belong in the Hall of Fame."

Watson had three more events to play to finish the year — a Champions Tour stop in San Antonio; the Champions Tour Championship the following week in Sonoma, California; and, finally, the UBS Cup in Sea Island, Georgia, the week before Thanksgiving. The UBS Cup was a team event, a sort of mini–Ryder Cup with twelve-man teams — six in their forties and six over fifty — representing the United States and the "rest of the world," competing with one another. Bruce was looking forward to working those first two weeks, especially after having had time off. He was hoping he would feel refreshed and rested, and that he and Watson could finish the season by winning again.

What he didn't count on was the fact that his speech made traveling more difficult than it had ever been and that, even rested, even working in a cart, he tired far more easily than he had in the past. Watson played reasonably well in San Antonio, considering the fact that he was coming off a long layoff. He finished in a tie for fourth place — seven shots behind winner Craig Stadler — and earned $64,500, which put him comfortably in the lead on the Champions Tour money list with one week left in the official season.

One of the things that had been lost in all the emotion surrounding the year was Watson's remarkable play. In his first three years on the Senior Tour, he had never been able to find the fire or inspiration that had made him the dominant player he had been at the peak of his PGA Tour career. Part of it, as he pointed out, was physical: He simply couldn't practice as long or as hard as he had been able to do when he was younger. But it was more than that. Playing in 54-hole tournaments, with no cut most weeks, on golf courses set up to give up birdies the way a hose gives up water, didn't exactly get Watson's competitive juices flowing on a regular basis. During his first three full years on the Senior Tour, he had finished 13th, 17th, and 8th on the money list, bolstered the first and third years by big-money victories in the Tour Championship — not coincidentally a four-round event with an elite field (top 31 on the money list) usually played on a reasonably difficult golf course. Watson wanted to play well, worked hard when he was out on tour, and always gave 100 percent of himself on the golf course. But he wasn't driven to play well, certainly not the way he had been driven as the young player Bruce had hooked up with way back in 1973.

In 2003 Watson was clearly driven again. He was driven by the understanding that the better he played, the more opportunities he had, as he had said in Chicago, to use the bully pulpit handed him when he was in contention, but even more so when he was in the lead. "Fame is fleeting — for everyone," he said one summer morning while leading the Senior Open. "Even now, I can feel the momentum from Chicago slipping. You have to grab it while you can, because it doesn't last long."

But his drive was more than practical. He understood, as everyone did, that the time he and Bruce had together on the golf course was now extremely finite. Prior to Bruce's diagnosis, both men had assumed that Watson would play into his sixties and that Bruce, who was in excellent shape when it came to walking golf courses, would continue to work for him until they both got around to retiring. That was no longer the case. Watson very clearly wanted to win for Bruce, wanted that hug they had at the Tradition, an old-time victory hug; not the kind of hug they had in Chicago, because that was entirely different. When they had their victory hug, made perhaps even more special because they were alone in the scorer's trailer, not on a green in front of thousands of spectators, Watson and Bruce didn't want even to think that it was the last one. But of course it crossed both their minds.

Watson had thought about that often as he watched his friend grow thinner and weaker. One day in San Antonio, when they had a moment alone during a practice round, he said to Bruce: "Is there anything, I mean *anything*, in the world that you haven't done that you want to do?"

Bruce looked at him, smiled, and said in words perhaps only Watson and Marsha could have understood at that point: "Tom, I've done it all."

Watson wasn't sure at that moment if he wanted to laugh or cry or do both. He was happy that Bruce felt that way. "If there's anything you think of," he said, "just ask."

He didn't have to say, "And I'll make sure it happens."

Bruce already knew that.

It was in Sonoma that Bruce finally crashed emotionally.

The week in San Antonio had been difficult. He was fully aware of the fact that even his close friends were having trouble understanding him when he talked, and the fatigue he felt at the end of each day reminded him that the disease was progressing rapidly. "People kept telling me that I looked good," he said. "Which is exactly what you say when you're worried about the way someone looks."

Friends who had not seen him for a while were stunned by how thin he had become. The crowds were as supportive as ever, but walking through the gallery ropes from the cart to the tees or greens, Bruce could hear people whispering about how he looked, wondering how much longer he would be caddying. On the first practice day at Sonoma, he and Watson were out alone. The day was beautiful and the golf course was too. It was the kind of afternoon they had both enjoyed through the years, a chance to get some work done but also spend some time talking, with no one to interrupt them. There was virtually no gallery, so it felt as if they had the golf course to themselves.

On the 13th hole, a par-five, Watson asked Bruce a question about yardage and what kind of contour the green had. Bruce gave him the yardage and said something about the way the green was tilted. Watson leaned forward, trying to understand what he was saying. Bruce tried again. Watson still couldn't understand him. That was when it all crashed on Bruce. Talking to Watson was an essential part of his job; not just giving yardages, but telling him what he thought about putts, encouraging him when he needed encouragement, kicking him in the butt verbally when he needed to be kicked in the butt.

"And now I couldn't do any of that anymore," he said later. "Tom and Marsha were the two people who always found a way to understand what I was saying no matter what. Now Tom couldn't understand me on something simple like yardage, and I knew he was trying as hard as he could to understand me. But he just couldn't. It all got to me and I lost it completely."

Watson understood exactly what was going on. He put his arm around Bruce and told him they would get through this too. "Listen to me, Bruce," he said. "Don't worry about it. We'll get done what we need to get done. If you have to write something down, write it down. If you need more time, take more time. This is *not* a problem. Get your head up, you're going to be fine, we're going to be fine. I'm not concerned about it, you shouldn't be concerned about it."

Bruce knew that Watson would never complain about his speech problems, that if he needed to take five minutes to write something down, Watson would stand and wait for five minutes. Writing wasn't very easy for him at that stage either, because the condition of his hands had deteriorated too. But he got the message that mattered: I don't care if you can talk. I want you here with me. This is where you belong. That was what mattered.

"Thank goodness it was just Tom and me out there," he said. "It gave me a chance to get myself together."

He did get himself together. In fact on other days Watson could understand a good deal of what he was saying. As had been the case from the beginning, his speech was better early in the day, when he wasn't tired. Watson played well once more that week but was again victimized by a brilliant performance. This time it was Jim Thorpe, long one of Watson's and Bruce's favorite people on the tour, who played superbly. He began the week with a nine-under-par 63 and ended up leading wire to wire. Watson did his best to chase him down on Sunday afternoon, getting to within one shot with three holes to play before Thorpe eagled the par-five 16th hole to wrap up the title.

Thorpe was extremely aware of the emotions his two friends were feeling that day. "At one point I asked Tom how Bruce was doing," he told reporters after receiving his trophy. "I could see the happy smile on his face fade. His mood changed."

Watson had gone into the week knowing that a solid finish would almost certainly wrap up the title as leading money winner for the year. He had told PGA Tour officials early in the week that if he did win, he was planning to announce that he would contribute the prize, a $1 million tax-deferred annuity paid by Charles Schwab & Company, to ALS-related charities. Commissioner Tim Finchem had asked if Watson would like to make the announcement during the awards ceremony on the 18th green and Watson said, yes, he would like to do that.

"I was really inspired by what Allen Doyle did a couple years ago," Watson said (Doyle had contributed the $1 million he had won as leading money winner in 2001 to six different charities). "Obviously after all that had happened this year and knowing how far ALS still needs to go in terms of research dollars, it just seemed to be the right thing to do."

By finishing second and making $254,000 for the week, Watson finished the year with $1,863,401 in earnings, the most money he had ever made in one year as a professional golfer. When Finchem presented him with the annuity during the awards ceremony, Watson, with Hilary and Bruce standing next to him, announced what he planned to do with the money. When Watson had told Bruce what he was going to do and asked him to be there for the ceremony, Bruce had thought he would be in the crowd, not out on the green. "Another adjustment," he said. "I forgot that at this point I was part of what Tom was doing."

Bruce was thrilled by Watson's gesture and yet, standing on the green in the fading sunlight of a late fall afternoon, he caught himself looking around, wondering if he had just caddied in the last stroke-play event of his career. It had been a long, difficult two weeks on the road, and he was looking forward to getting home. But he didn't want to think that this had been his last afternoon trying to help Watson win a golf tournament.

"If we had won, I wouldn't have felt any differently," he said. "I wish we had won, but Jim's a great guy and he played wonderfully. Either way, I was thinking I didn't want this to be an ending, but I knew, deep down, that it very well might be."

For the moment, he focused on going home to see Marsha and Brice and Avery and Nabby and the puppy they had gone out and bought a few weeks ago as a companion for Nabby.

Bruce had suggested naming the new dog Deuce, after Eagles running back Deuce Staley. Marsha had put her foot down on that one. One dog named after an Eagle was enough. They talked it over for a while and finally came up with a name that made everyone happy.

They named the new dog Hope.

18

"See You in Hawaii"

ON NOVEMBER 16, 2003, a warm Sunday in Ponte Vedra, Bruce celebrated his forty-ninth birthday. In all, it was a happy day, with a few friends, including Greg Rita and Mike Rich, over for a cookout and to watch the Eagles play the New York Giants. Not only did the Eagles win, but — for once — they won easily, 28–10.

"Pretty close to a perfect day," Bruce concluded.

Naturally there were certain thoughts he couldn't escape: Was he celebrating his last birthday? Would this be his last holiday season? And, more imminently, was he about to caddy for the last time?

The UBS Cup would be held only 90 miles from Ponte Vedra, on St. Simons Island, a lovely resort near the south Georgia coast. Bruce's parents were driving up from Vero Beach for the weekend, along with his aunt Joan. Chris, his older sister, was flying down from Annapolis. Marsha had made plans to have her son Taylor, who lived in Orlando, drive up to babysit for Brice and Avery on Saturday and Sunday so she could be there too.

The event itself was one that the players and caddies enjoyed greatly. It had only been in existence for three years, started by IMG, the giant international management firm, to capitalize on the popularity of the Ryder Cup. The PGA Tour had beaten IMG to the punch in 1994 when it launched the Presidents Cup, matching the United States against all the non-European players in the Rest of the World (thus the team name), and IMG had finally responded with the UBS Cup, which was named, rather crudely, after the corporate sponsor, the United Bank of Switzerland.

That aside, the site was stunning, the golf course scenic and challenging, and the accommodations, a place called the Lodge, right on the grounds of the Sea Island Golf Club, elegant. "It's rather embarrassing when they tell you not to hesitate to call on your butler," Hilary Watson said.

There were twelve players on each team. Arnold Palmer was the playing captain of the American team, which included, in addition to Watson, players like Hale Irwin, Raymond Floyd, Curtis Strange, and Mark O'Meara — all winners of more than one major title. The Rest of the World, captained by Tony Jacklin, included veteran Ryder Cuppers (in this case Rest of the World meant *everyone*) Nick Faldo, Colin Montgomerie, and Bernhard Langer. Each player received $100,000 for the week just for showing up (not to mention the butler), and the players on the winning team would receive an extra $50,000 apiece. Unlike the Ryder Cup, which involved two grueling days in which many players have to play 36 holes, starting near dawn and finishing at dusk, no one played more than 18 holes a day. There were six alternate-shot matches the first day, six best-ball matches the second day, and then the traditional twelve singles matches the last day. Everyone played each day, no one got their feelings hurt by not playing (as often happened at the Ryder Cup), and the atmosphere was far more fraternal than hostile. Even the fans understood that this was a competitive but friendly event. Not a single cry of "USA!" was heard all weekend.

Bruce was looking forward to the five days he would be spending on St. Simons. The only travel was a ninety-minute drive in his car, and he would be with friends and family all week. He had even figured out that if Watson got an early enough tee time on Sunday, he could make it home in time to see the second half of the Eagles-Saints game.

"As soon as it's over," he said, "I'm down the road."

The Eagles were part of the reason for that. The other part wasn't nearly as cheery: He didn't want any teary scenes, any lingering moments at the finish. If this was the end, okay, this was the end. He didn't want a pity party. Not now. Or ever.

Everyone had thought about the implications of the weekend. Watson would not play again until the last week in January, when he would fly to Hawaii for two weeks, first to play in the season-opening MasterCard Championship and then in the Senior Skins Game (a four-man, made-for-TV event). It was at the MasterCard in 2003 that Bruce and Marsha had been married. Given Bruce's condition, the notion of flying from Ponte Vedra to Hawaii in two months to work was a daunting one. He and Watson both knew that. Watson's approach was simple: "Tell me what you want to do," he said to Bruce. "You don't have to tell me until the last possible minute. If you want to work, come and work. If you can't, I understand."

Bruce knew Hawaii was a long way off. For the moment, he wanted to focus on getting through what he knew would be an emotional few days, enjoy every minute of it, and then deal with whatever came next whenever it came. He arrived on St. Simons on Wednesday morning, in time for the first of two pro-ams (remember, this was a corporate event), and met Watson, who had just gotten home after a vacation in Argentina.

"My golf game is a long way from being in any kind of shape," Watson said.

"Me too," Bruce answered.

So, as always, they were the perfect couple.

Bruce missed walking. "Half the fun is being able to walk down the fairways and talk to Tom and the other guys," he said. "I miss all that, the back-and-forth. Of course, as it is, I can't give that much back."

The good news was that he and Watson had worked out a system whereby Bruce could tell Tom what he needed to tell him, either with a few words, with hand signals, or by writing down what he needed to say. As Watson had predicted in Sonoma, they had both adapted. There were still times, especially early in the day, when Bruce wasn't that hard to understand. But trying to talk too much wore him out, as did raising his voice. At dinner each night, when he wanted to talk, he would usually address the person sitting closest to him and have them repeat what he had said to the rest of the table.

Bruce felt funny walking off each tee, getting in his cart, and working his way through the spectators until he could reach a point on the fairway where he would take the cart under the rope, ride over to Watson's ball, and wait for Watson to arrive. On the greens, it was usually the other way around, Bruce finding a spot to park the cart, then hurrying under the rope to get to Watson in time to clean his ball and help him read his putt.

For his part, Watson was determined to treat the situation as if everything was normal. He didn't hesitate to ask Bruce what he thought about club selection or about which way he thought a putt was going to roll, just as he had done in the past. When spectators heard Bruce's answers, the uninitiated would look at one another, because it sounded as if Bruce was answering in gibberish. More often than not, especially if he pointed to a spot on the green or nodded or shook his head in reply to a question about club selection, Watson had no trouble understanding him.

On Friday, Watson was paired with Curtis Strange in an alternate-shot match against Eduardo Romero, the Argentine he had played with during the first two rounds at Olympia Fields, and Vicente Fernandez, another Argentine, who had contended until the last nine holes in the U.S. Senior Open. Alternate shot means exactly that: The players on each team alternate shots from each tee to each green, taking turns hitting the tee shot to begin a hole. The match was never really close. Watson and Strange were two down early, rallied to get even, then fell behind when Romero nailed a 35-foot birdie putt on the seventh hole. They never got even again, and only a twisting 12-foot par-saving putt by Watson on the 14th green kept the match alive until the 15th hole.

"I told Tom the key was my great chip," Strange joked on the next tee, having left Watson the 12-footer with a (to be kind) mediocre chip shot.

"Maybe you can rally," said his wife, Sarah, who, like Hilary Watson, had turned her cap backwards to create a rally cap.

"Don't bet on it." Strange laughed.

He knew what he was talking about. The Argentines birdied the 15th to close out the match, and at the end of the day, the Rest of the World led by 3½ to 2½. Later that afternoon, when the captains announced the next day's pairings, Watson had a new partner — Rocco Mediate. Unfortunately he had the same opponents: Romero and Fernandez.

"They're both great guys," Bruce said at dinner that night. "Unfortunately they're also really good players. And Tom's game isn't that sharp yet."

Jay Edwards, being the belt-and-suspenders guy that he is, had made dinner reservations ahead of time at three different restaurants. By Friday night, Chris had arrived and so had Marsha — along with Taylor and Brice and Avery. At the last minute, Marsha had scrapped her plan to have Taylor babysit for the weekend and had brought all three of them along.

"I just decided this may very well be the last time Bruce is going to caddy and we should all be here for it and for him," she said. "I told the kids we were going to make it a camping trip, all five of us sharing a room together."

That was fine with Brice and Avery. The only one suffering was twenty-one-year-old Taylor, who, at 6-3 and 235 pounds, found himself scrunched into a corner of a double bed while his half-brother and half-sister, younger by a dozen years, flopped around happily looking for a comfortable spot to sleep.

Saturday was a lot like Friday. The weather was perfect — temperatures in the 70s, enough breeze to keep everyone comfortable but not enough wind to really affect the golfers. That was the good news. The bad news was that the results weren't any better. Romero and Fernandez were every bit as good the second day as they had been the first, and the team of Watson and Mediate wasn't any better than the team of Watson and Strange. In a familiar scene, the Americans conceded a birdie putt to Romero on the 15th green and everyone shook hands.

"The only good thing is, I know for sure we won't have to play *both* those guys again on Sunday," Bruce joked.

The two teams had split Saturday's six matches, meaning the Rest of the World led 6½ to 5½ going into the twelve singles matches Sunday. The United States would need to win 6½ points to retain the cup (it had won the event the first two years), since a 12–12 tie meant the defenders kept the cup. The ROWs (as they were called) needed 6 points to get to 12½ points and win the cup.

Palmer, who would play the first singles match against fellow captain Jacklin, decided to send Watson out in the third match on Sunday, against Colin Montgomerie. Bruce liked the matchup for two reasons: He knew that playing Montgomerie, the youngest man in the event (he had just turned forty), would ensure that Watson was fired up to play, especially after enduring one-sided losses the first two days. Second, with a nine-twenty tee time, the match would be over no later than one o'clock, meaning that Bruce would be able to get home in plenty of time for the second half of Eagles-Saints.

"I told Tom we need to win seven-and-six," he said. "That way I might be able to see almost the whole game."

A one-sided victory against Montgomerie wasn't likely. He was one of the sport's more enigmatic figures, a great talent who was as accurate off the tee as anyone in the game. He had almost won the U.S. Open twice, had lost the 1995 PGA in a playoff, and had been the dominant player in Europe for close to a decade. And yet he had never gotten around to actually winning a major and had never won at all in the United States, a sharp contrast to Europe, where he had won twenty-seven times. His greatest achievements had come in the Ryder Cup, where he had a 4–0–2 record in singles matches and had very much been the leader of the European team that had upset the United States in 2002.

His personality was as mercurial as his golf. One-on-one in the right setting, he was bright, charming, and funny, someone who was very popular with most of his fellow players. But he had the worst case of rabbit ears ever seen in golf, something fans knew and played on — especially in the United States during Ryder Cups — hounding him with often mean-spirited hooting and hollering, knowing he would not only hear it but was likely to respond to it. In dealing with the media, Montgomerie was also a Jekyll-Hyde. When he wanted to be, he was thoughtful and insightful. On other occasions he was known to simply storm off or to snap off one-word answers and *then* storm off.

Watson was going to be ready to play, regardless of his opponent. Whether it was the Ryder Cup, the UBS Cup, or the Member-Guest at Kansas City Country Club, the notion of being shut out for three straight days rankled. He and Bruce spent a solid hour on the putting green Saturday, searching for a clue to the greens, which had mostly baffled Watson (and almost everyone else) for two days. The greens on the Tom Fazio–designed Seaside Course at the Sea Island Golf Club were just about as enigmatic as Watson's Sunday opponent.

Dinner on Saturday night was alternately cheerful and quiet. Sitting across the table from Bruce, Jay Edwards watched his son entertain Avery, who had walked 18 holes that day and was looking like a very tired nine-year-old girl as she waited patiently for her food. Her older brother Brice had summed up the way a ten-year-old views an upscale restaurant a few minutes earlier: "You sit down and you wait. Then you order food and you wait. Then you get a little bit of food, you pay a lot of money, and when you leave you're still hungry."

Watching Bruce with Avery made the normally stoic father melancholy. "He's always been great with kids," he said softly. "He was a great big brother when he was a kid. Of course he's always been a people person, regardless of age. But he goes an extra step with kids."

Bruce had a huge smile on his face as he quietly entertained Avery, who had her eyes closed and a happy grin on her face. Watching that scene, Jay Edwards made a decision. He had planned to drive home the next morning, skipping the last day to avoid a long trip that might stretch until after dark on Sunday. "We're going to stay tomorrow," he said, turning to Natalie. "We should be here. I think Bruce would want us to be here."

When he leaned across the table to tell Bruce that he and Natalie and Joan were staying, the look Bruce gave him as he nodded his head told him he had been right. There was no need for anyone to discuss the reason why Jay had made the decision to stay.

It was warmer the next morning than it had been earlier in the week. Bruce was at the club by seven forty-five to have breakfast, keeping intact his streak of never having been late to work in more than thirty years as a caddy. Warming up on the range, Watson quickly worked up a decent sweat, noting that it was more humid than it had previously been. The ritual this day was no different than it had ever been: Watson working through his bag until he hit several drivers, with Bruce standing behind him to check his swing and positioning. He finished with a few wedges and then they went to the putting green. This was a little different. Watson walked; Bruce went to get the cart. Watson hit a few bunker shots, then putted for five minutes before they headed to the first tee.

Montgomerie was the first to arrive, and because this event was a lot more low-key than the Ryder Cup, he received warm applause. Watson arrived a moment later to another ovation. Seconds later, when Bruce carried his driver onto the tee, the fans applauded again. Bruce had grown accustomed to this sort of reception, but it still left him feeling gratitude, awkwardness, and sadness all at once.

Bruce and Jay had been able to round up a cart that morning for Natalie, Joan, and Jay (who could walk 18 holes if necessary but, having had hip replacement surgery two years earlier, thought that three straight days might be a bit much). That meant all three of them would be able to see the entire match. It also meant that Bruce wouldn't have to worry that his parents and aunt were pushing themselves too much to get around in the heat. Taylor and Brice were there, and so was Mike Rich. Avery had slept in, so Marsha would bring her to the golf course as soon as she woke up and had breakfast.

From the beginning, Watson was a different player than he had been the first two days. Except for a bad pull-hook that he hit into a water hazard at the fourth, he was driving the ball straighter and longer than on the first two days. Montgomerie, after a bogey at the first — which gave Watson the first lead he'd had all weekend — settled down and took the lead with back-to-back birdies at the fourth and fifth.

Watson had chances too. At the par-three third, he stood over a three-iron, uncertain if it was the right club with the breeze coming from left to right. "What do you think, Bruce?" he asked. "Do you like this?"

"I do," Bruce said, his words clearer in the morning than they might have been at night. "I think it's perfect."

When the shot floated down 12 feet left of the flag, Watson grinned and said, "Yup, just about perfect."

Unfortunately he missed the birdie putt. He did birdie the eighth hole, though, to even the match, and they arrived on the 10th tee even, or as the Europeans say, "all square."

"Last nine holes of the year," Montgomerie said on the tee.

Watson and Bruce looked at each other and said nothing.

Watson appeared to take control of the match on the next four holes. He had an eight-foot birdie putt on 10 that did a 360 around the cup and stayed out. Then he *did* birdie 11 to go one up, and when Montgomerie muffed a chip on 12 and made bogey, he was two up. The 13th was proof, if it was needed, of why Montgomerie is so tough in match-play situations. After Watson, rolling now, hit his second to six feet, Montgomerie hit an ordinary approach shot to 25 feet. Another Watson birdie seemed likely, as did a three-up lead with five holes to play. Montgomerie responded by coolly rolling his putt in. Watson made his too, but the lead remained two up. When Watson badly blocked his tee shot into a bunker at the 14th, Montgomerie knocked the lead down to one hole.

The match had been played exactly the way you would want a match to be played. The players had chatted pleasantly throughout. There had been numerous delays, since they were playing directly behind Curtis Strange and Nick Faldo. Strange was no speed demon, but he was the Roadrunner compared to Faldo, who played as if he were being paid by the hour. On one hole, Faldo spent a solid three minutes looking over a putt while Strange stood to the side literally tapping his foot as if to say, "Are you ever going to putt?"

Watson and Montgomerie are both brisk players. So throughout the match they found themselves waiting. On one tee, Montgomerie asked Watson how far outside of Kansas City he lived.

"Pretty far out," Watson said. "We live on a farm."

"Really?" Montgomerie said. "How much land?"

"About four hundred acres."

"You mow the grass yourself?" Montgomerie asked, deadpan.

They complimented each other's good shots and the crowd cheered good play by both men. It was a long, long way from the flag-waving rancor seen at Ryder Cups. The golf was very good, the mistakes few and far between. They both parred 15 and 16 and came to the par-three 17th with Watson still clinging to his one-up lead. Both players found the green with their tee shots, and after Montgomerie had missed from 25 feet for birdie, Watson had a 20-footer to win the match. He and Bruce looked it over carefully and Watson stroked it almost perfectly. Almost. At the last possible second the ball curled an inch to the right of the cup. Watson was still one up with one hole to play.

The 18th hole is a long, difficult par-four, an excellent finishing hole. Montgomerie's drive was perfect. Just as Watson was about to draw his club back, a little girl in the crowd got stung by something and let out a shriek of pain. Somehow Watson never lost his focus. He swung right through the shriek, and his drive ended up in almost the same spot as Montgomerie's.

"You really are amazing," Bruce said as Watson handed him the driver. "Nothing ever gets to you."

They had to wait one more time for Faldo and Strange to finish. By now Mark O'Meara, who had already won his match, had come out to the fairway along with Greg Rita to watch the finish. Watson's five-iron second shot found the middle of the green, about 20 feet left of the flag. Montgomerie knew that par wasn't going to be good enough, so he aimed his four-iron right at the flag. And hit a perfect shot. The ball took one hop and spun to a halt three feet from the hole.

"Great shot, Colin," O'Meara shouted, even though at that moment it was about the last thing he wanted to see. He knew his team needed the point. (The U.S. would retain the Cup after the teams finished tied at 12–12.) He also knew that wasn't what really mattered.

Watson walked briskly onto the green, looked at Montgomerie's ball, glanced at the hole, then picked the ball up and flipped it to him, conceding the birdie putt. "I made him putt a three-footer on seventeen, I wasn't going to do it again," he said. "Besides, I didn't want to win the match because he missed a three-footer. I wanted to make mine and win that way."

In the movies, Watson makes his putt and he and Bruce have one last victory hug as the putt rolls in. In real life, they studied it from all sides, Bruce pointing to the exact spot where he thought the ball had to go to get to the hole. Watson agreed. Just as at 17, the putt looked good for an instant but died an inch from the cup. Montgomerie's brilliant four-iron had won the hole and given him a halve of the match.

Everyone came on to the green for handshakes. Montgomerie put an arm around Bruce for a moment to tell him how much he had enjoyed being with him and to wish him luck. Watson and Bruce shook hands, and Watson put an arm around Bruce before someone dragged him away for a TV interview. As Bruce came off the green, Rita was waiting for him, fighting back tears. He threw his arms around Bruce and said simply, "I love you."

Bruce said nothing. At that moment his only goal was to escape. People in the crowd were calling his name, some asking for autographs, some simply shouting encouragement, and some echoed Rita's sentiment, shouting, "We love you, Bruce!"

Marsha, who had arrived with Avery on the sixth hole, was standing by the cart with the kids. Jay and Natalie and Joan had gone off with their driver to return their cart. Hilary Watson was there too, giving Bruce a quiet hug. Bruce signed a few autographs, then asked Hilary to tell Tom he would meet him in the locker room.

"I need to get going," he said, tapping his watch. "Eagles."

Hilary knew his need to leave had very little to do with the Eagles. She smiled, hugged Bruce again, and said she would tell Tom where he was. Marsha and the kids climbed into the cart, and Bruce was able to get away from the crowd. He had to get away, because he didn't want them to see him crying.

He almost made it to the locker room before he lost it. Then the tears came. Marsha put her arm around him and said nothing, knowing there was really nothing to say.

He was all business in the locker room, or so it would have appeared. Rita helped him take what was left in Watson's locker and put it into the golf bag and zip it up, since zipping had become all but impossible for Bruce. The players who had finished were sitting around tables in the middle of the spacious locker room, discussing their matches, glancing up at the Jets-Jaguars football game on the TV sets.

Bruce took a deep breath and looked around. "I have to get going," he said to Rita and a friend.

"Tom will probably be here in another minute, you know."

"I know," he said, the tears coming back into his eyes. "I'm going to go." He tapped his watch again. "Eagles."

He paused and took another breath. "When Tom comes in here, tell him something for me."

"Anything."

"Tell him I'll see him in Hawaii. I'll be there."

Bruce took about three steps and there was Watson. He had run into Marsha and the kids and Bruce's parents and aunt Joan outside the locker room and had come inside looking for him.

"Tom, I'll see you in Hawaii," Bruce said, putting his hand out as Watson approached.

"I know you will," Watson said, his eyes bright, smiling, but clearly very emotional at that moment. "Let's go sit down and have a beer, okay?"

Bruce's face lit up. "Sure," he said.

They walked across the locker room to the bar and sat down together, just the two of them, to have a drink and talk about the day.

Maybe Bruce would caddy in Hawaii. Maybe not. Caddying might be in his past. But the friendship was not.

They sat there together, in no rush to leave. Not just friends or even brothers.

Closer than brothers.

And that would never change.

Acknowledgments

Normally when writing book acknowledgments, an author thanks three groups of people: those who made it possible for him to write the book; those who helped him get the book written and published; and friends and family.

This book is no different from the norm in that those are the three groups of people I have to thank. What makes this book different is the thanks I owe to the people who made the book possible. It is one thing to ask people to give you their time to tell you stories; it is quite another to ask them for their time to tell stories that break their heart. That is what all the people who appear in this book did. For all of them, talking about Bruce this past year has been both exhilarating and excruciating. They greatly enjoy talking about the man they have known and loved. Talking about what has happened to him since January 15, 2003, is brutally difficult. And yet no one flinched, no one said they couldn't do it. As Bruce said of Tom Watson after the first round of the U.S. Open, they did it for him.

This is Bruce's book. It was his idea, something he wanted to do, I believe, because he knew there was a story to be told, but also because, like all of us, he wanted a legacy. What I found in doing the research was that he already had a legacy; a legacy built on being one of the first truly professional caddies, but beyond that a lifetime of loyalty to friends and an instinct for kindness that is a credit to him and to his family. As his best friend often says, "There's not a mean bone in Bruce's body." There are few people in the world for whom that is completely true. I can attest to the fact that Tom Watson has that one exactly right.

So I begin by thanking everyone who sat through the often painful interviews that made this book possible: Jay and Natalie Edwards, who doubted themselves for years as parents only to find out that they had actually done a wonderful job with all four of their children. Chris Edwards, Brian Edwards, and Gwyn Dieterle, Bruce's siblings, who have dealt with the heartbreak of this past year exactly as their brother would have wanted them to. Thanks also to their spouses — John Cutcher, Laurie Edwards, and Len Dieterle — and to all their children, who are probably still wondering who that stranger was at the family reunion in Boston last September. Let me not forget Joan Walsh, whose political leanings alone make her a heroic figure to me.

As you read this book, you will, I'm sure, be amazed by Marsha Edwards. Certainly all who know Bruce are amazed by her courage and strength, and so was I. She was also remarkably patient with me and the torrent of questions I kept sending her way since she and Tom Watson were the ones who knew the most about all the testing and medications Bruce was dealing with and with all that he was going through. Bruce's buddy Bill Leahey is convinced that Marsha isn't really one of us, that she's an angel sent from heaven to get Bruce through all this. I am not prepared to argue with him. Thanks also to Brice and Avery and to Taylor. I haven't met Marsha's other child, Brittany, but I can attest to the fact that the three I did meet are making their mother quite proud.

Of course this book would also not have happened without the help and cooperation of Tom Watson and his wife, Hilary. Tom was generous both with his time and with his spirit. Like the others, he sat and dealt with many questions he had no reason to want to deal with; delved into his memory bank for stories from long ago; and never flinched when it was time to talk about things that, understandably, made him cry. I'm also grateful to Chuck Rubin, not only for his efforts this year, but for his friendship dating back to 1982, the first time I wrote at length on the subject of Watson.

Bruce's other friends were invaluable resources to me, as they have always been to him, from start to finish: Greg Rita, Neil Oxman, Bill Leahey, Gary Crandall, Drew Micelli, Mike Boyce, Mike Rich, Mike Hicks, Jim Mackay, Tommy Lamm, Bob Low, Mark Jiminez, Lee Janzen, John Cook, Billy Andrade, Brad Faxon, Ben Crenshaw, Scott Verplank, Jeff Sluman, Davis Love III, Hal Sutton, Peter Jacobsen, Mike Hulbert, Jay Haas, Curtis Strange, and Dick Lotz. Special thanks to Greg Norman, who took a lot of time to discuss issues that weren't always easy to talk about, and to his assistant, Erin Moore, who did remarkable work in getting the two of us to the same place at the same time on the same day to talk.

A number of other people went out of their way to help me track down background information and some of the people I needed to find, notably Marty Caffey at the PGA Tour, Dave Senko at the PGA Tour, and Todd Budnick, also from the tour. I'm sure they all came to dread my phone calls and e-mails, but they always responded. Thanks also to the usual suspects at the tour: Mark Russell, Jon Brendle, Slugger White, Ben Nelson, Mike Shea, Dave Lancer, Denise Taylor, Commissioner Tim Finchem, and Cathy Hurlburt; and to Craig Smith, Pete Kowalski, and Suzanne Colson at the USGA; and to Steve Malchow.

Others in golf: David Fay and Frank Hannigan (I like putting them together); Tom Meeks, Mike Butz, Mike Davis, Margharete Saunders, Ellen McMahon, Kathy Whaley, Kathy Paparelli, Ellie Marino, Marty Parkes, Mark Carlson, Mary Lopuszynski, Patterson Temple, Romaney Berson (and her two sons), Tony Zirpoli, Roger Harvie, Steve Worthy, Frank Bussey, Ron Read, Pete Bevacqua, Mimi Griffin, Jon Barker, Robbie Zalznek, Jeff Hall, Glenn Greenspan, Craig Currier, and the still unsinkable Dave Catalano.

Michael Pietsch has now edited ten of my books. That alone should tell you how patient a human being he is. This book is like several others: It came out of nowhere at him and he agreed to publish it based on one thing — his trust for my instincts. A writer is very fortunate to have an editor like that. Michael is very fortunate to have a great staff at Little, Brown and Company, and I benefit from their presence. That would include Stacey Brody, Zainab Zakari, Heather Fain, Heather Rizzo, Marlena Bittner, and, at least in emeritus status, Holly Wilkinson.

Esther Newberg has been my agent for fifteen books and counting. A lot of this book is about loyalty and friendship. Those are two words that best describe who Esther is both professionally and personally. Thanks as always to her two fabulous assistants, Andrea Barzvi and Christine Bauch.

Like Bruce, I am blessed with wonderful friends, although I think it is fair to say they put up with a lot more than Bruce's friends do. They include, as always: Barbie Drum, Bob and Anne DeStefano, David and Linda Maraniss, Tom and Jill Mickle, Lexie Verdon and Steve Barr, Jackson Diehl and Jean Halperin, Jason and Shelley Crist, Bill and Jane Brill, Terry and Patty Hanson, Terry Chili, Tate Armstrong, Mark Alarie and Clay Buckley, Pete Teeley, Bob Novak, Al Hunt, Vivian Thompson, the great Bob Zurfluh, Wayne Zell, Mike and David Sanders, Bob Whitmore, Mary Carillo, Doug Doughty, David Teel, Andy Dolich, Beth Shumway (BEC), Beth Sherry-Downes (BWC), Erin Laissen, Jesse Markison, Bob Socci, Pete Van Poppel, Frank Davinney, Scott Strasemeier, Eric Ruden, Billy Stone, Mike Werteen, Chris Knocke, Andrew Thompson, Joe Speed, Jack Hecker, Dickie Hall, Steve (Moose) Stirling, Jim and Tiffany Cantelupe, Derek and Christina Klein, Bob Beretta and Mike Albright, Roger Breslin, Jim Rome, Travis Rodgers, Jason Stewart, Mark Maske, George Solomon, Tony Kornheiser, Michael Wilbon, Ken Denlinger, Matt Rennie, Mike Purkey, Jim Frank, George Peper, Bob Edwards, Jeffrey Katz, Ellen McDonnell, Ken and Christina Lewis, Bob Morgan, Hoops Weiss, Little Sandy

Genelius, Jennifer Proud-Mearns, Joe Valerio, Rob Cowan, Andy Kaplan, Chris Svenson, and the always gutsy Norbert Doyle.

Basketball people: Mike Krzyzewski, Gary Williams, Mike Brey, Tommy Amaker, Doug Wojcik, Mike Cragg, Billy Hahn, Rick Barnes, Dave Odom, the entire Patriot League from coaches to employees, Howard Garfinkel, and *still* the only honest man in the gym, Tom Konchalski. Special thanks to Jo-Ann Barnas, who dug through her Watson files from long-ago days in Kansas City, and to Ed Sherman of the *Chicago Tribune*.

Swimmers: Jeff Roddin, Tom Denes, Carole Kammel, Margot Pettijohn, Susan Williams, Mary Dowling, Amy Weiss, A. J. Block, Warren Friedland, Marshall Greer, John Craig, Danny Pick, Mark Pugliese, Peter Ward, Doug Chestnut, Bob Hansen, Paul Doremus, the gone-but-not-forgotten Penny Bates, and the members of the still exclusive FWRH club: Clay Britt, new dad Wally Dicks, and Michael Fell.

The China Doll gang: Red Auerbach, Morgan Wootten, Jack Kvancz, Reed Collins, Aubrey and Sam Jones, Hymie Perlo, Pete Dowling, Bobby Campbell, Stanley Copeland, Rob Ades, Dr. Murray Lieberman, Joe McKeown, Karl Hobbs, Bob Ferry, George Solomon, and the perennial rookie, Chris Wallace. Zang is always in our thoughts.

Then there is the Feinstein advisory board. None of these people are volunteers, although they are unpaid. If they were paid, regardless of how much, it would not be enough, since they take calls at all hours that usually begin with me whining, complaining, or desperately seeking help with a problem that is completely unsolvable (like, among other things, how to use the Internet properly). The board members, kicking and screaming, are: Keith Drum, Frank Mastrandrea, Wes Seeley, and Dave Kindred. They have my eternal gratitude. I'm sure they would prefer to have a way to block my calls.

Last, never even close to least, the family. The remarkable in-law group: Jim and Arlene; Kacky, Stan, and Ann; Annie, Gregg, Rudy, Gus, and Harry; Jimmy and Brendan. Dad and Marcia; Margaret, David, Ethan, and Baby Benjamin; Bobby, Jennifer, Matthew, and

Brian. Danny and Brigid are, of course, the smartest, handsomest/prettiest, and cutest children in the world. Just ask their dad.

Finally, this book was written because of the courage and patience of two people: Bruce, who showed me the definition of true courage: Never giving in to an opponent even when you are told that opponent can't be beaten. And my wife, Mary, who always has the right answers. Sometimes I even listen.

About the Author

John Feinstein is the author of fifteen books, including *Open, The Majors, A Good Walk Spoiled, A Civil War,* and *A Season on the Brink.*

He is a contributor to the *Washington Post,* writes a column for America Online, and is a commentator for National Public Radio and Sporting News Radio and an essayist for CBS Sports. He lives in Potomac, Maryland, and Shelter Island, New York, with his wife, Mary, and their two children.